Roar Sundby, Arno Heimgartner

The Welfare Society –
an Aim for Social Development

Soziale Arbeit – Social Issues

herausgegeben von

Univ.-Prof. Mag. Dr. Arno Heimgartner

(Universität Graz)

und

Mag. Dr. Maria Maiss

(Fachhochschule St. Pölten GmbH)

Band 20

LIT

Roar Sundby, Arno Heimgartner

The Welfare Society – an Aim for Social Development

LIT

Cover image: Friedrich Simon Kugi

Supported by the Norwegian University of Science and Technology,
University of Graz and ICSD, European Branch

Bibliographic information published by the Deutsche Nationalbibliothek
The Deutsche Nationalbibliothek lists this publication in the Deutsche
Nationalbibliografie; detailed bibliographic data are available on the Internet at
http://dnb.d-nb.de.

ISBN 978-3-643-90718-9

A catalogue record for this book is available from the British Library

© LIT VERLAG GmbH & Co. KG Wien,
Zweigniederlassung Zürich 2016
Klosbachstr. 107
CH-8032 Zürich
Tel. +41 (0) 44-251 75 05   Fax +41 (0) 44-251 75 06
E-Mail: zuerich@lit-verlag.ch   http://www.lit-verlag.ch
Distribution:
In the UK: Global Book Marketing, e-mail: mo@centralbooks.com
In North America: International Specialized Book Services, e-mail: orders@isbs.com
In Germany: LIT Verlag Fresnostr. 2, D-48159 Münster
Tel. +49 (0) 2 51-620 32 22, Fax +49 (0) 2 51-922 60 99, e-mail: vertrieb@lit-verlag.de

In Austria: Medienlogistik Pichler-ÖBZ, e-mail: mlo@medien-logistik.at
e-books are available at www.litwebshop.de

Content

Inclusion of disadvantaged groups

Introduction to the proceedings from the 14th Biennial ICSD European Conference

Roar Sundby and Arno Heimgartner

This presentation of articles are papers and presentations given at the 14th Biennial European ICSD Conference under the heading "The Welfare Society – an Aim for Social Development" 11th – 13th September 2014 hosted by the Sør-Trøndelag University College in Trondheim and ICSD (International Consortium for Social Development) European Branch.

The Harald Swedner award 2014 for promotion of Social Development was presented Sven Hessle, Professor of Social work – chair emeritus at Department of Social Work at Stockholm University Democracy. His presentation on the Relationship between Global North and Global South in Child Welfare Research is an important reminder that the best intentions of helping and doing social research in the poor parts of the global south may be part of the richer norths exploitation of the weaker part.

The International Consortium for Social Development (ICSD) is a network of practitioners, scholars and students in the social work and social development professions. The first ICSD Europe meeting was in 26 September 1989 in Heidelberg under the leadership and initiative of the founder of the European branch Dr Harald Swedener. In order to emphasize the need for cooperation and social work professions and research in the former Warsaw nations a number of the conferences in the 90ies were organized in the East European countries. ICSD has a strong focus on building networks for peace and social development. The tension between local belonging, community projects and global citizenship has been a focus through the history of ICSD. The vision of ICSD is to make a meeting point and a community of researchers, teachers and, practitioners' in the field of community work, social development and peace.

The Nordic countries, identified as models for the welfare state system have all a strong public sector and governmental regulations of social life. In contrast to the centralized understanding of welfare the concept of welfare society is including a broader definition of how non-governmental bodies, civil life, social relations, economic conditions, sustainable development and social commons plays a part in addition to, in cooperation with, as a supplement to or in opposition to public services as important factors for life quality Some of the challenges related to these shifts will be explored throughout these contributions.

Two main topics will be addressed in relation to the welfare society discussion and the contributions to this book are also organized under these heading.

The chapter *"Welfare: state policy or local solidarity?"* will focus on the design of social policy solutions, public services, and social work, social care and social actions in the frame of public sector, NGOs, community work or civil life as a basis for creating or solving social problems. One of the main problems connected with the welfare state as provider for social security and welfare is the obvious rigidity and control regime connected to these services. The paternalistic idea that the client is responsible for his destiny and that he should change or be treated by a special method in order to change his behavior, is central in this thinking.

The activity and participatory principles connected to community based social welfare and NGOs and interest groups are inherently more democratic. The shift from the concept of social welfare as provided by the state to the social client as a giver-receiver relationship to realizing the disadvantaged population as actors in their own life with the obvious right to express and define their own problems are main trends in the social development and democratization as experienced in today's society.

The same shift is reflected in the research were the objectified relationship between the researcher and the passive client as object for research towards participatory principles in the research process. The opening article by *Sven Hessle* is addressing some of the serious consequences of this traditional research paradigm on the international arena, as a part of the western imperialistic worldview.

The concept of welfare understood as an integral part of human rights is proposed by *Hans Kolstad*. Each human has fundamental human rights, which are considered as fundamental welfare rights where each person takes part in the forming of the welfare policy and thereby his personal future. The importance of local solidarity and communicative is underlined.

Liljana Rihter is discussing if the local community can substitute the role of the state in guaranteeing welfare by using the case of Slovenia as example. She strongly suggest that the communities are given responsibilities, but not the adequate resources to respond to these needs. The result is increasing inequalities between communities and between individuals as seen in the liberal societies.

The European influences on national welfare schemes are critically investigated by *Peter Szynka* with the "Social-Investment-Package (SIP)" as a case. The Schumpeterian term of creative destruction is used to analyze the outcome of this implementation as either a as a precondition for further development or a preparation for a lower level of social service delivery. He suggests that it rather "may be taken as an example for Schumpeter's long term prognosis that capitalism on the long run will destruct his social base instead of creating something new and sustainable." Szynka characterize the SIP as *New Feathers for an Old Hat*

The popular support of the welfare state is considered as a basis for social services. The Effect of Immigration on Attitudes towards Economic Redistribution is examined by *Isaksen and Jakobsen* in their paper on *Migration and the Welfare State*. By analyzing the survey data from 30 OECD countries they find that there is a threshold effect when it comes to attitudes to economic redistribution. When this threshold is reached further diversity will decrease the support in favor of redistribution.

The theory of recognition as forwarded by Axel Honneth has been increasingly central to the understanding of welfare as he is claiming that recognition is essential to self-realisation. *Knut Magne Sten* is exploring the connection between *Recognition and the symbolic value of work,* with examples from Norwegian job schemes for youth drug addicts. He claims that the connection between recognition, solidarity and social rights remains to be investigated.

Lucjan Miś from the Jagiellonian University in Krakow describes in his essay *"To be like Copenhagen... Central European city residents' dreams versus reality"* how the Social problems in the city are closely related to the city development, a city with a strong attraction to new residents. The population growth connects to both favorable and negative factors. In this context the term "Copenhagenize" has become a description of Young peoples dream a people-friendly city.

In the second part of the book, *Inclusion of disadvantaged groups,* the focus is turned towards inclusive processes and work with minorities, vulnerable groups and children.

In the article of *Baturina, Majdak and Berc, Framing the problem and challenges of dropouts in Croatia*, (Invisible people around us but not us) among high school students. They approach the problem of dropping out from school and how it is leads to unemployment, poverty and social exclusion. The focus on education is a crucial condition for social development both for individuals and for society. Initiatives and programs to meet these challenges in Croatia are encouraged.

Lasse Skogvold Isaksen is also drawing our attention to the importance of school and basic skills for Children in Residential Care. This article describes strategies to enhance collaboration between schools and residential institutions in order to improve children's basic academic skills and inclusion in the school. It is still a close correlation, between social economic background and school performance and these groups of disadvantaged children need special attention and continuous observation to improve their life chances.

The principle of User-Participation in social services is becoming more and more widespread. *Peter Szynka* addresses the challenges of involving homeless people in user-participation in the case of German services for homeless people. Szynka also gives examples of how this can be managed and recommendations how to support participation in homeless services. The recognition of the users as experts of their own situation and the clients taking back control over their lives is a trend in all parts of social services these days and represents a shift in the power structure in social work.

Anne Juberg is also addressing the young homeless adults in her paper *"Because I deserve it": Self-assured welfare claimant action amongst socially marginalized young adults (18–23) as an intake to current tendencies in the newer Norwegian welfare state.* The social services counts on self-reliance among its clients that these young adults find problematic to realize

Hyrve and Collin-Hansen are asking *How to include marginalized youth* using the case of motor-sport project in Trondheim as case. They stress the importance of the relational aspects provided by accessible and confident adult figures. The participation in the project provide status and self-esteem to the participants as well as social skills and new knowledge. The experience of being seen, heard and recognized is crucial.

The importance of participation is further developed in the paper of *Inger Sofie Dahlø* Husby in *The Children's Interview -From resistance to partnership.* From the point of view of the researcher in the open interview situation with children, gives access to more detailed information if the child can determine the content of the interaction, the resistance to share vulnerable information ends, and the dialogue is instead marked by cooperation and equality. Husby thereby underlines the importance of relationship also in the research process.

It is possible to see a trend in these papers that reflects a movement or a shift in social work and social services. The role of the client is changing from a passive receiver of services towards an active spokesperson defining his own life situation and needs. We welcome this development as a part of the general democratization of society

Traditionally suppressed groups defined as children, drug abusers, unemployed or women do not accept to be passively stigmatized, analyzed, defined or diagnosed but describe their own reality. We hope this book can contribute to this liberating trend. And thanks to Anneliese Pirs for her administrative support!

Roar Sundby
President ICSD Europe
Head of department
Social Education and Child Welfare Work Faculty of Health Education and Social
Work Sør-Trøndelag University College 7004 Trondheim Norway
roar.sundby@hist.no

Arno Heimgartner
Univ.-Prof. Mag. Dr. Arno Heimgartner
Social Pedagogy / Educational Sciences / University of Graz
Merangasse 70, A – 8010 Graz, Austria
http://erziehungs-bildungswissenschaft.uni-graz.at/

The Relationship between Global North and Global South in Child Welfare Research: Exploitation – Colonization – Subjugation?[1]

Sven Hessle

Abstract

With empirical evidence from different sources, it is shown that there is a risk that researchers from the Global North subject local resources to exploitation—by using the Global North's superior material resources, monopolizing the research questions, using the results to promote the researchers' own careers, and by neglecting practice and policy implementation. Three recommendations are suggested when considering child welfare research and practice in the Global South: (1) Build up a critical mass of locally based child welfare researchers in Global South; (2) Establish peer mentorship between the Global North and the Global South; (3) Establish collaboration between the knowledge banks of the Global North, the Global South and Global Action

There are intricate relationships between research and its practical implications as well as in the interaction between researchers, practitioners and policy makers. The more I have travelled to poverty areas around the world, these challenges have become increasingly interesting to me. They were even more articulated during my years as a board member of the *Swedish Agency for Research Cooperation with Developing Countries* (SIDA/SAREC).

I want to share with you my views on common challenges, regardless of where in the world the research is produced.

My main questions are formulated within my own area of interest, specifically child welfare. For many years, I have been involved with children in international contexts, especially children in poverty areas, and in countries that we sometimes categorize under the umbrella term "Global South."

---

[1] This article is based on the 2014 ICSD Harald Swedner Memorial Lecture which was presented in Trondheim 11th Sep 2014. An original version of this developed paper was given as the Hokenstad International lecture at the CSWE conference in Atlanta Nov 2011. The original version can be downloaded at http://www.cswe.org/File.aspx?id=55215

It has been estimated that every year, depending on the generosity of different donors, from 47 million to more than 500 million USD is spent on child welfare research in Sub-Saharan Africa (Mweru & Ng'asike, 2007).

This part of Africa, with a population of some 800 million inhabitants, is the most poverty-encumbered corner of the world; 50% of children here are younger than 15 years of age. More than 70% of the rural population live in absolute poverty. African children are the most disadvantaged in the world, with very limited chances for success in life; they are exposed to violence, HIV/AIDS infection, numerous diseases, malnutrition and have little access to education. Here, we find the lowest life expectancy in the world (in many countries, lower than 50 years of average life expectancy, and in Angola no more than 38 years; see Mweru & Ng'asike, 2007). Sub-Saharan Africa is the only region in the developing world where child mortality has increased (Macassa, Hallqvist, & Lynch, 2011). Considering that some of the countries in this region have the lowest GDP in the world, it is understandable that child welfare research funding depends on external resources (Mweru & Ng'asike, 2007).

My questions concern how research is conducted with children in their context, and by whom? What kind of research? Which content? How is the research implemented? By whom? So far, we can say that these questions are universal.

Additional questions concern the Global South, with a special focus on Africa. These are questions that we should ask ourselves more frequently in the Global North academic communities: Who finances the research? Who defines the research questions? Where are the results published? I ask these questions because they are of special importance for the Global South countries.

My point of departure is that research within this territory is necessary, and that it is preferably designed, conducted, and reported by researchers who are locally recruited.

My thesis is that there is a risk that research from the Global North subjects local resources to exploitation—by using the Global North's superior material resources, monopolizing the research questions, using the results to promote the researchers' own careers and by neglecting practice and policy implementation.

From the perspective of the Global South, we need to ask whether these are relevant accusations. Is the knowledge bank of Global South researchers being subjugated, as is claimed?

Sources underpinning the analysis

While I was sitting on its board, the Swedish Agency for Research Cooperation with Developing Countries along with Child Watch International initiated an investigation of the conditions for research in Sub-Saharan Africa. Three African research groups delivered a report for a symposium held in Stockholm in 2007 (Hessle, 2007). This report is my main source for the analysis to follow.

Second, I use a report from an evaluation carried out by a Norwegian institute on Swedish and Norwegian engagement in child welfare/child protection projects in the Global South (Tostensen, Stokke, Trygged, & Halvorsen, 2011).

Third, I increasingly find colleagues involved in evaluations of development projects in Global South countries. This "evidence-based projects fever" of our time, which even earlier in history contaminated developmental initiatives in the Global South, is reflected in the current inflation of evaluations of methods in social work in the Global North. My own experience of this situation underscores the tendencies I find among my other sources for this analysis.

Finally, I include among my sources some international articles on the subject.

Categories for the Analysis

The four categories in which I have organized the data are obvious against the background mentioned:
(1) the material conditions for establishing research;
(2) the negotiations that lead to formulation of research questions in an agenda;
(3) the process of publishing the results internationally; and
(4) following up the implementation of the results.

Main Actors in Global South Research and Implementation

Before we go into the reports from the African groups, we should make a distinction between three main actors involved in research in the Global South: *Global North researchers, Global Action researchers, and Global South researchers.*

Global North researchers are generally established scholars whose research platform is the academic environment. Quite common is the bilateral academic relationship between two universities or research departments, permitting the exchange of research projects involving graduate and postgraduate students.

Global Action researchers are established scholars whose research platform is the leading international nongovernmental organizations (NGOs). I call it "global action" within this contextual framework to include organizations with clear action-oriented objectives. Their work is to discover, analyze, and implement. This in turn means that one important characteristic of these organizations is their closeness to the stakeholders. Their action-orientation and advocacy-orientation will evidently result (or should result) in policies. Within the area of child welfare, many NGOs claim to have research capacity, which in most cases means that

they evaluate their own action. Large so-called IGOs (i.e., international govern-
ment organizations) are able to draw on their own research administrations, such
as the United Nations agencies UNICEF, the World Health Organization, United
Nations Research Institute for Social Development, and the International Labour
Organization, which finance and conduct research in the field of child welfare
(Axford, 2012).

Global South researchers are locally established academics conducting research in poverty-stricken regions. The research programs are mainly formulated
in universities and research institutions or centers.

Table 1 summarizes the main child welfare research actors and their agencies
of origin, classified in the categories Global North, Global Action, and Global
South. I combine them in the table with the categories for the forthcoming analysis.

Table 1: Child Welfare Research – Risks and Challenges

Agency Origin	Material Resources	Def. of Research agenda	Int. Publ. of Results	Policy Implem.	Risk
Global North					
Global Action					
Global South					

Basic Conditions for Research on Child Welfare in Sub-Saharan Africa

I now turn to the documentation of research activities in Sub-Saharan Africa with
the main source being the three reports, though I will also include my impressions
from the other sources mentioned earlier. How is research conducted with regard
to child welfare in this part of the world, what is the content, and by whom is it
reported?

The researchers who reported to the Swedish Agency for Research Cooperation with Developing Countries made a very detailed study of the research documentation in their region of Africa. Their mission was difficult due to the heterogeneous, sprawling and varying quality of the sources of the information. Through
document reviews, interviews, and surveys, the researchers have summarized 10

years of child welfare research in their part of the world. Here, we can only share a summary of the summaries. Let us first note that the analysis of more than a hundred reported and published research publications during a timeframe of 10 years shows that the projects are widespread and with few or no connections with each other. When we add that the research activities that are published by NGOs, such as Global Action, the impression of a fragmented body of research projects is reinforced. Most of the NGO projects are also not reported through international research publications; these reports end up in the hands of the donors.

The researchers comment that child welfare research largely depend on donor funding from governments of industrialized countries and international agencies (Axford, 2012). Prominent sources of funding are the United States and governments in Northern Europe. More than a hundred listed international non-government agencies add to the impression of the domination of the North over the South. Governments from sub-Saharan countries contribute very modestly, with what might be considered "pocket money," to child welfare research. The researchers further state that this uneven funding for child welfare research, of course, underscores the power relationship between the rich and poor. "African countries may not be capable of establishing strong institutions for research in child development," the researchers conclude, and therefore research will be externally controlled in line with the research design policy of international bodies (Axford, 2012: 62).

But what is child welfare research all about? The funding priorities are mainly focused on Millennium Development Goals and the Convention on the Rights of the Child (CRC) with issues of health as number one, with HIV/AIDS and malaria as dominant projects. Other prioritized areas are research on education, poverty reduction and nutrition. These are seemingly vital topics, of course. But what is interesting is the observation by our authors that the funds are directed toward focus areas that describe the African child as "vulnerable". The authors conclude that "the image of the African child is distorted," (Axford, 2012), and they recommend that priority is given to studies highlighting the resilience of the children in Africa!

Moreover, this way of concentrating the agenda on crisis themes tends to ignore the lives of the children living under normal circumstances. The authors call for research projects that respect what they term "culturally specific situations." One example they mention is the failure to take into consideration different perspectives on children and young people in the African context. Many of the mentioned projects did not even note the age of the children involved or relied exclusively on the UNICEF definition of a child as being a person under the age of 18.

CODESRIA (Council for the Development of Social Science Research in

Africa), situated in Dakar, Senegal, is an organization for the promotion of African research and publication. This organization is more explicit in its critique of the existing research in the area of child welfare. Having listed approximately 15 research programs as being of prime importance, CODESRIA concludes that the contextual factors defining the framework for marginalization of youth in society are underexplored:

"These factors are political, economic, social and demographic in nature and they speak to broader processes of transition and change in society that have impacted adversely on children and the youth... new factors connected with accelerated processes of urbanization that have generally gone hand-in-hand with the expansion of the boundaries of the informal sector, deepening of social inequalities in the context of the collapse of social policy, increased migratory flows within and across borders, and the massive and accelerated refraction of global processes and trends into local contexts, have emerged into significance and closer attention". (CODESRIA, 2007: 31)

The disciplinary background of child welfare researchers in the Global North is quite diverse and more subdivided in comparison with those from the Global South; for example, project involvement comes from departments of microbiology, public health, community health, medicine, political economy, pharmacology, anthropology, law, dentistry, education, geography, and even a few representing sociology and social work.

Their counterparts in the Global South tend to be located in academic institutions with multidisciplinary teams, including experts mainly from the field of health. Moreover, child welfare research was also found to be included in broader fields of studies, such as in the university departments of economics, development studies, pediatrics, and agriculture, where the main subject might be poverty alleviation. The authors of the report I am referring to seem to be inspired by this interdisciplinary collaboration of researchers in the field of child welfare: "The involvement of individuals from different disciplines in child research provided an opportunity to make use of different insights on African children and also on research more generally" (CODESRIA, 2007:50).

CODESRIA's conclusion regarding the analysis of the African research notes that:

"... it is important to shift the balance and invest in understanding the lives and situation ofthe normal African children in order to establish standards of well-being that have relevance and meaning in the context of the African child". (CODESRIA, 2007:45)

The NGOs walk hand-in-hand with the research institutions from the Global North, in their way of spending resources and defining the agenda. As international watch dogs their focus is of course on vulnerable children; the children at risk. Their job is both to be close to and support children affected by different kinds of disasters and to advocate and educate children in normal situations as well as children at risk. The research that is connected to this world of Global Action mostly relies on big surveys and small evaluation projects. NGOs usually work closely with government bodies and stakeholders in the communities and thus have an opportunity to influence policy development for the children, at least in the short term.

There are few, if any, connections between these kinds of projects and local or international universities or research centers, while the research reports are generally not published in international peer-reviewed journals; the results remain with the donors. The results are also owned by the donor, which means that the researchers involved get no academic credit for their work to add to their personal CVs to advance their academic careers. The highly influential Global Action agencies, such as UNICEF, have developed a quite advanced system for defining scientific concepts and disseminating social methods concerning the practice of child welfare/child protection around the world. This is often done with a qualified network of international experts, recruited from both practical professions and academic environments. But how often do these important steps become part of the academic discourse?

When considering the publication of child welfare research, researchers from the Global North are obviously in a winning position. Quite a lot of the research is financed by grants allocated to the funding of PhD and Master theses "...which then end up lying on the shelves of the dean's office" (Mweru & Ng'asike, 2007:39). Mweru and Ng'asike (2007:39) conclude that "...data generated by students is never used to address SSA children's problems, thus research funds are wasted". Moreover, Global South researchers go a step further and ask their Global North colleagues why the scientific work carried out by researchers in the South is ignored by the academic communities in the developed countries? "The only exception is when these research works have been carried out on instructions from individuals in the North" (ibid, p. 38). Subsequently, if local researchers from the Global South are to have a chance to be published in peer-reviewed journals, their work has to be connected to their colleagues in the Global North. And considering the money spent on research programs, we have to conclude that the results are far from acceptable. Over a 10-year period, the average number of published articles is ten per year. Health and medicine journals have a dominant position; a third of the articles were published in journals covering these disciplines. There were very few articles published in social science journals or journals specializing in child welfare issues (Mweru & Ng'asike, 2007).

Summary

To summarize the analysis, let us update Table 1 and complete it with answers to the key questions presented at the beginning (see Table 2).

Table 2: Child Welfare Research – Risks an Challenges

Agency Origin	Material Resources	Def. of Research agenda	Int. Publ. of Results	Policy Implem.	Risk
Global North	YES	YES	YES	No	EXPLOITATION
Global Action	YES	YES	YES	No	COLONIZATION
Global South	YES	YES	YES	No	SUBJUGATION

1. There is no doubt about the power relationship between the Global North and the Global South. The material resources for child welfare research are distributed from the North to the South. The South invests very few resources on its own. We understand this inequality in resource distribution from the South as a consequence of the fact that the nations in sub-Sahara are among the poorest in the world. So, in order to categorize the answer to the question of resource contribution as "yes" or "no," the answer for the Global North is "yes," for Global Action it is "yes," and for the Global South it is "no."
2. It does not follow that an uneven resource distribution is dominating and influencing the areas of research studies. But we found evidence that the research agenda is determined by the main donors, regardless of whether they are governments, research foundations, universities or international agencies. So if our question concerns the influence on the direction of research on children, the answer for the Global North would be "yes"; for Global Action, "yes"; and for the Global South, "no."
3. When considering the publication of research results, we found remarkably little evidence of the research, at least in terms of the money spent and the number of scientific articles published. Local researchers have to collaborate with colleagues from the North to be published in the peer-reviewed journals of the North. Global Action research seems to be hidden away in the desks of the donors.
4. Finally, with regard to the implications of the results, we recommended a larger presence of Global North researchers in the implementation of child welfare re-

search. We are aware that this is a universal problematic phenomenon. Implementation in Sub-Saharan Africa seems to have been monopolized by agencies outside the universities, the Global Action donors. Global South researchers seem to have the same kind of implementation problems as those in the Global North despite objectively being closer to the local civil society than even the Global Action agencies. A possible explanation is that being without a material resource base for research, not being able to influence the content during research project planning, and not participating in the international publication of the research results, makes them outsiders with respect to policy implementation. There is a term that well describes the position of the researchers from sub-Sahara: *Subjugated.*

Conclusion

We are returning to my initial statements. I claimed that there is a risk that the research from the Global North subjects local resources to exploitation
– by using superior material resources,
– by monopolizing the research questions,
– by stealing the results to promote their own careers, and
– by neglecting practice and policy implementation.
I think the review supports this statement, and we can add "exploitation" to the list of risks.

As far as the researchers in the agencies of Global Action are concerned, they seem to be in the same position as their colleagues at the universities of the Global North – they sit on the resources and the research agenda – but we found no academic dialogue concerning the results in scientific publications. They are closely connected to the local governments and stakeholders, so whatever the results of the evaluations, the Global Action researchers implement (or should implement) their results as policies. But due to a lack of transparency, there is an obvious risk of colonization through Global Action (see Hessle, 2007).

The Way Forward – Three Appeals

Research within this area is required, and it should be designed, conducted and reported by researchers who are locally recruited. It is obvious through this review that the basic conditions for research production are far from acceptable in the Global South (at least in Sub-Saharan Africa). Adding to these shortcomings is the migration of researchers from the South to the North, leaving the Global South with insufficient scientific capacity. In other cases, those who return after postgraduate studies in the North are overburdened with teaching responsibilities at the university, leaving little or no time for their own research. It is urgent that we contribute to their scientific capacity-building in the area of child welfare research.

And why should not social work/social welfare be the main contributors, given that our subject is academic and is practice- and policy-oriented? Being close to children is one of the fundamental traits of our profession. Why are so few of us involved in research-focused capacity-building in the Global South?

Below are some practical recommendations based on the analysis so far, when considering child welfare research and practice in the Global South. They could be summarized in three appeals:

1. *Develop a critical mass of child welfare researchers in the Global South.* One researcher in a university department is not enough. An optimal research environment needs enough researchers in a unit to establish, preserve, and expand the conditions for research in a research area of interest! A critical mass of researchers would be able to establish networks with colleagues and other research groups, domestically and internationally. They would also be able to attract new cadres of young researchers. Related needs include communication qualifications in ICT and foreign languages to stay up-to-date with the development of discipline and in touch with the scientific community at large. Also important is access to competence in qualitative and quantitative methodology, scientific theory and the reporting of results in scientific articles, as well as participation in regular seminars for discussing research projects at various stages of completion. An optimal research environment has competent teachers at the undergraduate level, enabling students to learn the conditions for research, and the significance of research for their own institution and the world at large. This could mean that students and teachers become able to visualize an academic career at their own institution of learning.

2. *Establish peer mentorship between the Global North and the Global South.* It follows from the first appeal that much support is required in child welfare research for the establishment of optimal research conditions in the academic world of the Global South. Besides the need for material support, the need for mentorship and coaching is obvious. Mentorship is not a new concept in the Global South; it is practiced among all actors that we have mentioned here. We should also emphasize a special need for peer mentors with a focus on publishing research articles.

3. *Establish collaboration between the knowledge banks of the Global North, the Global South, and Global Action.* It is obvious that Global Action researchers are more successful than their colleagues in the universities of the North and South in implementing their results as social policy, which might be partly explained by their closeness to the field of practice and the stakeholders. Even

if the research from Global Action is less subject to critical academic discussions, there is much to learn from their involvement with children at risk. An increased effort in supporting a holistic view of children, which the Global South advocates, could be a step towards acknowledging the local knowledge bank of the Global South.

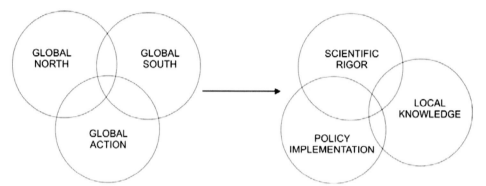

Figure 1: Consideration in child welfare – Resources für Development Research

Final words

What has been presented could be considered an example of circular reasoning: Researchers from the Global South are subjected to exploitation by their colleagues in the Global North, as I have discovered in my review. This criticism may be unfair, because I am aware that there are many examples of successful collaborations between Global North and Global South researchers. But I still cannot ignore the cries for help from my colleagues in the South: Support us, don't subjugate us!

References

Axford, N. (2012). Children and global social policy: Exploring the impact in international governmental organizations. *International Journal of Social Welfare*, 21,53–65.

The Council for the Development of Social Science Research in Africa (CODESRIA). (2007) In S. Hessle (Ed.). *Bridging Global North and Global South in child welfare and child protection research*. Stockholm, Sweden: Stockholm University.

Hessle, S. (Ed). (2007). *Bridging Global North and Global South in child welfare and child protection research* (Report to SAREC on the Peer–Mentor Network Symposium). Stockholm, Sweden: Stockholm University.

Macassa, G., Hallqvist, J., & Lynch, J. W. (2011). Inequalities in child mortality in sub-Saharan Africa: A social epidemiologic framework. *African Journal of Health Sciences*, 18, 14–26.

Mweru, M., & Ng'asike, J. (2007). Mechanisms and priorities in child research funding in Sub-Saharan Africa. In S. Hessle (Ed.) *Bridging Global North and Global South in child welfare and child protection research* (pp. 34–43) Stockholm, Sweden: Stockholm University.

Tostensen, A., Stokke, H., Trygged, S., & Halvorsen, K. (2011). *Supporting child rights – synthesis of lessons learned in four countries* (CMI Commissioned Reports, No. 10016). Bergen, Norway.

Author

Sven Hessle

Professor of Social work – (Chair Emeritus)

Department of Social Work at Stockholm University, S-106 91 Stockholm, Sweden

Research areas: Numerous research projects within the field of Family and Child welfare in poverty areas in different parts of the world as well as International social work

The Welfare State System Confronted with the Human Rights Principle

Hans Kolstad

Abstract

The paper discusses two different conceptions of the welfare principle. In the traditional way of understanding welfare, something is granted to individuals from the state or authorities. Welfare understood in this way becomes relative to political doctrines, ideologies or parties. Facing the different challenges which this conception of welfare raises, the paper proposes a conception of welfare understood as an integral part of human rights. According to this view, each human being has fundamental human rights, which are essential to one's personal life world. In this paper I try to clarify which these human rights are, and address the relation between human rights and welfare rights. Finally, I draw some conclusions regarding the necessity of introducing a system of unconditional basic income guarantees and the importance of local solidarity and communicative action as a condition for citizens to actively claim their fundamental welfare rights, stressing each person's role in shaping a future welfare policy and his/her own future life.

Introduction

The Social-Democratic Welfare State Model, which is known from the Netherlands and the Nordic countries Denmark, Finland, Sweden and Norway, is based upon the principle of universalism, with provisions that cover everybody, giving access to benefits and services based on citizenship. Such a welfare state is said to provide a relatively high degree of citizen autonomy, limiting reliance on family and market (Ferragina & Seeleib-Kaiser, 2011). However, the principle is one thing, how it is practiced is a different matter. In at least Denmark and Norway there is today a growing tendency to limit welfare rights normally granted by the state. Thus, on several points the Nordic welfare state system is not as liberal or even as universal as it would seem. There are exceptions to it, with groups of people today being excluded from parts of the national welfare system. Those people experience a limitation on their citizen autonomy.

Opposing this tendency, I will argue that the welfare concept is an integral part of human rights. According to this view, each human being has some fundamental rights, which are essential to his or her personal life world and hence crucial in order to understand the idea of welfare.

My point of view differs from theories of earlier philosophers. I do not see the welfare system as consisting *merely* as a means to close the gap between the poor and the rich, which very often has been an effect. On the other hand, I neither agree with the American political historian Alan Ryan, who writes that the modern welfare state does not set out to make the poor richer and the rich poorer, but to assist people in compensating for future sickness when enjoying good health and to put money aside for unemployment when working (Ryan, 2012a). I disagree with this understanding of the welfare concept because I think economic factors constitute an essential part of this understanding.

What I will argue is that the welfare concept has a deeper meaning and a more overriding importance than equalizing economic differences between people in society. In short, welfare does not mean to close the gap between the poor and the rich because this *feels right*, but because welfare primarily is a question of basic human rights *pertaining* to everybody as equal members of a universal mankind. In this paper, I will pursue this deeper or overriding meaning of the welfare concept.

Objections raised against the traditional welfare concept

In the traditional way of understanding welfare, something is granted to individuals from the state or authorities. This understanding reflects a socially just allocation of common benefits in society, guided by the principles of distributive justice. However, welfare understood in this way often becomes relative to different political doctrines, ideologies or parties. An example illustrates this point: Recently, the biggest political party in Denmark (Left, Denmark's Liberal Party) has stated that they are ready to renounce their adherence to the United Nations Convention on the Rights of the Child so that Denmark should not be "forced" to give citizenship to children of immigrants, even if these children are born and raised in Denmark, in cases where this is in the interest of Denmark (or the interest of the Left, Denmark's Liberal Party) for security reasons. Thus, these children are left without the protection of a national citizenship, which might be a serious handicap for them.

Such a conception of the welfare idea, where welfare rights become a question of short-term political interests of a minority of the citizens, is reprehensible in many ways. A general issue is that such a system treats people as passive recipients of welfare benefits. The question of what these rights are and to whom they should be allocated, is not decided by the citizens themselves but certain minority groups within the state. The problem is that if modern welfare provides what it pretends to do, a degree of citizen autonomy and the nature of this autonomy, remains outside the sphere of influence of the citizens themselves. This limitation on the individual's right to decide over his/her own life would be seen as normal under some political regimes. The paradox is that this also takes place in countries which understand themselves as enlightened democracies.

Among more specific objections raised against the traditional welfare concept, I will mention a few which can be illustrated by certain tendencies in the Nordic countries today.

The first issue concerns the administration of welfare rights. Of the total amount used by the state on welfare issues, an increasing share is spent on the administration of these rights, on research concerning the efficiency of different welfare programmes, on the organization of the programmes, or on monitoring citizens to whom the welfare benefits are allocated. The result is a high-cost welfare system which risks undermining the tax payers' will to fund it.

However, this issue is not only a question of budgets. It also points to a democratic challenge: In the twentieth century, opponents of the welfare state have expressed apprehension about the creation of a large bureaucracy required to administer it, possibly driven by self-interest and of a desire to strengthen its own position within the state, and which in many cases is operating outside the democratic monitoring of the welfare services (Ryan, 2012b).

Another tendency which can be witnessed today, for instance in Denmark, is the tendency to marginalize a growing part of the citizens by excluding them from fundamental welfare rights. An example of this is the introduction of the model of workfare instead of welfare. Under workfare, recipients have to meet certain participation requirements to continue receiving their welfare benefits. These requirements are often a combination of activities intended to improve the recipient's job prospects (such as training, rehabilitation, and work experience) and those defined as contributing to society (such as unpaid or low-paid work). One objection raised against this model is that it tends to keep people in poverty, so-called working poverty, through low wages and lack of education, and by directing the participants into "low-grade, high-turnover jobs" (Peck, 2003:83). It even creates new poverty as programme participants (e.g. in the secondary sector) obtain jobs at the expense of other workers and in this way push them out of the labour marked, causing endemic problems of displacement and substitution

(Solow, 1998). Another objection is that the regulatory project that is workfare functions in a compulsory and harsh way by "playing a part in shaping norms of labour-market socialization and participation" (Peck, 2003:82). "Workfare strategies are becoming normalized as a means of enforcing labour-market participation in a climate increasingly dominated by underemployment, low pay, work insecurity, and low-grade service employment" (Peck, 2003:81). In short, the objective of workfare strategies is not citizen autonomy, but rather a sophisticated form of citizen slavery. Finally, these programmes lead to absolute poverty for people who cannot find work within a fixed period of time: They are reduced to live on a strict minimum of social assistance, and in many cases not even that. In times where work is hard to find, these programmes tend to create new economic and social problems instead of helping to resolve them.

A report from Statistics Norway points out that in 2009 9.5 % of the Norwegian population was considered poor, i.e. about half a million people (Kirkeberg, Epland & Normann, 2012). Poverty is of course a relative concept and must not here be understood in an absolute sense as deprivation of basic human needs, such as food, water, sanitation, clothing, etc. Relative poverty is defined contextually as economic inequality in the community or society where people live. Relative poverty measures are used as official poverty rates by the European Union, UNICEF and the OEDC. The main poverty measurement used in the OECD and the European Union is based on "economic distance", which means a level of income set at 60 % of the median household income (Grødem, 2012; Kirkeberg et al., 2012).

Let me give an example to illustrate the poverty problem in the Nordic countries by looking into the case of children under 18 years. According to the United Nations Convention on the Rights of the Child, "all children have a right to an adequate standard of living regardless of their parents' financial situation. Children have a right to equal educational opportunities and safety, but also to play and recreation" (Vidje, 2013:75). However, reality is sometimes different. "There are children who grow up in poverty, have poor health and education, lack recreational activities and live in more precarious conditions than other children. A deepening poverty, with increased gaps between different groups of children, leads to children being excluded and forced to grow up at the margins of society" (Vidje, 2013:75). Children in the Nordic countries are not the most vulnerable ones, but there are clear signs that the gap between poor and rich children is increasing. The above mentioned report from Statistics Norway concludes that in the period from 2007 to 2009 8 % of all children under 18 years in Norway were living in families with income below the median household income (Kirkeberg et al., 2012). This is a significant increase since the period from 1997 to 2001, where the percentage of children living in poor families was 2 % (Kirkeberg et al., 2012). A report on poverty and social exclusion in Norway made by an independent and multidisciplinary research foundation focusing on social welfare and trade policy in Norway (Fafo Institute for Labour and Social Research) concludes that the percentage of poverty in Norway has been relatively constant over the last years, with a tendency to increase for children under 18 years (Grødem, 2012).

In Denmark, during the period from 2007 to 2010, 10 % of children under 18 years were living in relative poverty (TÁRKI Social Research Institute, 2010), whereas the number is significantly higher in Sweden (about 14 % in 2009) (Fløtten, 2013). A Finnish report shows that poverty among children under 18 years has increased from 5 % in 1995 to 12.5 % in 2005 (cited in Fløtten, 2013:14). Even if not high compared to child poverty elsewhere in OECD, the percentage tends to increase, and the rise *after the mid*-1980s and later has been more pronounced in some Nordic countries than the OECD average (Fløtten, 2013). It should also be noted that if we exclude the economic support given to families with children in Sweden, about 25 % of the children households would have an income below 60 percent of the median household income in the country (Fløtten, 2013).

The above-mentioned report on poverty and social exclusion in Norway identifies several inherent problems in the Norwegian welfare system concerning state versus municipal governance of welfare projects. One of them concerns frustration about grants from the Norwegian state meant to fight poverty and social exclusion becoming linked to a fragmentation of efforts both at the municipal and state level, "in the sense that several state bodies administer separate grants targeted in areas that are closely related. The reason for this pattern is that different state bodies want municipalities to implement targeted projects in 'their' area" (Grødem, 2012:16). Another problem is that the needs "the municipality may have, is normally not seen as relevant" (Grødem, 2012:17), though what the municipalities actually want, is "to apply for grants rooted in local needs" (Grødem, 2012:16). A third problem is that programmes offered by the state do not involve long-term commitment: Grants are limited in time, in some cases to only one year, and moreover they are awarded only late in the year (Grødem, 2012). According to the report, many municipalities have emphasized the need for more time to develop innovative projects. Instead, they continuously receive new projects, even if they ask "for the means to develop and strengthen what they already have" (Grødem, 2012:17). These objections point to a problem concerning the relations between state control and local requirements, and raise the more fundamental problem of the role of local democracy in welfare policy.

Welfare rights versus human rights

With the modern welfare state, the right to welfare or what is called welfare rights – have become a part of our vocabulary. The question is what kind of rights does this imply?

First, what do we mean by welfare? If it is true that the word "welfare" now has entered into so many and different combinations that hardly anyone reflects on its meaning, it is no longer a clear concept. Welfare has many elements emanating from a variety of disciplines and approaches, including economics, psychology, sociology, and philosophy, which can all be clearly defined. Understanding welfare in terms of just one discipline would still be to ignore central aspects of the concept.

In the following part, I will concentrate on the term welfare as used in connection with the concept of the state. Here, welfare implies a clear role for the state with regard to helping members of society towards a good life.

However, this can be understood in two opposite ways, depending on how we understand the concept of state.

Understood according to a top-down approach, welfare is for many economists mainly understood as "connected to [the] individual's perception and utility of the use of income" (Greve, 2008:53).

Or more precisely, the concept of welfare "includes the understanding of welfare in terms of economic aspects based upon the amount of money available for spending irrespective of how it is used" (Greve, 2008:68). This amounts to say that welfare depends on how much money each person has left after deducting taxes and public dues. The role of the state is here synonymous with the reduction of taxes and dues, and consists of the income transfer from the state to the individual through a reduction of the state's own income. This view serves as a basis for an extreme liberalist conception of the state and the reduction of its activities to the strict minimum requirements.

An obvious objection to this understanding of the concept welfare state is that it presupposes that people have an actual income, which is not always the case, and that the income is sufficient after deducting taxes and dues. Which is not always the case.

Subsequently, an opposite understanding of the welfare state is based on a bottom-up approach. Here, welfare is understood as the actual delivery of services and income transfers from the state to people who cannot afford to cover their basic material and social needs or do not have an income at all.

In my opinion, the first understanding does not concern welfare, but well-being, which is something quite different. Only the latter definition concerns proper welfare as it sees welfare as something shared by all citizens, and since it tries to respond to the inequalities in society. Well-being is on the other hand an individualistic phenomenon, emphasizing the individual as something subjective.

Therefore, I suggest the following definition of welfare when used in connection with the word state: Welfare is *the highest possible access to common economic resources for each citizen in the form of a guaranteed minimum income to avoid living in poverty and with the possibility of ensuring the individual a good life.*

The last part of the definition is important. It points to other values than mere economic values as part of the welfare state concept. Which are these values?

In the discussion of welfare today, a broader conception of welfare than mere economic values is often highlighted. Very often this aspect of welfare is summarized in statements that welfare includes more subjective features, including the individual's happiness, well-being or satisfaction (Greve, 2008). Still, these concepts are very vague and difficult to measure or even to define. Moreover, they tend to stress the individualistic part of the citizen's life, when welfare in my mind should focus on what is common between individuals.

In order to clarify this point, I want to base the welfare analysis on the concept of human rights. I think that a broader understanding of welfare than a mere economic one is an important element in the perception of the nature of welfare societies, and that a proper understanding of the concept of human rights may provide a foundation for such a broad welfare concept.

From a formal point of view, human rights are based on an idea of a universal brotherhood of human beings whose existence the very notion of human rights is supposed to promote. More specifically, a right indicates the disposition of an individual to realize this aim. This aspect of the human rights is what makes them truly human, i.e. what gives them their human meaning. In this sense, they are inclusive rights as opposed to exclusive rights, which separate individuals from each other, and accordingly only claimed by individuals.

This indicates an understanding of the concept "human rights" that emphasizes participation in a universal human nature. With "human nature", I understand the living and intuitive experience of being bound by an inalienable, interdependent and indivisible interconnectedness to other persons. Rights belong to the common human nature as such, and not to the individual: It is only by being part of a common human nature you can claim human rights, not by virtue of your individual interests. Or to put it differently: The subject of human rights is not the concrete individual, but the community consciousness within each individual.

Let us then think of human rights as embedded in the idea of a human community within each other, consisting of the inalienable, interdependent and indivisible interconnectedness that constitutes human nature, and which we want to realize in society. Such a notion of human rights implies several *conditions*, which then become *particular* human rights, including the right of each person to develop a universal, inalienable, interdependent and indivisible human community consciousness along with others (see for instance the United Nations Universal Declaration of Human Rights (1948), article 3: "Everyone has the right to life"), one particularly important condition is a formal duty which can be summed up as follows: Human rights condition that people take responsibility for their actions and thoughts in order to realize the universal human brotherhood. Neither an obligation to act nor insanity can claim to be human rights. Human rights presuppose a certain order in the society which permits people to take responsibility for their thoughts and action towards each other and their consequences, or at least that society should face the challenge of adapting itself to such an order. On an individual level, this duty, which prevails in every circumstance of life, may be transformed into a particular human right and a very material human right indeed: The right to be responsible for our thoughts and action towards the common human nature is the second human right. From the latter I think it is possible to deduce certain other fundamental human rights as conditions for realizing the inner community consciousness within each person.

In the first place, in order to be capable of taking responsibility for their action and thoughts people should be free to do so. From this deduction, *liberty* seems to be a fundamental human right (see the United Nations Universal Declaration of Human Rights (1948), article 3: "Everyone has the right to liberty").

The next human right is a social and economic one: In order to share the responsibility, people should share necessary material means and social services. Human rights presuppose a society of economic equals, which means that the same share of social and economic means on an individual level, i.e. the same right to food, clothing, shelter, medical care and necessary social services. Hence *equality* should be a fundamental human right (see the United Nations Universal Declaration of Human Rights (1948), Article 25: "Everyone has the right to a standard of living adequate for health and well-being, including food, clothing, housing, medical care and necessary social services").

Another human right concerns the law. In order for people to take responsibility, it is necessary with an objective application of the law. This means that everybody should be entitled to a fair process and for offenders to receive a fair assessment and rehabilitation into society. *Equity* or *justice* would be the fifth human right (see the United Nations Universal Declaration of Human Rights (1948), article 8: "Everyone has the right to justice").

Besides material human rights, we also have immaterial human rights. Formally understood, they can be summarized as the right to a meaningful life. The most fundamental components of this human right are: 1) The right to develop our mental or spiritual powers and skills. 2) The right to realize values outside ourselves, i.e. the possibility of engaging in activities that will be beneficial to others. I consider these human rights as perfect rights in the sense described above (see Seligman, 2002).

Earlier, I claimed that human rights belong to human nature itself, which is identical to the inner community consciousness in us, and not merely to individuals. At the same time, human rights can be regarded as a codification on the individual level of certain presuppositions linked to human nature, in order to bring about an inner community consciousness within each person. Therefore, human rights are considered *absolute, indivisible, universal* and *inalienable* or *necessary* in the strict sense of the word. When being absolute with no exception they are called perfect rights. Human rights that depend on different circumstances linked to a certain group of people or a country, I call imperfect, circumstantial or adventitious rights, according to a traditional philosophical classification of human rights. These rights are human rights in the sense that they under certain conditions contribute to realizing a universal, inalienable, interdependent and indivisible human community consciousness.

This analysis of human rights provides us with a basis for a better understanding of what is meant by welfare rights. The relationship between human rights and welfare rights can be illustrated by an understanding of welfare rights as decisions or provisions from the state that are required to realize fundamental human rights. In other words: A welfare state is a state that guarantees the necessary system of laws for the realization of those human rights that I have called perfect rights. Hence, welfare rights are the same thing as human rights – only considered from another point of view: Human rights are the ideals which provide substance to welfare rights, whereas welfare rights represent the materialization of legally based human rights at a certain moment in a specific country. Human rights should be considered an idea of welfare rights, and welfare rights the same idea put into practice.

However, a useful understanding of the welfare concept should not be restricted to include only material goods or services. The concept of human rights as understood above could likewise serve as a broadening of the welfare concept, where certain qualities of life are added to the material rights. Thus the welfare concept becomes tied to human rights in a double sense (i.e. both as the realization of human rights in daily politics and by including immaterial human rights, like the right to live a meaningful life).

Here, a philosophical problem should be noted concerning the legitimate use of the word "rights" in connection with welfare rights. In an article, the American jurist Tushnet (2004) argues that the word rights should only be used when somebody has a correlative duty with regard to the rights-holder: "I note, only to put aside," he says, "the objection made by some philosophers that it is wrong to describe the provision of social welfare as a right because, in their view, we should speak of *rights* only when we can identify an individual or class of individuals who have a correlative duty with respect to the rights-holder (usually, a duty to refrain from interfering with the exercise of the right)" (p. 2). This objection concerns both the word human rights and welfare rights. In each case the answer is the same: The state or the commonwealth is considered to be the "debtor" for dispensing the rights. It is responsible for the realization of the rights and enabling the citizens to access them. "I believe that these philosophical objections are misplaced," Tushnet in the same article asserts, "in part because as a matter of linguistic fact people do use the word *rights* to refer to the provision of social welfare, and in part because I see no insurmountable barrier to placing a duty on the public generally to provide sufficient resources for each person to realize the relevant social welfare rights" (p. 2; see also Fabre, 2000).

Furthermore, the recognition of welfare rights as an aspect of human rights refutes the objection made against welfare rights, i.e. that the right to shelter or the right to a minimum subsistence do not belong in a constitution and are accordingly not judicially enforceable. The argument presupposes that constitutional rights must be enforceable in the courts (Tushnet, 2004). However, human rights have been incorporated in many constitutions. Consequently, the definition of welfare rights, as proposed here, could serve as an argument for recognizing constitutional welfare rights.

Another consequence of my argument is that welfare rights as human rights have to be understood in a universal sense. Like human rights, welfare rights can be called perfect rights. Consequently, they are much more than a simple question of the individual's well-being or happiness. They concern the universal human aspect of each individual's life, where each person is entitled to the same living standards and fundamental values based on their common human nature.

Welfare rights could also be what I call imperfect rights. They may be accompanied by special provisions in order to meet certain requirements in a community. They then depend on these conditions and are not absolute in the sense of being perfect rights, i.e. they are not universal within a society, but relative, targeting a particular group of people or aimed at preventing a deterioration of society.

How to realize welfare rights

The traditional welfare concept and the problems that it raises, is based on the idea that welfare is something granted to somebody from the state or politicians as a result of good will. This is illustrated by the history of the concept: Originally, welfare issues were a question of charity given by rich to poor people, with the church and volunteer agencies providing the bulk the aid. In this perspective, the right to welfare could be questioned. Even when an organized system of state welfare provision for the first time was introduced in Europe (particularly in Germany) in the middle of the 19th century, being the origin of the modern European welfare state, this programme was something that the state *could* do, and was not obliged to do because the citizens had the right to the allocations. This understanding of the welfare concept was reflected in the principle that governmental benefits represented a privilege and not a right.

As a result of the understanding of the concept of welfare as a human right it follows that welfare allocations have to be understood as proper rights, and that these rights belong to the citizens by virtue of them being part of a universal human nature. Subsequently, it is wrong to ask how the state can *provide* the citizens with welfare goods or services. Instead, we should ask: How can citizens *claim* welfare benefits?

One solution would be a system of unconditional basic income guarantee (citizen's income), a system of social security in which all citizens or residents of a country regularly receive an unconditional sum of money from the government or some other public institution, in addition to any ordinary income. This idea goes back to the Renaissance humanists. It has been revived by philosophers in both the 18th and 19th centuries. Today it has become an issue in several countries in the world. Without going deeply into the matter, I think such a system of guarantees could be one solution to many of the problems that people have endured in the aftermath of the global financial crisis of 2007 2008. The system of a basic income guarantee could also be a way to limit the expensive bureaucratic system that has become necessary in order to organize welfare in the classical sense of the word.

Another way to solve the problem of how to ensure welfare rights for those who are in need of economic help would be to strengthen the awareness of the citizens at the local level about claiming welfare rights as part of their human rights. Here, we deal with democracy in the proper sense of the word, i.e. with local, participatory democracy or democracy at the grassroots level (and not representative democracy).

Democracy at the grassroots level enables people to participate in the government of public affairs in a much more direct way than what is conceivable in society at large. In order to be efficient, it must be based on solidarity and communicative action between local citizens. At the same time, participatory democracy educates the citizens to political life. Finally, by admitting the citizens local decision-making, the politicians, who should be the local people's representatives, also educate themselves. By educating the individual, you also educate his or her representatives.

Participatory democracy at a grassroots level does not only take into account welfare in general, but also focus on real needs among those who depend most on a strategy for local solidarity and communicative action. In other words, it is based on a bottom-up approach to the question of how we realize welfare rights.

One way of establishing an efficient welfare policy is to involve the individuals themselves and not only their representatives. The principle of this idea is that the people affected by human rights deprivation are best able to reinvigorate the human rights discourse, unleashing its energy and transformative power. It is not up to the politicians – even not the local ones – to decide what the welfare needs are, and who are the worthy recipients. As a matter of fact they in many cases do not see the needy ones, according to the aforementioned report on poverty and social exclusion in Norway (Grødem, 2012), which requires the people themselves to take charge in order to enlighten their representatives or politicians about their real needs. The same report emphasizes the necessity of the welfare system to heed the local voices and concludes that this does not always happen in Norway (Grødem, 2012).

One condition for such a programme is a local platform where people can meet and decide their requirements. An active and local participatory democracy based on solidarity and communicative action would represent such a platform. Another condition is the possibility for people to become aware of their rights and of the importance of active participation in claiming fundamental human or welfare rights. A third condition is the introduction of a progressive learning process where agents of change (or mentors/monitors) may act as sources of information, learning people to identify, analyse, and document their needs. This process could enable identification and analysis of causes and symptoms regarding violations of fundamental rights, the identification of *poverty causes* and effects of poverty, and help designing ways to secure the sustainability of the community as a viable, creative and caring society within a human rights framework.

An important step in this direction has been achieved by the organization the People's Movement for Human Rights Learning (PDHRE), which was founded by Shulamith Koenig in New York in 1988 in an effort to respond to the demand for Human Rights Learning at the grassroots level in today's world Here, the most important project is the idea of human rights cities. This concept is based on the metaphor of traffic regulation and the comparative advantage of those, she writes,

who know the 'rules of the road'. In a perfect world, villages, towns and cities would have in place a regulated traffic system and red, green and yellow traffic lights would function according to a thorough analysis that considers the actual needs of the people, thus providing safety for the young and old, women and men, youth and children of all religions and cultural affiliations. These traffic regulations enable humanity to travel the roads as they choose, by foot, or by any other means of transportation. In reality, people in many villages, towns and cities of the world move on the roads of their lives without being instructed about the traffic regulations and how these enable them to move safely to destinations of their choice, maintaining their dignity without being hurt or hurting others. [...] This project seeks to do the equivalent of allowing every village, town and city to enable all people to learn these traffic regulations, or, in our case, to know and own human rights as a way of walking in dignity. [...] The aim is for people to belong in society in dignity in community with others, taking the roads for a better future. Our goal is for people to walk the roads of their communities recognizing the green, yellow and red lights of the Universal Declaration of Human Rights, of the rule of law, of economic and social justice, in sum, to enjoy life in a community where human rights are respected, where all women and men actively participate in the decisions that affect their daily lives and work to overcome fear and impoverishment. [...] A further aim pursued is to advance human security, access to food, clean water, housing, education, healthcare and work at liveable wages, where all these resources are equitably shared with all citizens not as a gift, but as the full realization of human rights. Without owning this knowledge, people find themselves exchanging equality for survival. The question we want to answer is: How do people own this knowledge and act upon it? The human rights framework provides us with ratified guidelines of a well-designed way of life for a heavily populated world; it enables us to travel free from fear and free from want, as was the road from slavery to freedom. Such a road for the future can be travelled by people with newly gained practical knowledge about living in a human rights-based society. This is what this project aims to demonstrate by designing with people an ongoing process of learning human rights as a way of life (2014:12).

The human rights cities project understands human rights as synonymous with welfare rights in the sense I have explained above. It is based on a bottom-up approach where the people themselves participate in claiming their human or welfare rights, and which is based on the premise "that all people wish and hope for social and economic justice, to move from charity to dignity" (Koenig, 2011, para. 3). Moreover, the project also addresses all those "working on the issues of women, children, workers, indigenous peoples, poverty, education, food, water, housing, healthcare, environment and conflict resolution, and non-affiliated inhabitants, joined in the learning and reflecting about human rights as significant to the decision-making process" (Koenig, 2011, para. 5). In her presentation at a meeting at the United Nations on Human Rights, as part of discussions on the Post-2015 Development Agenda, 9 December 2013, she states:

Having analyzed the limited reach of human rights education – hardly 5 % of the world population in the last 20 years – several civil society organizations moved to define this necessary process as 'human rights learning'. It is an ongoing, never-ending, process of integrating the learning, dialogue and discussion about human rights as relevant to people's daily concerns, to become cross-cutting through all issues attended by all sectors of society as a powerful tool for action and a meaningful strategy for development. It is also a strategy of self empowerment that is consistent with the dignity of women and men of all ages and that takes into account the different segments of society to learn, know and own human rights and to participate meaningfully in the decisions that determine their lives, and thus to belong to a community in dignity in with others (2013:1).

Though the project underlines the need for teaching people to claim their human or welfare rights and what these rights are, the objective of the project is to make individuals aware of their human rights and assist them in claiming their rights, in order to establish a more efficient welfare policy. In other words, the project combines learning about human rights and participatory democracy as a necessary condition for an efficient welfare policy.

Such a programme emphasizes the importance of moving on from formal perfect rights to more definite and specific imperfect or circumstantial rights, which have to be effectuated in order to establish a true welfare policy. This, I think, can only be achieved by raising the awareness of the citizens at the local level.

An active local commitment would be important for the welfare rights question in a state where welfare rights are not acknowledged. However, this would also be important in developed welfare states in order to adjust them to new or more complex conditions than those addressed by the perfect human rights. This would respond to a lack of awareness among politicians who try to undermine actual welfare rights, a challenge which we face even in the context of the social-democratic welfare model of the Nordic countries.

In my opinion, the only way to implement a coherent and humane welfare system would be to combine the two solutions proposed above, i.e. the idea of a basic income guarantee and the idea of an active local engagement at the grassroots level. While the first implies realizing the fundamental social and economic human rights in the absolute sense of the word, i.e. as perfect human rights, the latter responds to the need for fulfilling economic welfare rights that target a particular group of individuals or particularly vulnerable people (i.e. welfare rights reflecting what I have called imperfect or circumstantial human rights). Together, these two solutions may resolve the problem that we face due to the increasingly more complicated structures of poverty and the effects of poverty in today's society. At the same time, an active, local participatory democracy would be a powerful tool for reinvigorating other perfect human rights (e.g. the right to liberty, justice or equity, as well as the right to live a meaningful life) than merely the social and economic ones. The necessity of transforming these other perfect human rights as well as circumstantial human rights into welfare rights makes an active participatory democracy based on local solidarity and communicative action a fundamental principle in practical politics.

Conclusion

In this paper, I have presented another approach to the welfare concept than the traditional or almost classical understanding of welfare. I have based this approach on several objections raised against the traditional concept of welfare, stressing the tendency in the Nordic countries to move towards a system that has become exclusive and not inclusive, and the relatively high percent of people in the Nordic countries that today is defined as poor. This situation is particularly grave with regard to children, and presents a danger for the future democracy.

In order to propose a way out of the dilemma, I have decided to rethink the welfare concept as an aspect of human rights, i.e. rights that belong to the people as human beings, and which consequently must be claimed instead of granted from politicians with a superficial notion of the welfare concept, causing it to be misunderstood and misused.

In an effort to reinvigorate an efficient welfare policy, I have proposed a basic income guarantee and an active participatory democracy at the grassroots level, stressing the necessity of local solidarity and of communicative action as a means for the citizens to actively claim fundamental welfare rights. From this latter point of view, welfare is also a question about the rights of the citizens in relation to the public authorities.

Another intention of this paper has been to expand the understanding of the welfare concept beyond the economic sphere, via the perception of the nature of welfare societies, and towards the rights to liberty, justice and a meaningful life, in addition to rights that are imperfect or relative to the individual or to social circumstances at the local level.

Such an understanding of welfare also has implications for welfare state interventions. The welfare state should not only ensure access to classical welfare benefits and services, but also enable the citizens to participate in forming the future welfare policy. The issue is not what the representatives of the people decide at the local level, or how they become aware of the real needs among the common citizens, but how the citizens become active players in determining their own future lives.

References

Fabre, C. (2000). *Social rights under the constitution: Government and the decent life.* Oxford: Clarendon Press.

Ferragina, E. & Seeleib-Kaiser, M. (2011). Welfare regime debate: Past present, futures. *Policy & Politics*, 39(4), 583611.

Fløtten, T. (2013). Nordisk barnefattigdom – et problem å bry seg om? In G. Vidje (Ed.). *Barnfattigdom* (pp. 919). Stockholm, Dronninglund, Helsingfors: Nordens Välfärdscenter. In Norwegian.

Greve, B. (2008). What is welfare? *Central European Journal of Public Policy*, 2(1), 50-72.

Grødem, A.S. (2012). *Statlige tilskuddsmidler mot fattigdom og sosial eksklusjon. Hvordan fungerer de lokalt?* Oslo: Fafo Institute for Labour and Social Research. Report No. 2012(24). In Norwegian with a summary in English.

Kirkeberg, M.I., Epland, J. & Normann, T.M. (2012). *Økonomi og levekår for ulike lavinntektsgrupper 2011*. OsloKongsvinger: Statistics Norway. Report No. 2012(8). In Norwegian with a summary in English.

Koenig, S. (2011). *The human rights cities program*. Retrieved December 8, 2014, from: http://www.wunrn.com/news/2011/05_11/05_02/050211_human.htm.

Koenig, S. (2013). *Why integrating the learning of human rights is relevant to people's daily lives worldwide in the21ˢᵗcentury. Presentation at a meeting at the United Nations on Human Rights as part of discussions on the Post-2015 Development Agenda, 9 December 2013*. Unpublished paper.

Koenig, S. (2014). *Learning from learners: Applying human rights in people's daily lives based on local agenda-setting. Proposal submitted by PDHRE, People's Movement for Human Rights Learning*. Unpublished paper.

Peck, J. (2003). The rise of workfare state. *Kurswechsel. Zeitschrift des Beirats für gesellschafts-, wirtschafts- und umweltpolitische Alternativen*, 18(3), 7587.

Ryan, A. (2012a). *On politics: A history of political thought. Book two: Hobbes to the present*. New York: Liveright.

Ryan, A. (2012b). *The making of modern liberalism*. Princeton, NJ: Princeton University Press.

Seligman, M.E.P. (2002). *Authentic happiness: Using the new positive psychology to realize your potential for lasting fulfillment*. New York: Free Press.

Solow, R.M. (1998). *Work and welfare*. Princeton, NJ: Princeton University Press.

TÁRKI Social Research Institute (2010). *Child poverty and child well-being in the European Union. Report prepared for the DG Employment, Social Affairs and Equal Opportunities (Unite E.2) of the European Commission, Budapest*. Retrieved December 8, 2014, from: http://www.tarki.hu/en/research/childpoverty/index.html.

Tushnet, M. (2004). *Social welfare rights and the forms of judicial review (draft)*. Retrieved December 8, 2014, from: http://politics.as.nyu.edu/docs/IO/4742/tushnet.pdf.

United Nations. (1948). *The universal declaration of human rights*. Retrieved December 8, 2014, from: http://www.un.org/en/documents/udhr/.

Vidje, G. (2013). Summary. In G. Vidje (Ed.). *Barnfattigdom* (pp. 7577). Stockholm, Dronninglund, Helsingfors: Nordens Välfärdscenter.

Author

Hans Kolstad, PhD
MAS, is associate researcher at Aarhus University
Business and Social Sciences, DK
Research area: European continental philosophy, philosophical analysis, theories of knowledge and education, methods and models of understanding, human dignity

Can Local Community Replace the Role of the State in guaranteeing Welfare: Case of Slovenia

Liljana Rihter

Abstract

In the years of economic crisis neo-liberal ideologies have appeared in Europe as a guiding role model in guaranteeing welfare. In Slovenia the role of the state and public services in guaranteeing welfare have been criticized as the main obstacle to economic progress and the expenditures of public sector have been seen as costs that the state cannot afford any more. The European Unions' guidelines or recommendations are in favour of emphasizing persons' own obligation for guaranteeing social security ('activist policies') and also local solidarity. In the article we present the possible consequences of the changes in social policies for the most vulnerable groups of citizens on the case of Slovenia. Slovenia is an exemplary case of these changes since in the past (when Slovenia was one of the ex-Yugoslav republics) the role of guaranteeing welfare was mainly state responsibility, now we can see the diminishment of the role of the state. In the analysis of the data on services that are provided and financed by the local communities we have revealed the paradox. It is obvious that the principles of availability of the services and accessibility of the services were abused. The state has shifted more and more services to the responsibility of local communities (without providing additional finances) with the argument that they can better respond to the needs of the people. And nowadays economically weak communities indeed detect more and more needs yet they are not able to respond to them. Almost the same trends can be noticed when analysing the situation of the individuals. More and more responsibilities and obligations are shifted towards individuals and they are no longer able to bear additional burdens.

Introduction

Social security and the welfare of citizens can be guaranteed in various ways and researchers have developed diverse typologies or models explaining the role of actors in different countries. The majority of the models are based on Esping-Andersens' (1990) typology differentiating liberal welfare states, conservative-corporatist welfare states and social democratic welfare states. The major difference between them is the extent of the role of the state in providing social security or welfare. The state and public finances have an important role in social democratic welfare states, yet in liberal welfare states they have only a residual role (Rihter, 2011).

While in the 'golden years of welfare' social democratic welfare states have been seen as a guiding or 'role model' at least in Europe, in the years of economic crisis neo-liberal ideologies have appeared. The role of the state and public services in guaranteeing welfare has been criticized as the main obstacle to economic progress and expenditure in the public sector has been seen as costs that the states cannot afford any more. Even if The European Union does not have a common social policy, the guidelines or recommendations were in favour of emphasizing persons' own obligation for attaining social security (so named 'activist policies') and also local solidarity (The Social Protection Committee 2010). Member states have responded in various ways. Some of them have taken the recommendations very seriously, others less. So nevertheless analyses based on the data even before the latest economic crisis show that a scenario of neoliberalism prevailed (Powel & Hendriks, 2009).

In this article possible consequences of changes in social policies for the most vulnerable groups of citizens in the case of Slovenia will be discussed. We argue that Slovenia can be an useful example since in the past (before independence, when Slovenia was one of the ex-Yugoslav republics) the role of guaranteeing welfare was mainly a state responsibility, yet in 2014 at the least in the national documents and also on the basis of data trends we can see the diminishing of the role of the state. Therefore we can analyse how the supposed best solutions of changed guidelines can affect citizens and how they can fulfil obligations to assure their own security or welfare.

Type of welfare state in Slovenia: a brief history of development in Slovenia

There are various typologies of welfare states that apply different criteria. The majority of them are based on Esping-Andersen (1990) typology, which distinguishes liberal welfare, conservative-corporatist welfare states, and social democratic welfare states. Leibfried (in Deacon, Hulse & Stubbs 1997:39) has added a southern-European type, While Deacon, Hulse and Stubbs (1997) differentiate also special type of welfare state in East European countries and the former Soviet Union.

Since the majority of these typologies involve the first three types of welfare state it is possible to identify principal criteria for differentiation among them: prevailing principle of redistributive justice; prevailing measures that assure social security; the extent of the role of the state in providing for social security and the kind of resources that are used by the state for providing for social security. One possible summary of differences is presented in Table 1 (Rihter, 2011, Esping-Andersen, 1990, Deacon, Hulse & Stubbs, 1997, Pierson, 1998, Clasen & Van Oorschot, 2001).

Table 1: Differences of welfare states

	Liberal welfare state	Conservative corporatist welfare state	Social democratic welfare state
Prevailing principle of redistributive justice	Principle of means- tested needs	Principle of reciprocity	Principle of equality (universal)
Prevailing measures that assure social security	Social assistance / Voluntary private social insurances	Programmes of Social insurances / obligatory systems of social insurances	Universal transfers and services provided by public institutions / national insurances
Extent of the role of the state in providing for social security	Residual	Medial	Universal
Kind of resources that are used by the state for providing for social security	Financial social assistance	Compensation for lost income	Services

Some Slovenian authors (Kolarič, 1990, Rus, 1990, Črnak–Meglič, 2000) argued that the Slovenian welfare system after the Second World War (Slovenia was a part of ex-Yugoslavia) was similar to the social-democratic type with a dominant role for the state in all areas of social policy (with the ultimate aim of egalitarian social stratification). Some foreign authors (as for instance Deacon 1993) have emphasized similarities to corporative type of welfare state (the social security system was based on employment status).

In Slovenia the system of social protection was well developed and therefore expectations of citizens were focused on the state as the main provider of social services. After the independence of Slovenia (in year 1991) due to new social problems (unemployment, early retirement, new types of addictions,...) and harmonization with the European Union the system has changed to be more in line with a corporatist type (Črnak–Meglič, 2000). In the years before and after entering European Union Slovenia has followed some of the guidelines developed in various projects that aim at harmonizing social protection approaches in Europe.

Analysis of basic acts in the field of social assistance that are in force in Slovenia from the year 2012 (Enforcement of Rights from Public Funds Act (ZUPJS 2010), the Social Financial Assistance Act (ZSVarPre 2010), and Proposal of Social Assistance Activities Act) show a neoliberal trend. As a prevailing principle of redistributive justice the means-testing has become most evident and prevailing measures of social assistance can be characterised as means-tested assistance programmes. There is more room for private organizations in implementing social assistance programmes and the role of state in providing for social assistance has apparently narrowed. Yet there is no clear evidence about the prevailing kind of resources that are used by the state for providing social assistance – on the one hand there is financial social assistance and on the other, some services are available to all in need. (Rihter, 2011)

From a social work perspective some of the basic purposes and aims of new legislation in the field of social assistance could be criticized as perverse principles (as Goodin pointed at in 2001) that transferred the burden of assuring well-being to the pillars in the society that are not able to carry it (more responsibility is turned from the state to individuals, who are already in a disadvantaged social position).

A variety of researchers (Powel & Hendricks, 2009) dealing with the welfare state in post-industrial society have presented similar picture to that seen in the social assistance field in Slovenia in respect to legislation. We are facing an imprudent utilization of neoliberal ideologies while social welfare policies are being reshaped. Bode (2009) argues that welfare states have been diminished due to the creation of welfare markets, entrusting welfare provision to market actors. This has unfavourable consequences for people with various handicaps since they are neglected due to higher costs and resources needed to work with them; quasi-markets increase social segregation

One of the important documents that emerged in preparation of the recent programme for social protection in Slovenia forward to 2020 was A Voluntary European Quality Framework for Social Services (The Social Protection Committee, 2010). We will now analyse what are or can be impacts of consistent implementation of European guidelines without considering local (national) circumstances, needs and possibilities that are available in the particular national setting.

The impact of European quality framework for social services on the Slovenian social protection system

How is the European Quality Framework for Social Services reflected in the Slovenian National Programme for Social Protection?

According to the Resolution of the National Programme of Social Protection (2013) the state and local communities are responsible for assuring that all can have a quality of life and to assure human dignity when people cannot themselves secure their wellbeing. Both state and local communities have to assure preventive, curative and maintenance services and programmes.

While preparing the Resolution (Resolution of National Programme of Social Protection (2013), the main guidelines from A Voluntary European Quality Framework for Social Services (The Social Protection Committee 2010) were strictly followed without discussing advantages or disadvantages or possible impacts.

In A Voluntary European Quality Framework for Social Services (The Social Protection Committee, 2010) the following quality principles for social services provision are anticipated: availability (access to the wide range of social services), accessibility (social services should be easy to access, including information and communication), affordability (services provided for all persons who need a service regardless of their financial situation), person-centred services (services should address the changing needs of individuals), comprehensive (services should be conceived and delivered in a way which reflects capacities and multiple needs of the users), continuous (ensure continuity of service delivery according to the duration of needs), outcome-oriented (focused on the needs of users). Another group of principles deals with the relationship between service providers and users: service providers should respect the users' rights and their dignity (providing users with clear, accurate information; ensuring access for people with disabilities to information; implementing advice and complaint procedures for users; regulatory frameworks and control mechanisms; adequate training for workers and volunteers; promoting users' inclusion in the community; confidentiality and security of data); participation and empowerment (ensuring involvement of the users; dialogue with organizations representing the users; periodical review of users' satisfaction with services). Quality principles that focus on the relationship between service providers, public authorities, social partners and other stakeholders are: partnership (active involvement and cooperation of all stakeholders, establishing synergies; promoting proximity of services, supporting coordination among service providers); good governance (openness, transparency, respect for legislation, efficiency, effectiveness, accountability). The last group are quality principles for human and physical capital, which are mainly in line with working conditions, investment in human capital and adequate physical infrastructure.

Because the Slovenian Resolution of National Programme of Social Protection (2013) follows the main guidelines, emphasising principles such as accessibility, partnership between users and providers (also local communities), person-centred services that are driven by the needs of the users, etc. politicians have decided that is necessary to transfer responsibility for some services to local communities with the aim of applying those guidelines with fewer obstacles. This is not problematic in itself yet there are some obstacles or risks that can endanger realization of other principles of the above mentioned quality framework (The Social Protection Committee, 2010), especially affordability of services and there is a question of how we can guarantee social justice for all inhabitants. Slovenia has 2.062.623 inhabitants (2014; Državni portal Republike Slovenije) and 212 local communities (municipalities). In more than half of Slovenian municipalities there are less than 5000 residents (all together 15 % of Slovenian residents). Two of them have less than 500 residents (Statistical Office of the Republic Slovenia 2014). Small municipalities are less capable of organizing all kinds of necessary services and often, due to severe financial restraints, less able to finance them.

In the Resolution of National Programme of Social Protection (2013) it is expected that local communities will be responsible (to organise and finance):
– Home care for the elderly
– Home care for the handicapped people and long-term ill people
– Home care for children and young people with difficulties
– Family assistant.
They should also participate by guaranteeing financial resources for:
– Verified public social programmes
– Development of experimental programmes
– Additional programmes
– Self-help groups for the elderly.
When preparing the Resolution of National Programme of Social Protection (2013) several advantages of shifting services from state to local communities were anticipated. It was expected that accessibility and availability of services would improve. If services are available in the local setting users will not have additional costs for instance for transport. In evaluation of former national programme of social protection it was emphasized that some services are only available in the biggest cities and users with fewer financial resources will have limited access. It is also important that in the local communities various programmes that respond to the potential needs of the people are available (for instance types of programmes that "fits" particular problems in the local community: violence, addiction,...) and also various providers for each type of programme, so that users

can choose among them. Another expectation was that services in the local communities will provide more person-centred help, since the community can respond to the needs of the people that are evident. All the above-mentioned principles can be easier to accomplish if more services in the home environment are available. It is also planned that more measures should be available that will offset differences in regional/local development and effectiveness in guaranteeing more social programmes besides already existing social services that are the responsibility of local communities. Partnership of state, local communities, services providers and users are assumed in defining the network of public services and programmes in local communities.

Potential and existing risks of shifting services from state to local communities

All of the intentions and principles in the Resolution of National Programme of Social Protection (2013) are in favour of users. Yet before planning and implementing such changes and shifting the responsibility for some important services from the state to the local communities at least the existing services and programmes provided by local communities should be evaluated and possible risks or/and disadvantages identified.

One of the most outstanding risks based on current data that are presented below concerns the regulation of home care services that are provided by local communities. They have a long tradition and are of great importance. On the one hand this is an important service which can shift the trend of services from institutional care towards community care (which is one of the main goals and also a criterion for assessing the effectiveness of Resolution of National Programme of Social Protection); due to population ageing and growing needs of elderly people more such services will be needed in the future. At the moment the proportion of users of institutional care and users of community care services is about 2:1 and it is expected that it will be changed to 1:1 by the year 2020 (Resolution of National Programme of Social Protection.

Home care is according to Social Security Act (2007) available for elderly persons, handicapped persons, chronically ill persons and long-term ill persons, and for children and young people when it can be a substitute for institutional care. It is the most widespread and important service in social protection at community level (Nagode et al., 2014). Local communities have a competence (Articles 43, 44, 99, Social Security Act, 2007) to organize and partly finance home care service. It is provided by public institutions (mainly centres of social work or of homes for the elderly – as a special service) or private providers who have a licence for it. The tasks that are usually implemented can be: help in everyday functioning (help by putting on clothes, washing, feeding,...), household help (delivery of daily rations, buying foodstuffs, washing dishes, basic cleaning,...) help in establishing social contacts (volunteers, relatives, escort). Home care is carried out within the scope of a maximum of 20 hours per week. Home care is a professionally guided process with organized practical help by professional workers and co-workers; other participants are carers, users and family members. The price for the service is set according to the regulations. Local communities have to pay at least 50 % of the costs of the service; the rest is paid by the user. If the user is in lower income groups or is without income, he or she can be exempted payment and local communities then have to provide it for them.

In 11 (out of 211[1]) local communities in Slovenia there were no users in the year 2013. The main reasons were that some of them didn't manage to organize the service, some of them didn't have any users or the responsible person in local community said that there is no need for such a service (Nagode et al, 2014:16–17). From the year 2006 (5328 users) till the end of 2013 (6540 users) the number of users increased initially and after the year 2011 (6624 users) it has declined due to legislative changes (ZUPJS 2010) which were brought into force in 2012. Users with lower (or no) income that have the right to be exempted from payment now have to contribute if they have any property. Therefore some of them (mainly those who for instance have been living in their homes their whole life) prefer to waive the right and to not lose the property they want their relatives to inherit. There hasn't been any comprehensive research yet on how these non-users compensate for the loss of assistance.

The majority of the users are elderly (nearly 90 %), 60 % users are aged 80 or more. Two thirds of all users are women (Nagode et al, 2014:20–23). Slightly more than half of the users (56,5 %) receive less than 3,5 hours of help per week and about 16 % 7 hours or more per week.

The costs for users are from 9,69 EUR to 0 EUR per hour and are regulated. In some local communities there are no costs for users (Brezovica, Ig, Odranci, Škofljica) – these are economically well developed. In the last year there was a decline in costs for users even in the economically less developed communities, yet users in these communities still have higher costs than the average for Slovenia. The differences in price (for the services and not for the users) between local communities have declined in the recent years. This may be due to systematic monitoring of services by The Slovenian Institute for Social Protection (Nagode et al; 2014:37). On average local communities have covered 75, 8 % of all costs which is slightly less than in the preceding years (Nagode et al; 2014:43).

The biggest risks according to the above mentioned data are how to assure

---

[1]   In the year 2014 one new municipality was established by ODCEPITI from former one.

regional accessibility and availability of services. Local communities in Slovenia that according to the Act on local communities (2007) must guarantee quality of life for all citizens are economically not equally developed, also some of them have a small population. Those that are economically and financially weak will have a problem in financing various programmes in a variety of fields. They have problems in financing (or have highest prices) for the existing services they are responsible for. Yet it is to be expected that social problems are more evident in these communities. People have lower incomes compared to other economically well-developed municipalities and therefore are less able to pay for services needed.

Therefore more cooperation between different local communities is necessary, but this has not emerged so far.

Conclusion

After the year 1991 when Slovenia became an independent state we have seen many changes in social policies. Pluralisation of social security providers was seen as a main principle even in the first National Programme of Social Protection in 2000 yet the role of the local community or local solidarity was only predicted for some defined services (i.e. home care services, payment for institutional care for the elderly who have lover incomes). Even if the pluralism of providers of welfare services was promoted and various NGO's and private providers have appeared, they were, and still are mainly dependent on public (state) funds. In the last Resolution on National Programme of Social Protection forward to 2020 (2013) there is even more emphasis on the role of local communities, based on an assumption that local communities can better respond to the needs of the people, and on the pluralisation of service providers. Data on services that are provided and financed by the local communities (for instance home care for the elderly) reveals a paradox. In the communities where economic conditions and available funds for financing social services are scarce there are many people who do not have enough resources to pay for the services themselves and are therefore left without any possible formal support, and so are dependent on local or in-formal solidarity. The state which declares itself as a social state and has provided national programme on social protection on the basis of principles following a voluntarily European Quality Framework for Social Services (agreed in the Social Protection Committee in 2010) should not overlook the possible consequences. In Slovenia it is obvious that the principles of availability of the services and accessibility of the services were violated in the sense that the state has shifted more and more services to the area of responsibility of local communities (without providing additional finances for them) with the argument that they can better respond to the needs of the people. And nowadays economically weak communities detect more and more needs yet they are not able to respond to them. Almost the same trends can be noticed when analysing the situation for individuals. More and more responsibilities and obligations are shifted towards individuals and they are no longer able to bear additional burdens. How can we then secure welfares for all?

References

Act on Local Communities (2007): *Official Gazette of the Republic of Slovenia 94/07, 76/08, 79/09, 51/10, 40/12*, Ljubljana.
Bode, I. (2009). On the Road to Welfare Markets: Institutional, Organizational and Cultural Dynamics of a New European Welfare State Settlement. In J. L. Powell, J. Hendricks, J. (Eds.). *The Welfare State in Post-Industrial Society: A Global Perspective* (pp. 161–177). Dordrecht, Heidelberg, London, New York: Springer.
Clasen, J. & Van Oorschot, W. (2001). Changing Principles and Designs in European Social Security. Retrieved from http://www.sefos.uib.no/eiss, 5.10.2001.
Črnak-Meglič, A. (2000). *Vpliv (tipov) države blaginje na obseg in vlogo neprofitno-volonterskega sektorja v sodobnih družbah, doktorska naloga (Impact of (types of) welfare state on the size and role of non-profit voluntary sector in modern societies)* (doctoral dissertation). Fakulteta za družbene vede, Ljubljana.
Deacon, B. (1993). Developments in East European Policy. In: C. Jones (Ed.). *New Perspectives on the Welfare State in Europe* (pp. 177–198). London: Routledge.
Deacon, B., Hulse, M. & Stubbs, P. (1997). *Global Social Policy: International Organizations and the Future of the Welfare.* London, Thousand Oaks, New Delhi: Sage.
Državni portal Republike Slovenije: Retrieved from https://e-uprava.gov.si/e-uprava/osl oveniji.euprava, 31. 10. 2014.
Esping-Andersen, G. (1990). *The three Worlds of Welfare Capitalism.* Cambridge: Polity.
Goodin, R. E. (2001). Perverse Principles of Welfare Reform. Retrieved from http://ww w.sefos.uib.no/eiss, 5.10.2001.
Kolarič, Z. (1990). *Socialna politika in družbene ter prostorske spremembe, doktorska naloga* (Social Policy and Changes in the Society and Living Space, doctoral dissertation). Ljubljana: Fakulteta za sociologijo, politične vede in novinarstvo.
Nagode, M., Lebar, L. & Jakob Krejan, P. (2014). *Izvajanje pomoči na domu, analiza stanja v letu 2013* (Home care assistance: analysis of implementation in the year 2013). IRSSV, Ljubljana.
Pierson, C. (1998). *Beyond the Welfare State: The New Political Economy of Welfare.* Cambridge: Polity Press.
Powell, J. L. & Hendriks, J. (Eds.) (2009). *Beyond the Welfare State: The New Political Economy of Welfare.* Cambridge: Polity Press.
Predlog zakona o socialnovarstveni dejavnosti (Proposal of Social Assistance Activities Act): Retrieved from http://www.mddsz.gov.si/fileadmin/mddsz.gov.si/pageuploads/ dokumenti_pdf/word/zsvd-04012011.doc, 20.1.2011.

Resolution of National Programme of Social Protection (2013). Ministry of Labour, Family and Social Affairs, Ljubljana.

Rihter, L. (2011). Slovenian social assistance legislation in the era of paradigmatic changes of social work concepts: incentive or obstacle. In P. Salustowicz, (Ed.). *Sozaiale Arbeit zwischen Kontrolle und Solidarität: Auf der Suche nach dem neuen Sozialen* (pp. 171–192) Warszawa, Bielefeld: Societas Pars Mundi.

Rus, V. (1990). Socialna država in družba blaginje (Social State and Welfare State). Domus, Ljubljana.

Social Security Act (officially consolidated text) (2007). Retrieved from http://www.md dsz.gov.si/fileadmin/mddsz.gov.si/pageuploads/dokumenti__pdf/zsv_upb2_en.pdf, 20.1.2011.

Statistical Office of the Republic of Slovenia (2014). Retrieved from http://www.stat.si/ novica_prikazi.aspx?id=6644, 31. 10. 2014.

The Social Protection Committee (2010). A Voluntary European Quality Framework for Social Services, SPC/2010/10/8 final. Retrieved from http://ec.europa.eu/social/keyDocuments.jsp?type=46&policyArea=0&subCate gory=0&country=0&year=0&advSearchKey=&mode=advancedSubmit&langId=en, 22.1.2011.

ZUPJS (2010). Zakon o uveljavljanju pravic iz javnih sredstev [Enforcement of Rights from Public Funds Act]. *Official Journal of the Republic of Slovenia* 62/2010, 9339–9357.

ZSVarPre (2010). Zakon o socialnovarstvenih prejemkih [Financial Social Assistance Act]. *Official Journal of the Republic of Slovenia* 61/2010, 9195–9219.

Author

Liljana Rihter, Ph. D.
Senior lecturer and researcher
University of Ljubljana, Faculty of Social Work
Research areas: evaluation, social policy, vulnerable groups, poverty, methodology of research

New Feathers for the Old Hat: The "Social-Investment-Package" and the German Welfare Tradition: Innovation, Creative Destruction or something else?

Peter Szynka

Abstract

The author examines European Initiatives like the "Social-Investment-Package" (SIP). It will be asked, what outcomes could be expected when ideas from the European level are to be confronted with national welfare systems and traditions, especially with the German welfare tradition, where subsidiarity and strong welfare organizations have played an important role so far. In Schumpeterian terms: Would there be innovation, would there be creative destruction as a precondition of innovation and further development or would there be merely a destruction of social services in order to have another, weaker level of social service delivery. With this background, the goals and the theoretical and empirical base of SIP will be critically examined.

German Welfare System

The starting point is this: Welfare regimes or welfare cultures are organized at national level so far. They are part of a given, historically evolved redistribution system and guarantee a certain level of production and reproduction. Doing so, they reproduce a certain level of commodification of the labor force. I will begin with a description of the welfare culture in Germany, then come to some European social policy initiatives and draw a preliminary conclusion.

The German Term "Daseinsvorsorge"

The German term "Daseinsvorsorge" is commonly translated as "Services of General Interest". Services of General Interest include social and technical services as well and there is broad discussion about whether economic these interests are "general in general" or if – for instance – general interests should better be served by non-profit organizations, which devote themselves to common values instead of private economic interests. Therefore they should be privileged for instance by tax reductions without disturbing the competition and developments of the markets.

So the German term "Daseinsvorsorge" means more than Services of General Interest. The term was coined in order to explain the necessity to work rather towards the common good than to private interests. It refers also to the legitimacy of the state, which is constituted in post-war Germany as a Social State, based on laws (Sozialer Rechtsstaat).

The state is obliged to conduct social planning and has the responsibility of guaranteeing sustainable and accessible Social Services of General Interest according to the needs and in time. Regarding social work and social services the German Book of Social Laws (SGB) Book I § 17 states that "social services have to be established in proper time and in sufficient quantity." The government has to register the development of needs continually and react in advance. So "Daseinsvorsorge" could be translated as something like "provident care for the well-being of people"

Subsidiarity

Another characteristic of the German Welfare System is the special understanding of subsidiarity. Originally coined in the social teachings of the Catholic Church, the term subsidiarity recurred to Germany during the dark times of Hitler Fascism when Pope Pius XI wrote his encyclical writing "With Burning Concerns" ("Mit brennender Sorge"). The core of this text is to remind the totalitarian regime of the value of the individual, the family and religious institutions and their relation to the state and the then so called "People's Community" ("Volksgemeinschaft"). At that time German totalitarism stated that the individual is worth nearly nothing compared with the "Volksgemeinschaft". According to the national-socialist ideology every single member had to serve the "Volksgemeinschaft" especially by securing and developing the cleanliness and purity of the nordic race. The encyclical writing tried to rearrange this relation between the individual and the society. The state was called to serve the communities, the communities to serve the families and the families to serve the individual: the so called "onion-model" of subsidiarity.

After World War II German Social policy reestablished the Bismarck System with strong elements of subsidiarity and self-regulation. State activities in the social field were restricted to liability and supervision. The operational business was left to social insurance controlled by employer's- and worker's-organizations.

Social Work was left to the traditional welfare organizations which in part had strong ties to the Christian churches like Diaconia and Caritas, or had strong its roots in the worker's movement, like Arbeiterwohlfahrt. Others were founded at the margins of the European battlefields like the Red Cross. The list of recognized postwar German umbrella organizations in the social field is not complete without Paritätischer Wohlfahrtsverband and the Jewish Welfare Organization.

In German Social Laws we find important privileges for the German Welfare Organizations. They are supported by different means. There are tax reductions, there are rights to participate in relevant decision-making processes at local, regional and national level. If new social services are necessary, the state or communal bodies should not create their own services but enable recognized welfare organizations to do so. On the other hand, the state can control the finances and bookkeeping of welfare organizations. The non-profit sector is sharply divided from the profit sector by the rigour of the financial administration.

The establishment of a strong third sector was a consensual reaction to the experience of totalitarism and their bureaucratic operation of welfare during German fascism and German socialism. In contrast to the Scandinavian model a strong role for communal bodies was neglected by the Christian Democratic Party, which was in power during the early 1960s. A "municipal socialism" in those cities and counties where the Social-Democrats were ruling at that time, should be avoided. So the welfare organizations were established as a third sector or even a third power operating between political and economic interests.

Labor Market "Reform"

Whether these fears of a "municipal socialism" could have been justified, cannot be addressed here. But since the 1990th a new trend occurred in German welfare policy. Welfare organizations should be privatized; they should be turned over from the non-profit to the profit sector. A new kind of competition and managerialism should keep the social costs under control. This development was strongly supported by the Social-Democrats and it has begun with the so call Schroeder-Blair-Paper, called "The Third Way". It was inspired by the British sociologist Anthony Giddens, who stated the maxim "No rights without obligations" as a way to renew social democracy (Giddens 1999:81). The "Third Way" was the starting point for a series of deregulations and what we call "the Neoliberal Agenda". Dumping prices, lower wages for social and health workers, de-qualification of social work was the result. In this decade social- and health workers lost some of their worker's rights by means of outsourcing and union-bashing. On the other hand, the expected minimization of state expenses for social security, the main goal of the reform, was not realized. The neoliberal strategy has failed as Colin

Crouch states (Crouch, 2011). In Germany the failure of neoliberal "reform"-strategies could also be illustrated with some scandals of mismanagement.[1]

The peak of the neoliberal agenda in Germany was the so called "Labor Market Reform" in 2005. The labor market reform provided deep cuts into the state expenses. Meanwhile it led to a cessation of active labor market policy. It also questioned the social rights of the individual. Human rights are no more seen as inalienable (unveräußerlich). They seem to be regarded as something which could be added to the individual by the state according to the obligations, he or she is able to take. They were given to those individuals, who were fulfilling predefined duties. In this way the "contracting out" of young jobless people led to an increasing number of young homeless people. At this time the German High Court still considers whether parts of the labor market reform of 2005 are violating human rights laid down in the German Basic Law (Grundgesetz) and if they show some kind of discrimination against young people. Since the Labor Market Reform, critical observers of the German welfare system are skeptical in general about reforms and innovations that do not bring any improvement for people.

Before the deregulation of the German Welfare System had begun, welfare organizations had to face a campaign with several forms of criticism. The criticism ranged from unprofessional management to a critique of the too prominent role and influence of the churches, a lack of evidence for their methods and a lack of competition.

In his discussion of Esping-Anderson's Typology of welfare capitalism, the German scientist Philip Manow traced the existing European welfare traditions to their religious origins. Like Esping-Anderson he also delineated three welfare cultures and named them comprehensively: "the Good, the Bad and the Ugly".

Manow criticizes Esping-Anderson on some points, such as the missing differentiation between the continental and the Mediterranean welfare systems. He demands more attention for the confessional differences in the history of social welfare, which also led to differences in the welfare cultures established during the industrial revolution. In a simplifying terminology he distinguishes the "Good", the "Bad" and the "Ugly" to underline his argumentation. The "Good" in this sense is the (meanwhile historic) social-democratic system, based on a strong engagement of the state. The "Bad" is the Anglo-Saxon system, based on self-help and hard competition. And we, the Germans with the continental or corporatist model were in his view the "Ugly". But things are not always what they seem to

---

[1] Notorious was the so called "Maserati-Affair" which took place in Berlin 2009. The head of a number of homeless-shelters tried to attract donors and wealthy people by taking them to the slums with his used Maserati. Before, and with support of internationally recognized counsellors, he "created" fantastic "rates" of return of social investment.

Table 1: Religious Origins of Welfare Traditions in Western Europe according to Philip Manow (2008)

Skandinavian	Anglo Saxon	Continental	Mediterranen	
Social Democratic	Liberal	Conservative	Conservative	Esping Andersen
"The Good"	"The Bad"	"The Ugly"		
Lutheran	Calvinist	Lutheran and Catholic	Catholic	Philip Manow
Wittenberg	Genf	Berlin	Rome	City of Origin

be: the "Good" is not always as good as it seems and the "Bad" is not as bad as it seems.

But what's about the "Ugly"? In my view the German or Corporatist Welfare System only then is ugly, when its key persons behave like fools and when the umbrella organizations are disorganized. It is ugly, when there is no understanding of the value of a corporate model and there is no strategy to defend subsidiarity against the "divide et impera" attacks of the liberal agenda. It is ugly, when its key leaders support disorganization and prefer short term profits instead of keeping a good system running.

Today the welfare organizations and politicians slowly recognize, which structures and long term traditions are at risk and what the social cost will be: not only in terms of money, but also in terms of sustainability, peace and quality of life. The welfare organizations try to remember their values, their roots in civil society and strengthen their ties to their users. They form a critical public sphere, an organized third sector, watching critically the development of national social policies and the development of a Social Europe. After some hard struggles between the Unions and the Christian welfare organizations a new coalition was built against "outsourcing" and towards a common tariff for workers in the social and health sector.

European Social Policy Attempts

The Social Investment Package (SIP)

Against the background of the so called German Labor Market Reform, the SIP comes along like an old and well known companion. The SIP was launched in June 2013 (Europäische Kommission, 2013, 2013a, 2013b). The reasons for the SIP seem very clear: the financial crisis brought a lot of debts to the states and led to austerity politics and cuts into the social security budgets. At the same time the European states face a second crisis: demographic development. This will lead to older societies and societies of the elderly. A decreasing younger part of the population will have to care for a growing older part of the population and for themselves. The security of the systems of elderly care is in question. The states will have lesser means to guarantee the same quality in the future. The conclusion of the Social Investment Package is as follows: we need more money from the private sector in the social welfare system. But how will we get more private investment into this realm? The magic word is the "Social Bond". Investors should be attracted by returns on investment of between 7% and 10 %.

Investors should invest in Innovations which will improve the welfare system. This needs clear evidence and statistics. We need ciphers to measure the impact and results of social care. Will the number of school drop-outs decrease by 10%? Will the Re-Imprisonment of offenders decrease about 12 % or less. Will homeless people have to wait for a home only 10 month instead of 12 years? Will the mortality of new born babies sink? Will criminality in problematic city districts decrease?

Goldman Sachs already offered an amount of money, to be part of this new game. According to the "mortgaged backed securities" which have already devastated many parts of our cities we will probably tomorrow have a new financial product for our investments, called "public obligations backed security" (POBS).

To what extent can the public bodies get rid of their obligations without causing a new social crisis and uprisings of the poor? This seems to be the major contradiction of the SIP: The state tries to lower the costs of its social responsibility and tries to pass the burden on to private shoulders. So far, the investment brokers do not show much interest to this offer. If we look to the empirical base of "social bond" – activities we can see that in the case of London benevolent Foundations but not Goldman Sachs signed the bond. So far the results are not very encouraging: in this case there will be no return on investment, because the attained results were some points below the predefined goals of improvement. So maybe we will be know better in the coming years when the expected innovation is realized. In order to play down the difficulties, the German Government in its social investment guidelines emphasizes not a quick return on investment and says that the predicted rates of returning investment could be expected to be very low. This underlines, that the risks cannot be calculated properly yet. But the real risk is, that even desirable innovations will not be achieved in this way.

The Social Business Initiative (SBI)

The Social Business Initiative, also launched in 2013, backs up the activities of social entrepreneurs. A social entrepreneur should embody a new type of entrepreneurship. His business is aimed to a social goal as well as to financial goals. And the social goal should be the more important goal. But social entrepreneurship should not be a non-profit-business as it is in the German Social System.

The SBI is looking for young and motivated activists who are well trained in finance and should somehow also have some expertise in social work (Rummel, 2011:23–28). But they should not have a critical distance to the national economy and at least should have no feeling for social contradictions and class conflicts. They should be, to use a term from sociologist Max Weber: "charismatic".

They should be creative, should develop innovations and are expected to be dismissive about seemingly useless "traditional" solutions (to use another Weberian term). This is also expected from the so called social entrepreneurs in contrast to the more traditionally based German welfare organizations.

But will this happen? The case of the Social Bonds in Great Britain actually shows, that the social bond was not signed by creative social entrepreneurs of the charismatic kind, backed by Goldmann Sachs. It was signed by traditional, value oriented charitable foundations. So where can we find a common ground between these value oriented and charismatic players?

A survey on social innovation, done by the INNOSERV project shows a lot of "old hats". Among them were policy proposals of the traditional welfare organizations which would have been innovative if they had been accepted by the political bodies in time (Innoserv 2012). Also the theoretical base of the survey is interesting: "… Innovations need not necessarily be original, they must be new to the user, context or organization" or "… Innovation is as much about applying an idea, service or product in a new context, or in a new organization, as it is about creating something new" (Hawker and Frankland, 2012:12–13). So what kind of innovation are we talking about, when it is "not original" or "not new" except to some antiquated organizations, isolated regions or disinterested politicians?

Some Schumpeterian Terms and Conclusions

Political economist Joseph Schumpeter coined the terms innovation and creative destruction (Schumpeter, 2005). Schumpeter describes economic development as an ongoing process of innovation and imitation. Innovation is a creative process, which sometimes destroys or destructs traditional modes of production. The carriers of development in Schumpeter's theory are creative entrepreneurs, who are trying to improve their economic position. They invent new methods of production, financing or service delivery. He distinguishes the creative entrepreneur from the money-grubbing capitalist. The money grubbing capitalist or the arbitrage-entrepreneur is not creative but merely imitating. He is not creative in the original sense, but using the differences he finds in currency, prices and methods in different places and on different markets. In the long run, these differences will be less and less, because innovations, good practices and progress in production, financing and service delivery will be disseminated also without arbitrage-entrepreneurs. The arbitrage-entrepreneur does not create innovation but he copies and pastes procedures and techniques from one context to another and calls it "innovation". And sometimes he even fails, while applying his well-known solution to problems which may be unfamiliar to him.

So here is my conclusion: What we see in the Social Business Initiative is not a creative approach to improvement and coordination of the social systems in Europe but a phenomenon of arbitrage in the Schumpeterian sense. It makes use of different modes of production and financing of social services in the EU. In Schumpeterian Terms it is not a creative process but money grubbing one. It is more destructive than creative and may be taken as an example for Schumpeter's long term prognosis that capitalism on the long run will destruct its social base instead of creating something new and sustainable. The innovative destructivity of the Social Investment Package is not directed to old and useless techniques and methods, but to the solidary base of a cohesive society. It regards the human rights of the individual not as inalienable, but as added to the individual by "creative" government administration.

In this way the Social Investment Package is not able to reach honorable goals or a solution.

On the other hand, the Social Business Initiative has to take account of the traditional structures. If Social Business is able to find "real new" solutions and generate "original innovations" it may serve as a supplier to the existing welfare systems. But this should really be the task for Social Work Research than for free-lancing entrepreneurs. At least they should apply scientific standards.

Where Social Business is located in the German Welfare System can be shown in the next table. Also in the future, Social Services of General Interest should stay a task for the public bodies, which should guarantee the sustainability of services.

References

Europäische Kommission (2013). *Sozialinvestitionen für Wachstum und sozialen Zusammenhalt – einschließlich Durchführung des Europäischen Sozialfonds 2014–2020.* COM (2013) 83 final.
Europäische Kommission (2013a). *Investition in ein Soziales Europa.* Brussels.
Europäische Kommission (2013a). *Soziale Agenda Nr. 33, 06/2013.* Brussels.
Giddens, A. (1999). *Der dritte Weg.* Frankfurt am Main: Suhrkamp.
INNOSERV (2012). Work Package 2. Retrived from http://www.inno-serv.eu/de.

Hawker, Ch. & Frankland, J. (2012). *Theoretical trends and criteria for 'innovative service practices' in social services within the EU.* In: INNOSERV (2012). Work Package 2.

Rummel, M. (2011).: *Wer sind die Social Entrepreneurs in Deutschland.* Wiesbaden: VS College.

Schumpeter, J. (2005 [1947]). *Kapitalismus, Sozialismus und Demokratie.* Tübingen und Basel.

Author

Peter Szynka (Dr. phil, Social Scientist) works for Diaconia, one of the big German welfare umbrella organizations. The areas of interest are Services for Homeless People, Community Organizing (Saul D. Alinsky), the Relevance of Sociology for Social Work (Max Weber).

Migration and the Welfare State: Examining the Effect of Immigration on Attitudes towards Economic Redistribution

Joachim Vogt Isaksen and Tor Georg Jakobsen

Abstract

Is ethnic diversity associated with negative attitudes towards economic redistribution? To address this issue we employ a theoretical perspective to explain patterns in individual attitudes towards the welfare state. We suggest that there is a threshold effect when it comes to attitudes to economic redistribution. Our postulate is that up until a certain point more intergroup contact leads to more positive, or leftist, attitudes to redistribution. However, when this threshold is reached, any further diversity will lead to decreased willingness to redistribution. We use data from the last four waves of the World Values Survey combining the survey data from 30 OECD countries with country-level statistics. The models reveal a threshold effect, where individuals in ethnically polarized societies are the most positive towards economic redistribution.

Introduction

Immigration can influence factors other than ethnic tolerance. The increase of immigration in Western welfare states has generated new political pressures and new policy issues. One important issue is the influence immigration may have on the welfare state. Further, an important question is whether diverse societies are less likely than relatively homogeneous societies to invest in redistributive welfare programs. If so, this may lead to new challenges where governments must manage tensions between cultural majorities and minorities, and find their way through potentially explosive issues embedded in immigration and refugee policies, anti-discrimination programs, and the integration of newcomers. Immigration may also lead to an even broader transformation of policy regimes such as tax levels and the distribution of wealth. The aim of this paper is to investigate the link between the ethnic composition of 30 OECD countries, and their population's attitudes to economic redistribution.

Heterogeneity is often seen as a threat to the existence of liberal democracies because it challenges the consensus on – and the legitimacy of – its basic institutions and its redistributive instruments (Hjerm & Schnabel, 2012). Some studies have shown that relatively homogeneous societies invest more in public goods, indicating a higher level of public altruism. For example, the degree of ethnic homogeneity correlates with the government's share of gross domestic product as well as the average wealth of citizens. Case studies of the United States, Africa, and South-East Asia find that multi-ethnic societies are less charitable and less able to cooperate in the development of the public infrastructure. Moscow beggars receive more gifts from fellow ethnics than from other ethnicities. A recent multi-city study of municipal spending on public goods in the United States found that ethnically or racially diverse cities spend a smaller portion of their budgets and less per capita on public services than do the more homogenous cities (Rushton, 2005). However, empirical research on the impact of heterogeneity is inconclusive: While it could be shown that ethnic heterogeneity in the USA results in a lack of support for welfare measurements (Alesina & Glaeser, 2004; Sears & Citrin, 1985; Soss, Schram & Fording, 2003), little support for this relationship is found outside the USA – even though more elaborate controls were in use (Myles & St-Arnaud, 2006; Taylor-Gooby, 2005). What has been investigated in previous research about the relation between ethnic diversity and the welfare state is the impact of immigration on the welfare state as such, for example the size of the welfare state and public support for the welfare state (Alesina & Glaeser, 2004; Banting & Kymlicka, 2006; Crepaz & Damron, 2009).

In the present paper we explore the degree to which a country is heterogeneous and the attitude of the population towards redistribution of welfare. Our theoretical contribution is to show the explanatory power of the two grand theories of migration studies, i.e. Intergroup Contact Theory and Group Threat Theory. We have tested these assumptions with multilevel modeling. The main contribution of this paper is to test the effect immigration on attitudes towards economic redistribution in OECD countries, employing new data on ethnicity and modeling for a proposed squared effect.

Theory

What effect does heterogeneity have on the modern welfare state? Heterogeneity is widely seen as a threat to the existence of liberal Western democracies because it challenges both the consensus on, and the legitimacy of redistributive practices. Public support for social spending and redistribution is an important constituent of the legitimacy of mature welfare states. Welfare states today vary considerably with regard to the scale of the public redistribution. One important approach within the study of welfare investigates variation as a result of the historic power divide between the economic classes in various states (Esping-Andersen, 1990). The political power of the working class is considered especially decisive. Large welfare states were first established in countries with strong workers' movements and powerful social democratic parties (Korpi, 1983; Freeman, 1986).

Intergroup contact theory and group threat theory are concerned with mechanisms that seem to be at play when a majority population comes into contact with ethnic minority groups. We build on these theories in our study, assuming that the same mechanisms also have an effect on attitudes towards economic redistribution. In brief, the intergroup contact theory is based on Allport (1954) who stated that a lack of interaction between individuals belonging to different groups creates a hostile environment while an increase in intergroup contact leads to more ethnic tolerance. Intergroup contact has two dominant measures: individual behavior, which refers to personal contact between members of different groups, and context, that is, the size of a minority group within a specified geographic area (e.g., neighborhood, municipality, region, country). This argument has received support in several studies (e.g., Amir, 1969; 1976; Forbes 1997; Rothbart & Oliver, 1993).

The opposing group threat argument was first proposed by Blalock (1967), which for the purpose of this study implies that an increase in diversity will lead to more people being in direct or potential competition over resources across group boundaries. This competition will again lead to more negative attitudes towards redistribution of wealth to other ethnic groups. Prejudice and hostility towards subordinate groups are expected to increase among members of the majority group. Thus the basis of group threat theory is economic and/or political threat, which can lead to ethnic conflict or intolerance. In summary, the arguments proposed by different mechanisms and the findings supporting the two main theories of ethnic relations, seem to be at play in different settings. In other words, the findings are expected to be related to the type of ethnic composition that is studied. In this study, we investigate 30 countries, enabling us to go deeper into the mechanisms that lie behind the divergent results shown in the literature. The effects of the mechanisms are expected to vary according to the type of ethnic structure involved. The ethnic composition of a country can have implications for how loyal people are towards the welfare state.

Is there threshold effect in welfare attitudes?

Several studies argue that the dominant group perceives other group's sizes from the narratives they receive – whether they are false or correct perceptions. This has important implications for ethnic attitudes (Blumer, 2003; Lewis 2002). Up to a certain point, more diversity can be expected to lead to increased levels of tolerance. This can be explained by the logic of intergroup contact theory: increased interaction between different groups leads to more ethnic tolerance. Schelling (1978) argues that each individual has a threshold point when it comes to ethnic tolerance (which would be the mean threshold point of all its individual members). He provides a micro level explanation of this: a person might very well want to sit at a mixed-race table in a cafeteria, but the same person will be hesitant to sit down at a table where everyone belongs to the opposite ethnic group. This example can be applied to the country-level when individuals feel that their group is being threatened, either numerically, culturally, financially, religiously, or through a combination of these. For this particular study, this is a relevant point since an individual may feel less inclined to share resources across ethnic boundaries. For a smaller group, it could arouse a fear of becoming too small and to lose its identity vis-à-vis other groups within that country. Parallel to Schelling (1971, 1978) and Granovetter's (1978) modeling of a chain effect, it can be assumed that decreased loyalty towards the welfare state could be an effect of this threat. We assume that this is a threshold effect determined by a country's ethnic composition. In ethnically polarized societies, the effect of intergroup contact mechanisms will be at its highest, before group threat mechanisms surpass the effect. Figure 1 illustrates the different types of ethnic composition encountered in society. We assume that up to a certain point there is little effect of group threat mechanisms. However, the effect of intergroup contact increases the more ethnically diverse a society is. We argue that beyond a certain level of fractionalization, group threat mechanisms will increase in importance.

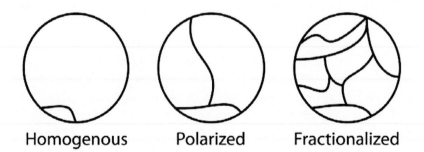

Homogenous   Polarized   Fractionalized

Figure 1: Categories of ethnic composition

Our research hypothesis is:
Individuals in ethnically polarized countries are most in favor of redistributing income.

Data and methods

For individual level variables, we used data from the last four waves of the World Values Survey (WVS),[1] combining the survey data from 30 OECD countries with country-level statistics. The data are nested into three levels: (1) individuals; (2) country survey-years, and (3) countries. Since we test the effect of country level on individual level attitudes, we rely on hierarchical modeling. The object of a multilevel analysis is to account for variance in a dependent variable measured at the lowest level by investigating data from all levels of analysis (Steenbergen & Jones, 2002:219). Multilevel modeling also enables us to investigate data structures that are hierarchical where the sample data can be viewed as a multistage sample from this hierarchical population (Hox, 2002).

Multilevel analysis is the statistical analysis of hierarchically and non-hierarchically nested data. The simplest example is clustered data such as a sample of students clustered within schools. Multilevel data are especially prevalent in the social and behavioral sciences and in the bio-medical sciences. The models used for this type of data are linear and nonlinear regression models that account for observed and unobserved heterogeneity at the various levels in the data (Leeuw, 2008). We employ random intercept models and find no theoretical reason for assuming that the regression slopes for the different countries or country survey-years should vary significantly.

To establish how much of the variation in the dependent variable is situated at each level, we have divided each level's variance component (in an empty model) on the total variance. Most of the variance is, not surprisingly, at level-1, which stands at 91.2 percent. The figure for level-2 is 6.2 percent, and for level-3 it is 2.5 percent. Even if most of the variance is at level-1, our main interest is to explain the level-2 variance, as the former has been the subject of much previous research.

Variables

Our dependent variable INCOME EQUALITY ranges from 1 to 10, and we thus ran random intercept three-level models. In addition, we ran random intercept two-level models where individuals are level-1 and country survey-years are level-2 to check for robustness. High values on the dependent indicate pro-welfare state attitudes. The exact wording of the question is as follows: "Incomes should be made more equal versus We need larger income differences as incentives for individual effort."

---

[1]   More information about WVS can be found at http://www.worldvaluessurvey.org. These datasets are made available through the Norwegian Social Science Data Service (NSD). Neither Ronald Inglehart, WVS, or NSD are responsible for the analysis or interpretations made in this article.

$$ELF = 1 - \sum_{i=1}^{n} s_{i,}^{2} \qquad (1)$$

Our main independent variable is ETHNIC FRACTIONALIZATION. This variable has its origin in Fearon and Laitin's (2003) updated ethnolinguistical fractionalization index (ELF). It indicates the probability that two randomly drawn individuals from the population will belong to different ethnolinguistic groups (Fearon & Laitin, 2003:78). si is the proportion of group i out of n groups. The groups are defined by their roles, their descent, and their relationship to other groups (Taylor and Hudson, 1972:215). The index is based on the formula for the Herfindahl index,[2] and data from *Atlas Naradov Mira* (Department of Geodesy and Cartography, 1964) and other sources (Fearon and Laitin, 2003).[3]

There are many caveats associated with this Fearon and Laitin measure. The latest data used is from 1990, and many ethnic groups, especially in OECD- countries that have seen a large influx of recent immigrants are thus underrepresented. We have chosen to use the updated measure provided by Bakkan (2012), where she has used various sources, including the Joshua Project,[4] to establish more reliable numbers of ethnic groups for OECD countries. This variable has been interpolated, filling in the missing data points from Fearon and Laitin's last observation up to Bakkan's 2011 observation. Generally, linear interpolation takes two data points, the interpolant being given by:

$$y = y_a + \frac{(x - x_a)(y_b - y_a)}{(x_b - x_a)} \qquad (2)$$

For country-years before 1990, the values provided by Fearon and Laitin are employed. We have also included the country survey-year-level control PER CAPITA GDP (World Bank, 2012). This is a variable that has outliers, something that can create statistical problems such as heteroskedasticity and too large an influence from outliers. We have thus chosen to log transform this variable in order to give a more correct statistical representation of the relationship between PER CAPITA GDP and INCOME DISTRIBUTION. The relationship is linearized by reducing the influence of extreme values (Hamilton 1992:148).

---

[2]   The Herfindahl index is used in economics as a measure of the size of firms and their competition for the market share.

[3]   Fearon and Laitin filled in missing values based on sources such as the CIA fact book, Encyclopedia Britannica, the Library of Congress Country Studies, and other country-specific sources (Fearon and Laitin 2003:78).

[4]   The Joshua Project is a project commenced in 1995, seeking to identify the world's ethnic groups in order to serve mission agencies, denominations, churches, and individuals around the world in their quest to reach the groups of the world with the fewest followers of Christ. www.joshuaproject.net

Thirty countries are included in the study, giving a country survey-year level N of 64. These include Argentina, Australia, Austria, Belgium, Canada, Chile, Czech Republic, Estonia, Finland, France, Germany, Iceland, Ireland, Italy, Japan, Mexico, Netherlands, New Zealand, Norway, Poland, Serbia, Slovakia, Slovenia, South Korea, Spain, Sweden, Switzerland, Turkey, the United Kingdom, and the United States. Also, dummy variable for Waves 3–5 are included as time controls.

Table 1: Descriptive Statistics for the individual level variables

Variables	Range	N	Mean	Std. dev.
IncomeEqu.	1–10	130,698	5.385	2.886
Woman	0–1	169,794	0.525	0.499
Age	14–101	164,916	43.511	17.056
Income	1–10	143,417	4.915	2.545
PeopleTrust	0–1	163,809	0.338	0.473
ConfGov	1–4	74,845	0.268	0.849
Education	1–3	100,793	1.856	0.757
LR-selfpos.	1–10	138,845	5.503	0.211

The skewness value of the dependent variable is 0.143, while its kurtosis value stands at 1.865. In a perfect normal distribution, the skewness coefficient is zero. A positive value is obtained where the distribution has a longer 'tail' to the right. A kurtosis value above zero indicates a pointy distribution. In both instances (skewness and kurtosis), values greater than 1.96 are considered problematic. In sum, and taking into account the high N of our study, we choose not to transform the variable.

As we see from the descriptive statistics, there is a very large level-1 N. The dependent variable, INCOME EQUALITY is not perfectly normally distributed (see Figure X). The dependent variable in hierarchical modeling should ideally be normally distributed.

Table 2: Descriptive Statistics for the country survey-year level variables

Variables	Values	N	Mean	Std. dev.
GDPpc	8.66–12.41	64	9.858	0.518
Ethfrac	0.01–0.77	64	0.265	0.194

It can be seen that it is a relatively (at least for the standard of many multilevel analyses) large level-2 N. This allows for the inclusion of level-2 variables without running out of degrees of freedom.

Models

We present four models. The first two models employ three levels; the latter has two levels. Models 1 and 3 test for the linear effect of ethnic fractionalization on people's economic attitudes, while models 2 and 3 test for a curvilinear effect of ethnicity on the dependent variable. We see that the trends for the individual level variables are the same in all four models; women, older people, those with a relatively low income, those with high trust in other people, low education, and those belonging to the left-side of the political spectrum, tend to have leftist views on INCOME EQUALITY.

Our models are formally presented as:

[1]

$$income\ equality_{ijk} = \beta_0 + \beta_1 woman_{ijk} + \beta_2 age_{ijk} + \beta_3 income_{ijk}$$
$$+\beta_4 peopletrust_{ijk} + \beta_5 confidencegov_{ijk} + \beta_6 education_{ijk} + \beta_7 lrscale_{ijk}$$
$$+\beta_8 lnGDPpc_{jk} + \beta_9 ethfrac_{jk} + e_{ijk} + u_{0jk} + v_{0k}$$

[2]

$$income\ equality_{ijk} = \beta_0 + \beta_1 woman_{ijk} + \beta_2 age_{ijk} + \beta_3 income_{ijk}$$
$$+\beta_4 peopletrust_{ijk} + \beta_5 confidencegov_{ijk} + \beta_6 education_{ijk} + \beta_7 lrscale_{ijk}$$
$$+\beta_8 lnGDPpc_{jk} + \beta_9 ethfrac_{jk} + \beta_{10} ethfrac_{jk} * ethfrac_{jk} + e_{ijk} + u_{0jk} + v_{0k}$$

[3]

$$income\ equality_{ij} = \beta_0 + \beta_1 woman_{ij} + \beta_2 age_{ij} + \beta_3 income_{ij} + \beta_4 peopletrust_{ij}$$
$$+\beta_5 confidencegov_{ij} + \beta_6 education_{ij} + \beta_7 lrscale_{ij} + \beta_8 lnGDPpc_j$$
$$+\beta_9 ethfrac_j + e_{ij} + u_{0j}$$

[4]

$$income\ equality_{ij} = \beta_0 + \beta_1 woman_{ij} + \beta_2 age_{ij} + \beta_3 income_{ij} + \beta_4 peopletrust_{ij}$$
$$+\beta_5 confidencegov_{ij} + \beta_6 education_{ij} + \beta_7 lrscale_{ij} + \beta_8 lnGDPpc_j$$
$$+\beta_9 ethfrac_j + \beta_{10} ethfrac_j * ethfrac_j + e_{ij} + u_{0j}$$

The effects of all individual-level explanatory variables in our mode were statistically significant. However, one must take into account the very large level-1 N, as the p-value is a function of the standard error and the slope, and the standard error is again a function of the standard deviation and the N. A high N, in this case 62,056 observations, makes the standard error small, and thus gives significant values. This does not necessarily mean that there are substantive differences between groups or different values on the independent variables. It is therefore also important to look at the standardized z-score, which shows that the variables with the most effect are INCOME, EDUCATION, and LEFT–RIGHT-SCALE.

Table 3: Random intercept three-level and two-level model, ETHFRAC on IN-COME EQUALITY, 1989–2007

Income Equality	1	2	3	4
Constant	6.793***	6.151***	6.180***	5.324***
	(2.207)	(2.162)	(1.736)	(1.691)

Level-1 variables

	1	2	3	4
Woman	0.159***	0.159***	0.159***	0.159***
	(0.021)	(0.021)	(0.021)	(0.021)
Age	0.002**	0.002**	0.002**	0.002**
	(0.001)	(0.000)	(0.001)	(0.001)
Income	-0.120***	-0.120***	-0.120***	-0.120***
	(0.005)	(0.005)	(0.005)	(0.005)
Trust in people	0.082***	0.082***	0.082***	0.082***
	(0.024)	(0.024)	(0.024)	(0.024)
Confidence gov.	-0.117***	-0.117***	-0.116***	-0.116***
	(0.014)	(0.014)	(0.014)	(0.014)
Education	-0.248***	-0.248***	-0.250***	-0.249***
	(0.016)	(0.016)	(0.016)	(0.016)
LR-selfposition.	-0.200***	-0.199***	-0.199***	-0.199***
	(0.005)	(0.005)	(0.005)	(0.005)

Level-2 variables

	1	2	3	4
Per capita GDP	0.186	0.227	0.244	0.298*
	(0.230)	(0.223)	(0.184)	(0.177)
EthfracInterpol	-0.333	1.889	-0.075	3.475*
	(0.565)	(1.748)	(0.474)	(1.486)
EthfracInterpol2		-3.197		-5.272*
		(2.400)		(2.103)

Time controls

	1	2	3	4
(Wave 2 refer.)				
Wave 3	-0.961***	-0.995***	-0.900*	-1.027**
	(0.330)	(0.333)	(0.525)	(0.503)

Wave 4	-0.683**	-0.722**	-0.799	-0.883*
	(0.337)	(0.339)	(0.527)	(0.504)
Wave 5	-0.923***	-0.946***	-0.908*	-0.986*
	(0.353)	(0.354)	(0.548)	(0.524)
Variance				
Level-1 variance	7.105	7.105	7.105	7.105
	(0.040)	(0.040)	(0.040)	(0.040)
Level-2 variance	0.141	0.144	0.460	0.418
	(0.036)	(0.037)	(0.083)	(0.075)
Level-3 variance	0.296	0.267		
	(0.097)	(0.091)		
Level-1 N	62,056	62,056	62,056	62,056
Level-2 N	64	64	64	64
Level-3 N	30	30		
Log Likelihood	-149,009.82	-149,008.98	-149,022.28	-149,019.28

Note: Significance levels: *=10%, **=5%, ***=1%. Countries included in models 1–4: Argentina, Australia, Austria, Belgium, Canada, Chile, Czech Republic, Estonia, Finland, France, Germany, Iceland, Ireland, Italy, Japan, Mexico, Netherlands, New Zealand, Norway, Poland, Serbia, Slovakia, Slovenia, South Korea, Spain, Sweden, Switzerland, Turkey, United Kingdom, United States.

As already mentioned, our main concern is with the country survey-year level in general, and with the effect of ethnic fractionalization in particular. We see quite clearly from models 1 and 3 that there is no linear effect of ethnic fractionalization on economic left–right attitudes. We had theoretical reasons to expect that there is a curvilinear effect, and thus chose to include a squared term of ETHNIC FRACTIONALIZATION. From models 2 and 4 we see that there is a tendency (in model 2) for an inverted U-shape, and both the original and the squared terms are statistically significant in model 4. The difference in significance can easily be explained. When modeling with two levels, much of the explanatory power at the third level is transferred to the second level. In a two-level model, 8.8 percent of the variance is found at the second level as opposed to 6.2 percent in a three-level model.

It can be seen from Figure 3 that it is the ethnically lightly polarized countries which score highest on the dependent variable. We have calculated the exact top

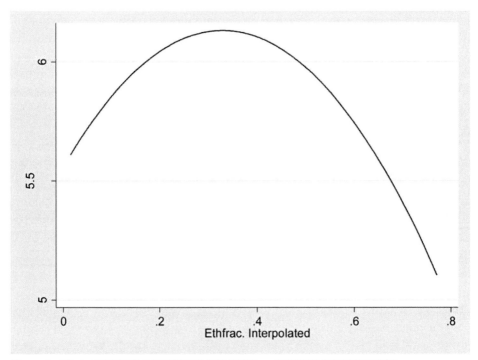

Figure 3: Effect of ETHNIC FRACTIONALIZATION on INCOME DISTRIBUTION
Note: The graph is calculated by using the sample mean of INCOME EQUALITY as the starting
point, and the ETHNIC FRACTIONALIZATION coefficients from model 4.

point of the graph to be at 0.33. The countries in the dataset that are closest to this value are the United Kingdom and Mexico.

The effect of the control variable, PER CAPITA GDP, was not significant in models 1, 2, 3, and only significant at the 10 percent level in model 4. The sign was positive, implying that countries with a high value on PER CAPITA GDP have more left-leaning attitudes than those residing in poorer countries.

Discussion

In this paper, we have investigated an assumption which states that people in countries with a high percentage of immigrants are more skeptical towards economic redistribution. Some of the earlier literature has suggested that there is a link between increased heterogeneity in a society and a weaker support among people for economic redistribution. In the final model,we find support for the hypothesis that the most ethnically fractionalized societies hold the most negative attitudes towards economic redistribution. The reason that the results are only significant in the level-2 modeling is that level-3 models are more conservative since more of the variation in Y is explained at level-2 when modeling with only two levels.

In this study, we tested the explanatory power of intergroup theory and group threat theory. The models included commonly used variables in research attitudes, such as gender, education, and left–right attitudes. The individual level variables were the same in all four models; women, older people, those with a relatively low income, those with high trust in people, low education, and those belonging to the left side of the political spectrum. All these groups tend to have leftist views on INCOME EQUALITY. The strength of the two theories was tested against a broad set of countries. The study shows that ethnically homogeneous societies are generally positive to economic redistribution. Polarized societies are the most positive, while the most ethnically fractionalized societies are the less likely to support economic redistribution. The results can be explained by a combination of the three different theoretical approaches. Since homogeneous societies are positive to economic redistribution, this could lend support to the group threat theory, where ethnic altruism is higher when people do not feel threatened by another ethnic group. We also find support for the threshold argument where polarized countries hold the most pro-welfare attitudes. A composition of ethnic groups which are relatively similar in size can reduce feelings of threat. The results show no support to intergroup contact theory since more contact between ethnic groups is correlated with negative attitudes towards economic redistribution. In sum, the findings show that societies that are lightly ethnically polarized are pro-welfare. Societies that have traditionally been homogeneous and have recently become more heterogeneous, such as the United Kingdom, are still positive to economic redistribution. Although based on the patterns we see in other countries there is a possibility that traditionally homogeneous countries will become less pro-welfare in the long run since group threat mechanisms may become stronger. The findings indicate that the two main theories of ethnic relations seem to be at play in different settings when it comes to the study of ethnicity and welfare attitudes. We argue that up to a certain point, more diversity will lead to increased positive welfare attitudes. However, when this threshold is reached, any further diversity implies less positive attitudes. Thus, the countries that hold the most positive attitudes are those from ethnically polarized societies. One explanation for this is that these countries enjoy a substantive positive effect of intergroup contact, without being exposed to the full extent of group threat mechanisms.

Conclusion

In this paper, we investigated assumptions in the literature that immigration and increased heterogeneity in society may weaken the support for a re-distributing welfare state. Our main finding is that in OECD countries a rise in ethnic diversity up to a certain point leads to more pro-welfare attitudes, but when this threshold is reached any further diversity is associated with more negative attitudes. Societies that are ethnically homogenous are positive to economic redistribution. This renders support to group theory which states that more ethnic contact leads to more ethnic competition over resources. We argue that group threat mechanisms lead to a lower degree of ethnic altruism, as seen in attitudes towards economic redistribution. Countries that are ethnically polarized are the most pro-welfare. These countries are characterized by ethnic demographic balance where the limited number of ethnic groups are similar in size. Here, the effect of intergroup contact is clearly present, while the effects of group threat mechanisms have not made their mark.

The possibility of economic decline in Western societies could lead to an increased struggle over resources. Quillian (1996) found that especially during a recession when the economic conditions are tough, the perceived threat in the majority group is likely to expand. This threat is connected to competition among the ethnic groups for jobs and other economic resources. There is a possibility that the present economic decline in many Western societies could strengthen the importance of group threat mechanisms. This could lead to more negative attitudes towards the welfare state. Our intention has been to map out the connection between diversity and welfare attitudes. A strength of the data is that it includes both Western and non-Western countries. One caveat concerning this study deserves to be mentioned: the sample included only 30 countries and one should be wary of drawing conclusions on a general basis. Further research would be well advised to include more countries in order to draw stronger conclusions concerning the connection between a country's ethnic composition and welfare attitudes.

References

Alesina, A. & Glaeser, E. (2004). *Fighting Poverty in the US and Europe. A World of Difference*. Oxford: Oxford University Press.

Allport, Gordon W. (1954). *The Nature of Prejudice*. Reading: Addison-Wesley.

Bakkan, H. (2012). *Unpacking Ethnicity and Civil Conflict*. Student Paper.

Banting, K. & W. Kamlycka (2006). *Multiculturalism and the Welfare State*. Oxford: Oxford University Press.

Blalock, Hubert M. Jr. (1967). *Towards a Theory of Minority Group Relations*. New York: John Wiley & Sons.

Blumer, H. (2003). Race Prejudice as a Sense of Group Position. In Ch. A. Gallagher (Ed.). *Rethinking the Color Line: Readings in Race and Ethnicity*, 2nd ed.,. New York: McGraw Hill: 111–7.

De Deleeuw, J & Meijer. E. (Eds.). (2008). *Handbook of Multilevel Analysis*. New York: Springer.

Department of Geodesy and Cartography in the State Geological Committees of the USSR(1964). *Àòëàñ Íàðîäîâ Ìèðà/Atlas Naradov Mira* [Atlas of the People of the World]. Moscow: Glavnoe upravlenie geodezii i kartografii.

Esping-Andersen, G. (1990). *The Three Worlds of Welfare Capitalism*. Oxford: Blackwell.

Fearon, J, D. & Laitin, D. D. (2003). Ethnicity, Insurgency, and Civil War. *American Political Science Review* 97, 75–90.

Forbes, H. D. (1997). *Ethnic Conflict*. New Haven, CT: Yale University Press.

Freeman, G. P. (1986). Migration and the political economy of the welfare state. *The Annals of the American Academy of Political and Social Science*, 485–51.

Granovetter, M. (1978). Threshold Models of Collective Behavior. *American Journal of Sociology* 88, 1420–43.

Hamilton, L, C. (1992). *Regression with Graphics: A Second Course in Applied Statistics*. Belmont, CA: Wadsworth Inc.

Hjerm, M. & Schnabel, A. (2012). How Much Heterogeneity can the Welfare StateEndure? The Influence of Heterogeneity on Attitudes to the Welfare State. *Nations and Nationalism*, 18 (2), 346–369.

Hox, J. (2002). *Multilevel Analysis: Techniques and Applications*. Mahwah: Lawrence Erlbaum.

Korpi, W. (1983). *The Democratic class struggle*. Boston: Routledge and Kegan Paul.

Lewis, A. (2002). Whiteness Studies: Past Research and Future Directions. *African American Research Perspectives* 8, 1–16.

Myles, J. & St-Arnaud, S. (2006). Population Diversity, Multiculturalism, and the WelfareState: should Welfare State Theory be revisited? In K. Banting & W. Kymlicka (Eds.). *Multiculturalism and the Welfare State*. Oxford University Press.

Quillian, L. (1996). Group Threat and Regional Change in Attitudes toward African Americans. *American Journal of Sociology,* 102, 816–60.

Rothbart, M. & Oliver, P.J. (1993). Intergroup Relations and Stereotype Change: A Social-Cognitive Analysis and Some Longitudinal Findings. In *Prejudice, Politics, and the American Dilemma*, edited by P. M. Sniderman, P. E. Tetlock, and E. G. Carmines. Stanford, CA: Stanford University Press, 32–59.

Rushton, J. P. (2005). Ethnic Nationalism, evolutionary psychology and Genetic Similarity Theory. *Nations and Nationalism,* 11 (4), 489–507.

Schelling, T.C. (1971). Dynamic Models of Segregation. *Journal of Mathematical Sociology,* 1, 143–86.

Schelling, T. C. (1978). *Micromotives and Macrobehavior*. New York: W. W. Norton.

Sears, D. & Citrin, J. (1985). *Tax Revolt. Something for Nothing in California*. Cambridge, MA: Harvard University Press.

Soss, S., Schram. J. & Fording. R. (2003). *Race and the Politics of Welfare Reform*. Ann Arbor, MI: University of Michigan Press.

Steenbergen, M. R., & Bradford, S. J. (2002). Modeling Multilevel Data Structures. *American Journal of Political Science*, 46, 218–37.

Taylor-Gooby, P. (2005). Is the Future American? Or can Left Politics Preserve European Welfare States from Erosion through Growing Racial Diversity? *Journal of Social Policy* 34, 661–72.

Authors

Joachim Vogt Isaksen
Assistant Professor
Norwegian University of Science and Technology
Department of Applied Social Science
Faculty of Health and Social Science
Research areas: ethnic relations, sociology of health and illness, sociology of the media

Tor Georg Jakobsen, Ph.D.
Associate Professor
Norwegian University of Science and Technology
Trondheim Business School
Research areas: political behavior, ethnic relations, peace research

Recognition and the symbolic value of work[1]

Knut Magne Sten

Abstract

The study reports from three different cases, an open prison, a "one-day-work" centre, and the selling of street magazines. Although different, they all reflect work outside the ordinary labour market. "Work" is an important social institution, and symbolic value is connected to every activity that can be considered work. The identification of action and the management of social identities are intimately and causally related. When action identity is communicated to others, it has the potential of affecting the image of the actor in society. The study is explorative both in the empirical description and theoretical basis, although a starting point is the theory of recognition of Axel Honneth.

Introduction

There are basically four different approaches when helping people to achieve change. To change the context by giving people new opportunities, to give people a new interpretation of what the possibilities are, to change their behaviour by acquiring new skills, or by understanding themselves in a new way.

The motivation for change could be extrinsic or intrinsic, being rooted in social connections, deliberation or emotional life. A combination gives six different possibilities, which will be illustrated later.

I do not call these and other statements a theory. In my words, it is more of a general theoretical wrapping. As such, it provides a background for my interpretation of efforts in social work. This effort could be organized in a programme, as informal ideas and guidelines among social workers, or as an open opportunity for

---

[1] Diana-Maria Bîzgan, Mâdâlina-Octva Buzdugâ, students at Universitatea Alexandru Ioan Cuza, Romani, have written the description of "Dagsverket", except for the interviews. Most of the interviews are translated from Fjær (2006). Apart from my own observations and interviews the section about Leira draws heavily on Trygve Steiro et.al (2013). In the section on "Sorgenfri" I have translated the interviews from interviews published in several editions of Sorgenfri.

the needy. Three examples, or cases, illustrate these three different settings. The underlying theory is that there is – if successful – some common grounds. One of these is supposed to be appreciation (acknowledgment, recognition), another is reciprocity. I will concentrate on the first one in this essay.

Acts of recognition affect many aspects of our lives, such as receiving a round of applause, being spotted in a crowded street by a friend, having an application for a job rejected because of your criminal record, enjoying some words of praise from a professor, being stopped at customs because you belong to a minority group, and fighting to have your same-sex marriage officially sanctioned. Evidently, the various ways we are recognized (and recognize others) play an important role in shaping our quality of life. Recognition theorists go further than this, arguing that recognition can help form, or even determine, our sense of who we are and the value accorded to us as individuals.

Axel Honneth (1995, 2007), the successor of Habermas and contemporary leading figure in critical theory, has produced a very extensive discussion of recognition. Like Charles Taylor, Honneth says that recognition is essential for self-realization. He draws on the early Hegel in order to identify how this is achieved, as well as establishing the motivational and normative role recognition can play in understanding and justifying claims made by marginalized people. Apart from Hegel, Honneth turns to Mead and Winnicott to find some empirical basis for the three 'patterns of recognition' necessary for an individual's development of a positive relation-to-self. These are love, rights, and solidarity (Honneth, 1995, 2007):

(i) the demand for love, confirming the reliability of one's basic senses and needs and creating the basis for self-confidence, (ii) the demand for rights, through which one learns to recognise others as independent human beings with rights like oneself, creating the basis for self-respect, and (iii) the demand for recognition as a unique person, the basis for self-esteem and a complex and tolerant social life"[2]

Recognition is instrumental in creating self-confidence, self-respect and self-esteem, and in this way contributes to form an individual's self-conception. A positive self-conception and a belief in one's capability, i.e. the self-efficacy of a person, is necessary for change. In order to explore this we will consider three different cases. By doing so we will approach the empirical reality instead of just referring to Mead and others (who could also more correctly be considered theorists rather than empirical researchers).

The cases are an open prison, a one-day-work service, and the selling of street magazines. The cases are different but there are similarities, and the unifying theme is promotion of self-efficacy. To develop self-efficacy could be an explicit

---

[2]   quoted from http://www.iep.utm.edu/recog_sp/#SH3b

goal (the prison), a most welcome by-product ("a day of work") or not considered as such, but acknowledged if asked (selling magazines).

Our three cases are in some way related to work. Work is paradoxical in many respects. It is something you think you should do, you have your obligations towards society and your community, it is a rational thing to do, you get paid and you can have decent life because of it, you do something you master and maybe you put a part of yourself, your identity, into it. Yet, you can read comments like

... you're probably not very excited to get to the office in the morning, you don't feel much appreciated while you're there, you find it difficult to get your most important work accomplished, amid all the distractions, and you don't believe that what you're doing makes much of a difference anyway. By the time you get home, you're pretty much running on empty, and yet still answering emails until you fall asleep.

The idea of working

The idea of working has a grip on our minds. Even if not valued by the worker, work carries symbolic value. Even if you do it first and foremost for instrumental reasons you would add symbolic value to what you choose to do. The money you could earn as a seller of a street magazine could be substantial in a very limited economy, but the value of showing others that you are more than a drug addict is equally important. By carrying out a day of service or serving in an open prison, one also participates in many other activities with the same opportunity to prove yourself. That is one important lesson for clinical practice, and the next important thing is to incorporate this insight into the theory of social work practice. The social pedagogy of Jens Bay (2005), the pedagogy of consequences, could be a valid response to this challenge.

The approach is a humanistic approach based on self-creation. This pedagogy and this kind of thinking is, as I see it, deeply rooted in symbolic interaction (Charon, 2001, Mead, 1934, Blumer, 1969). However, work as such – including in a clinical setting – must be understood from a sociological point of view through different categories. One of these is symbolic interaction: By performing normal work, you signal the meaning of being a person like any other who works for money. By working for some kind of external pay-off (i.e. not only the recognition) you are involved in social exchange, which is another category. These two categories are on the individual relational level, it is facework. But there is also a contextual level. First, there is the institutional level. The institutional level gives meaning to symbolic value, as this is what everybody does and is supposed to do. Second, there is the structural-functional one. In this case, it is the opportunity structure enabled by policy. For ordinary work, this is the labour market. You will

find these categories in a table, where they represent outcomes of a combination
of incentives (motivation) and the social level:

Motivation and achievements: Social level "everybody" or just "me and you":	External	Internal
Context (society – "everybody else")	Structure-functional "Everybody do have their place"	Institutional "Everybody thinks so"
Relations ("face to face")	Social exchange "What's in it for me"	Symbolic interaction "This is me"

This table illustrates the theoretical space for action as most kinds of action
do have connections to all these categories. The types of action are embedded in
the actor's position (in some structure), his social roles and the relevant social
norms, the meaning of the action and what the actor gets out of it. "Work" easily
illustrates this, if we consider the institutional category.

Ideas of work also stem from the Old Testament. Work is seen as punishment
from God, rightly so because of the sin introduced into the Garden of Eden. Not
to work with no acceptable excuse is seen as a rejection of man's subordination to
God – not to work is therefore – according to Foucault – the cardinal sin. Although
work could be necessary to achieve a good life, work in itself was not considered
a good thing. Things changed during the Reformation, as Martin Luther saw work
as a duty (Beruf), something called upon to do by God or a mission in life. Skills
in work was therefore of high moral value. This "work ethic" was also typical
of the 'treatment' institutions. Later, during the 1800th century, work was seen as
something good. You should have the right to paid work and a salary to sustain
yourself (Midre, 1990). Work as an evil or a virtue is blurred unless you draw
a line between meaningful and meaningless work. Though drawing the line is
not necessarily up to the individual. In social policy and social work, work is
considered a means to achieve goals. First, paid work brings people out of the
welfare queue. Second, there is the therapeutic value of work. Third, work is a
disciplinary tool and (a part of) punishment. Work as a means and a moral issue
are intertwined.

On the structural-functional side, new policies are introduced as Active
Labour Market Policies (ALMP). This means active measures rather than passive

(income maintenance); restricting the access and the level of benefits for unemployment, sickness, rehabilitation, disability, etc.

This is also combined with workfare:
– To compel able-bodied recipients to work
– To do work in return for benefits
– The terms are inferior to comparative work in the labour market
– The lowest tier of income maintenance

Welfare to work, yet another distinction, indicates something between ALMP and workfare. It is connected to social assistance, but unlike workfare offers training and new competences.

The goal of ending poverty is now more in the background; "we" should reinforce the work ethic and reduce the caseloads in the welfare system.
– The citizen has a right and a *duty* to work or prepare for work.
– The connection between personal responsibility and rights should be clear and perceptible for the young
– We expect necessary life styles changes (e.g. "the clients should learn to get up in the morning")

Welfare institutions are not only instrumental. They also include considerations of moral and social justice. It has been argued that this is not only moral, but moralistic and something resembling the view held in the Old Testament. Anyway, this short discussion of work promotes a broad agenda for work as part of social work, with clients outside the ordinary job market, and where morality and targets spill over.

Recognition

The methodological approach taken is explicitly social constructionist. In this context, the self or personal identity is formed dialectically through interaction with a social reality.

In her dialectical understanding of relations, the Norwegian psychologist Anne-Lise Løvlie Schibbye (2002) describes how the self develops in interaction with others. If you feel excluded or pain this is often because of a shortage of recognition. A person in need has both problems with receiving recognition and recognizing others. Recognition in the understanding of Løvlie Schibbye (2002) is first and foremost internal recognition, not praise and measurable valorization, which is external recognition. What matters is internal recognition. Internal recognition is when your deeper feelings and experiences are seen, shared and confirmed. If the other (it could be the therapist) manages to adapt to this attitude, it creates the necessary mood or atmosphere for a dialectic dialogue.

It also contributes to self-closure; being a self-determined person, open to, but still separate from others. Persons in need often lack the courage or self-efficacy to self-closure. Recognition is a building block to achieve this and to achieve self-understanding, to become wise when considering yourself. Instead of interpreting the person, the person is invited to wonder about herself – together with the other. Of course, the therapist does use some mild form of interpretation by wondering ... *has be it occurred to you that...* This is intended to strengthen the ability to reflect and the feeling of autonomy. Feelings are the foundation of the self, thoughts are necessary but not sufficient. Feelings are associated with moments of change.

Like Honneth (1995), Anne-Lise Løvlie Schibbye's (2002) thoughts are rooted in Hegelian and humanistic philosophy. The same issues are thoroughly examined in *practice* by the Norwegian sociologist Astrid Skatvedt (2010), and in a more Goffmanian way. As she says:

Goffman shows how we attempt to avoid loss of face, how we can preserve our dignity in interaction with others and at the same time contribute to a respectful presentation of the Other. In this way, the selves can be confirmed as worthy. Collins has developed the logic of Goffman's theory. His central point is how people move from situation to situation and discover the emotional energy developed in interaction with others. In this perspective, interaction situations are viewed as events that when "successful" generate feelings and symbolic messages that "recharge" people.

Some of these interactive situations are based on interaction between the client and staff, and some are among the clients themselves.

A Norwegian sociologist, Geir Hyrve who has studied many treatment programmes for drug addicts, youngsters with behavioural problems, etc. state that it is very important that the clients form relations outside therapy. Without group relations, the treatment tends to fail. If group relations continue after treatment, it will also increase the possibility for change. The clients need recognition on a broad scale. This also reflects the message by Skatvedt (2010).

Her practical context is "The house", which is a Norwegian state-run rehabilitation institution. The clients are male and female adults with drug-related addiction problems. Astrid Skatvedt is a participant observer. This is one of her stories:

Arne (employee) has finished his night shift and is about to go home. Kristian (resident) is about to begin his daily work with the other residents. Kristian asks Arne, "Why haven't you gone home yet?"
"Why weren't you up at 7.00 am?" answers Arne with the same obviously studied brusqueness.
"Residents are supposed to be up by then."

"I was up at 7.00! If you'd been up then you'd have seen me!" Replies Kristian.
"It's too laid-back here," says Arne, and stares out into mid-air.
"Goddamn, now you're getting to be grey-haired!" Kristian remarks and leans in close to Arne, squinting at his sideburns.

Her interpretation: This example can serve as an illustration of a typical informal interaction – small talk about nothing, but which has the capacity to move the identity of the resident in new directions while functioning as a confirmation of closeness in the relation. This situation generates emotional energy through camaraderie and trust despite the actors being staff member and client in an institution. Powerful symbolic signals of inclusion among the "straight" and worthy are communicated.

Incidents of reciprocity, in which residents communicate with staff members as equals, are identified by residents as particularly significant. They are given the possibility to present themselves as competent people. Another observation by Skatvedt (2010) is telling. Aimee, a mother of several children but without custody of any of them because of problems with drug addiction, shares such a moment with Karin, a staff member who is several years younger and pregnant with her first child. "How's it going then, are you tired? When did you say the due date was?" Karin looks at Aimee calmly and trustingly and sits for a long while quite still – it is almost as though she nods off to sleep in between talking to Aimee. They sit together for quite a while, but do not talk very much. There is an unspoken alliance between them that has developed spontaneously; they are two mothers sharing a bond that has not been created through words, effort, planning or structure, and is therefore easier to perceive as real and true than if it had been constructed as a carefully broached point of resonance in a therapy session. The roles are reversed; the resident is the one who gives a safe, relaxed moment to the staff member. If the chat had been between two residents it would not have had the same effect because residents cannot label one another as ordinary people. It is only the staff, representatives of ordinary people, who have authorization to do this.

This "flavour of reality", argues Schibbye, is something that lays the foundations for change (Skatvedt, 2010). I think this idea is confirmed in the next three cases that follow. The first one is from "Leira open prison".

Leira Open Prison

Leira Prison is situated in rural surroundings approximately seven kilometres outside the city of Trondheim. It works as a relatively small, open prison with a maximum of 29 inmates. There are several buildings located on the property: Apart from houses for dwelling and visiting, there is a barn, a stable, a garden centre, and a house for car repairs. You have the possibility of acquiring skills.

There are no fences around the property, the prison boundaries are indicated by crossroads and buildings. A prisoner moving beyond these limits is considered to be attempting escape. Nothing symbolizes a prison. A small event, much to the amusement among the prisoners, was shared with me. A car with Polish jobseekers was passing by. Leira looked like a good opportunity and they drove into the institution. They had a big laugh when they understood they found themselves in the midst of a prison.

Leira practices consequence pedagogy, an approach grounded in humanistic and existential thinking developed by the Danish philosopher and psychologist Jens Bay (2005). Central aspects of consequence pedagogy are freedom, choice, action, consequence and responsibility.

The staff do not wear uniforms. Managers, employees and inmates are on a first-name basis. This conveys a message of equality between inmates and staff, in marked contrast to the traditional division between prison staff and inmates in most prisons (Steiro et al., 2013) A key aspect of Leira is that inmates apply for admission to the prison, which can only be done after serving at least three years in a traditional prison. Leira is subject to the same laws and regulations as Norwegian prisons in general, but the institution has the opportunity to develop its own approach within the legislative framework. Their existential viewpoint is that each individual has a free will and therefore will have to take responsibility for his/her own actions and the ensuing consequences (Bay, 2005). The following beliefs are stated in their documents and reported by Steiro et al. (2013:13);

'When we say that humans are "thinking, willing and acting" we need to have in mind that this is meant subjectively – through dialectic relations to other people. In order to be able to understand how each inmate thinks, we need to be in a dialogue with each person and refrain from judging the other by applying our own unfounded beliefs.'

Consequences are not considered to be mere punishment or sanctions, but are rather viewed to be the logical results of one's actions (Steiro et al., 2013). Such a paradigm gives the individual a choice and provides each inmate with an opportunity for personal development by learning new and more constructive modes of behaviour. Steiro et al. (2013) observed the following: Staff members are conscious to not give advice but rather, through dialogue and the use of questions, empower inmates to find their own solutions. Staff and inmates work together on an everyday basis, and participate in mutual activities during their spare time. The staff is expected to take part in free time activities outside the working hours. The inmates must meet the same requirements at work as any other employee in the general population. They are expected to take responsibility for their job, and are not permitted to call in sick without a good reason. In addition, in focusing on job training, Leira concentrates on helping the inmates to develop social skills. The inmates themselves have signed a written agreement to take part in the social community at Leira.

The inmates viewed the applied consequence pedagogy as positive and feel that they were responded to as human beings. They regarded it as a good and fair framework that was easy to understand. They knew what to expect should they break the rules and had no problems with the methodology. Many inmates considered the mandatory physical activities to be a positive requirement, and used this as an opportunity to increase their physical exercises in order to change and grow as individuals. During the interviews, former drug addicts were particularly eager to report that they found this activity helpful, both mentally and physically, in order to keep living without any intoxicating substances. Furthermore, the management explained that, over time, a number of inmates at Leira improved their physical condition. The staff always expressed their appreciation of these accomplishments and often rewarded the prisoners who reached their goals with prizes. Management and staff emphasized that the prizes are not the crucial factor, but serve more as a means and symbol to maintain the system. The inmates thought that the entire staff worked in the inmates' best interest, although not all staff members were equally esteemed by the inmates. The inmates typically described the wardens as humane and wise, but at the same time quite realistic. The inmates felt that those characteristics were important in such a place. For their part, the wardens emphasized that they needed to be genuinely committed to the inmates' well-being and future. Otherwise, the inmates would soon view them as insincere. This point was also stressed as a condition for the staff's chances of influencing the inmates at all.

Work is important for recognition. Two conditions apply: One should be physically able to perform work and participate in activities. Next, one should have the motivation to do so. If motivation is missing two things happen: The other inmates try to convince the newcomer that the rules and obligations are to the benefit of the newcomer and the community. The staff hold talks with him or her, and if that does not help they make some kind of deal: They explain what the inmate has to do in order not to be transferred back to the ordinary prison. The message is: You always have a choice. A couple of newcomers had to return last year because they could not adapt. Altogether, about 10% of the new arrivals have to return, and the risk is slightly increasing. Leira does not pick their inmates, they accept whoever applies and is sent by the system. It is a kind of democratic opportunity, but it is a challenge and a possible threat. The development is illustrated by bicycling. Bicycling in teams has been a major activity, and in the beginning they joined a big competition of 550 kilometres. With less fit inmates they had to switch to an-

other (but also very popular) race, about 80 kilometres of mountain biking. But as
it turned out that this was also too demanding, they had to be content with more
simple biking on ordinary roads. The frequency of cognitive and psychiatric diagnoses has also been increasing. The approach at Leira is cognitive-behavioural,
generating rules of conduct that shape the attitudes of the inmates, who consider
their possibilities of action and make a psychological contract with the prison. If
you do not have the mental capacity to handle this philosophy, you do not have
much of a future at Leira. You must be able to participate in a community that in
return gives you recognition. Exchange is a requirement.

"DAGSVERKET" – "A day's work"

That is different at Dagsverket ("A day's work"), which is the second case. You
will find "Dagsverket" in Trondheim and Bergen (Fjær, 2006), and similar opportunities in Oslo (Bogen, 2007). At Dagsverket, people with social problems, such
as drug or alcohol addiction and sometimes with a criminal record, psychiatric
problems etc., can find daily work of four hours a day. At the end of the day, they
receive NOK 200, tax-free. Private people or organizations, businesses etc. who
want something done could buy the services from Dagsverket. The jobseekers
are free to come whenever they wish, from Monday to Friday without making an
appointment.

   Dagsverket occupies the ground floor of a tall building in the city centre. It
consists of two offices, a kitchen area, a place to sit, rest or have meetings, and an
area for small-scale production.

   On a regular day, people looking for work come between 8 and 9 a.m., sign
a contract, put their names on a list and have breakfast and coffee together with
the full time employees. At 9 a.m. the list is taken inside the office and the people
are assigned to 3 or 4 teams, depending on what jobs are available that day and on
how many have turned up for work. A beneficiary says:

It must really be something if a drug addict bothers to get up in the morning and work
four hours for a salary of 200 kroner. You must really be dedicated to something, you
can't have lost the hope... There are many drug addicts who don't have any hope in life.
They just enter the race and don't give a shit. Such people don't come, you must have
some hope...

On average, there are about 13 beneficiaries every day. The number varies between
8 and 20. At 9.30 a.m., after the teams have been formed, they all go to the clients'
sites, along with the team-leader and begin work. At 11.30 a.m. there is a lunch
break and each worker receives three pieces of bread, coffee and juice. At 13.00
p.m. all teams return to the headquarters, have another coffee and chat about their

day. The manager then takes the list that was written in the morning, calls the name of each worker and hands them 200 kroner (about 25 euros) each. The payment is little, but important:

I would rather earn the 200 kroner at Dagsverket than steal something in a shop and re-selling it. That means a lot. But I believe it might have been the reason to be here in the first place but it's not the reason for being here every day, five days a week. It's because I learn something by joining and because of the sense of community.

I am using Dagsverket only for the extra money. It's legal money right into the pocket every day. It is so fantastic, we are standing outside freezing waiting to come inside. Of course I think it is nice to be there, otherwise I wouldn't come...

After this, they are free to leave, but the team-leaders and the manager remain for a little longer to discuss the events that occurred during the day.

For people who can handle a permanent job, Dagsverket tries to help finding a job. Around 10 to 15 people receive a permanent job every year. This is not a small achievement.

In order to get the possibility to work at Dagsverket, in addition to having a drug or alcohol addiction, a beneficiary has to be registered in the official welfare support system (the Norwegian Labour and Welfare Administration, NAV). Dagsverket also acts as a bridge between the beneficiaries and NAV, as many conflicts and frustrations may arise in between. Discontent may appear on both sides: The beneficiaries are unhappy with the system controlling them, making them account for the money they spend or provide documents, and the workers at NAV are unhappy with the beneficiaries missing their scheduled meetings, showing up under influence of substances, or being loud or impolite. The workers at Dagsverket help the beneficiaries by reminding them about their meetings or sometimes keeping them at the headquarters, explaining to them what they need to do and keeping them up to date on the continuously changing rules of the system.

The activities at Dagsverket, production at the headquarter or work at clients' sites, include:
– Making a kind of ball for a local sport, "basse", that is sold to local stores
– Painting houses
– Cutting trees, chopping and selling wood.
– Doing laundry for some institutions
– Cleaning parking lots
– Gardening
– Transporting furniture
– Transporting objects to recycling factories
– Making packages with sterile utensils for the Overdose Team
– One to three people stay inside to clean the headquarter

– Collect food for the Salvation Army from two chain supermarkets.

As payment for the services and the transportation costs for collecting food, the food is divided fifty-fifty with Dagsverket. This list is not exhaustive, but reflects the main activities.

The activities do not require a lot of hard work, and everyone is allowed to work at their own pace. Even if they do not have a full working capacity, it is better to do what they can than do nothing at all. Except for the last two mentioned, all activities are a source of income for Dagsverket. With the money they make from these activities they manage to pay the rent and the administration costs of the headquarters. What is important for beneficiaries to know is that the work they do is valuable and supports the institution they work for. But of course these activities cover just a small part of the costs, like for instance the salaries of the permanent staff.

The rules at Dagsverket state that the participants are not allowed to use any substances when working and that they have to be sober enough to work. Therefore, the use of drugs and alcohol is reduced. However, they are not asked to stop using substances completely or undergo treatment in order to be able to work here. This is just the first step in their rehabilitation, with a low threshold, giving people a starting point. It is up to the workers to decide if they want to continue and they are free to do so at their own pace whenever they think they are ready. Some of the participants have been working there for years with little or no hope of finding a permanent job, which they are not forced to.

An important aspect of this opportunity is to give people in distress a first chance to improve their lives – giving them a job and a way to make some money – though it is also a way of becoming part of a community, to make friends, to find people who share their problems, to have the feeling of doing something useful, to learn team work and responsibility, and to become aware that they can contribute to society in a positive way. People come there to seek work, but the idea is to give them more than that, and to help them find a new direction in life.

It is easy to see how relationships are forming between the participants and between the participants and staff. The people have breakfast and lunch together, laughing and chatting, small groups of friends form and meet outside working hours, and there are is also the inevitable bickering and disagreements. Oivind, the manager, said there had been only one case of violence during all these years. What is more remarkable is the solidarity they show in times of trouble. Recently, a former beneficiary of Dagsverket committed suicide. Those who knew him gathered and had a memorial service to show support for his relatives.

All the work is carried out in teams, where the participants, team-leaders and interns are working side by side. This defines the relationship between all actors involved in a particular way: They are equal, ordinary workers do not view the team-leaders as an imposing authority that tries to do something for the beneficiaries against their will. They are rather considered co-workers with similar challenges. We heard some of the beneficiaries say that they did not see any difference between Oivind and them. This facilitates the development of closer connections and improves communication.

Work also raises a person's self-esteem, helping him/her to appreciate the activity. One of the participants said: "My children are so proud of me, I pay my bills with the money I make here." Responsibility and reciprocity is behaviour and thinking that can be learned. It is enough to consider the fact that they have to wake up in the morning and be at Dagsverket before 9 a.m., rather than just living on social support. The sense of responsibility becomes even more pronounced at the jobs that are contracted by Dagsverket for the beneficiaries to carry out.

"Many drug addicts don't have self-confidence, they believe it's written drug addict in their face. But, when they are dressed in the working clothes and do a piece of work, they meet people's enthusiasm, looks and gratitude. And they can almost not believe this to be true".
(One of the participants)

The beneficiaries are diverse; 30% female, 70% male, from 20 to 70 years old, some of them well educated, some who have not finished high school, some have families, some do not, some have children in foster care, some have spent time in prison, some are well travelled, some love Kafka, some love football, they are people who smile all the time or people who hear voices, people from Norway, Ukraine, Ethiopia, Somalia and Afghanistan.

It is fun at Dagsverket ....I do really need those 200 kroner, but the main reason is the social thing...I can make use of myself, I will sleep during the night, I don't need the sleeping pills...

...it is good to know that you have been here all week and know that you have contributed something good, not something terrible....

The opinions differ regarding some types of work. Picking garbage is one of them. Both team-leaders and participants think that this work could be degrading. People with an earlier job often do not want this work, not because of the job itself, but because they can run into people from their former life and make their fall in social status visible. Those who do pick garbage, on the other hand, do receive a lot of recognition from people passing by:

"You are doing one of the most important jobs in the city"

"Ordinary people give us a lot of praise. It is very encouraging. They see us as ordinary people. When we go around with our trolleys there are only positive words".

Selling street magazines

My third case is about selling street magazines. It is a fruitful activity in many respects, though it is not a programme for rehabilitation. Rather it is an opportunity, but how you interpret it is up to yourself. The effect of becoming integrated into society is more of a side effect along with the income.

The idea behind the street magazines is a simple, but effective one. The sellers buy the magazines they want to sell, and sell them for double the original price. It started with *Street News* in NY and *The Big Issue* in London as the first European magazine. Now you can find them worldwide, in more than 40 countries and more than 80 different versions. They also have their "The international network of street papers, INSP".

In Trondheim the magazine is called "Sorgenfri" ("Free of sorrow")

The job gives the sellers positivity and joy. They become more concerned about how they present themselves to others, which motivates a reduction in the drug consumption, as they wish to do their job with style. They want to be seen as members of society with useful work, which they feel they have. They do not only sell a magazine they think people should read but they also offer the buyers a broader perspective on life by talking to them. And many buyers seem to need this small talk, as the sellers are people with experiences from a troubled life, which may be similar to that of relatives or friends of the buyers. Through these meetings on the streets, the sellers' ability to cope, as well as their identity and belonging to the community is improving. Quite often, the magazines publish pictures showing the seller being embraced by a buyer, sometimes vice-versa, or, they close the deal with a handshake.

The handshake is a powerful symbol of belonging and respect. For most of us, it will surely boost our self-esteem. As in the case of Christer, one of the sellers. He wants one thing more than anything else, respect. That people look at him in the eyes without contempt and dislike. The importance of nonverbal behaviour in drawing inferences about others is estimated to have five times the impact of verbal messages concerning a person's friendliness towards another man (Dolcos et al., 2012). Dolcos et al. have examined the impact of the handshake. Not only the judgment but also the neural correlates.

Some of the sellers are well educated. Siri is one of the most experienced sellers. She is a trained social worker, (BSw), carpenter, taxi driver and a bachelor student in theatrology. Though sometimes she is out of work. She says:

If you need help, but are on your own, the only possibility is the public services. Then you are a "case", "a problem" – you are one of a category. What you really need is to be seen and understood as the person you are. Instead, you become involved in a long struggle with the services. If you stumble and fall, you will be misunderstood and punished. All have their talents and resources. What is needed is motivation, support and encouragement. Everybody wishes to contribute (do their share). It is not lack of motivation that is the problem, but real possibilities. To be engaged is the tool that helps you the most.

There are many stories, all with their characteristic turns. Apart from some common problems, the sellers are different persons. This becomes clear if one listens to each one, and I present a number of them below. Still, we should look for similarities.

Lars is 50 years. Apart from two months as an assistant to a truck driver he has never had a job, taking drugs all his life. Now he sells Sorgenfri. Lise is deaf. She does not use drugs at the moment and wants to stay clean to get custody of her daughter who is in foster care. As a deaf youngster it was not easy to get proper assistance, and she stayed in a number of foster homes and institutions. Anyway, being deaf is not as big a hindrance for a seller. 24 year-old Pavla is from Siberia but has stayed in Trondheim since she was twelve. Her mother got married to a Norwegian. She is a girl in a man's body, but she is struggling to change her gender – she has taken surgery (some done by herself). She needs the job and the money. Jan Ivar is another person who does not use drugs, instead he is a part-time actor, assists at the theatre and carries out voluntary work organized by the church. He says that selling Sorgenfri is his real job, and his main income.

Maria is a former nursing student, but too much partying and too much work for the student association etc. made her burned out. For a period drugs became her "medication".

Sorgenfri is an opportunity to be exposed to the world. Many people believe the magazine is only sold by heavy drug addicts. "You look quite healthy" they say to me. Some of the buyers with personal relations to someone with drug problems say that it is nice to see a seller who looks so healthy. The income is a good supplement. It means a good dinner every day.

Kenneth sells Sorgenfri as an alternative to criminal activity. He is trying to change his life. He has been in jail, but now he is a part-time student, doing exercises and turned into an outspoken Christian. Geir has been a seller since the beginning, seven years ago. He has been very steady and has his own favourite spot. Geir thinks that the most important thing is to have something to do and be a member of a working community. The money is ok, but not the main reason for selling. He has noticed that local stories are popular, and the customers also say this is the most interesting thing to read about.

For others, the road to become a seller has been much longer. Sebastian felt ashamed by the thought of selling. He started to use amphetamine and heroin after he got a cancer diagnosis. Now he seems to be cured, and has stopped most of his drug consumption. Rather than a drug addict, he likes to see himself as a musician. Before he got cancer, he had a decent job and made music during his spare time.

Berit is middle-aged. She has been in psychiatric hospitals several times. But after she started selling the magazine she has been there for only shorter periods. Selling helps her self-confidence and gives her an extra income. A good thing about being a seller is the flexibility – you can stay away for several days and always come back. Mats, 35, has been a seller for five years. He has been a decent guy, doing sports and worked as a bricklayer and a taxi driver. He has occasionally been a psychiatric patient, his main problem being gambling addiction. Of course, you sometimes win but in the long run you lose and build up heavy debts. For years, he has also been a vagabond, living in Denmark, Spain and other countries. He wishes to go back to Barcelona.

Some make social relations, enjoy new contacts and show involvement. A woman drops into the Sorgenfri office; she has knit a scarf for one of the sellers, Anita. Anita is a drug addict, but she also has Bechterew's Syndrome. She is a mother of three children in their twenties and one of about ten. She really needs the money.

A meaningful relation, made meaningful by the symbolic value of the hand-shake, is a benefit. But the money earned is also important. With some extra money, they are able to do more of the ordinary things people do, having a meal in a restaurant, enjoying a holiday, giving some money to their children and so on.

Values like being independent, doing a day's work, performing your duty – in this way they felt in line with social norms and roles. This is their institutional context. "Street trade, not street aid" and "I don't beg for money for the bus and the food for the cat".

When it became known in 2014 that "Sorgenfri" was struggling to make ends meet, rock musicians in Trondheim and the nearby counties launched an initiative. For the benefit of Sorgenfri, they recreated the legendary concert "The Last Waltz" by The Band, selling out a big concert hall. Everybody played for free, making a huge donation to the magazine. As the original concert, the whole event was filmed and in cooperation with the national broadcasting company made into a documentary about Sorgenfri and its sellers. Of course, all this is was a symbol of recognition, producing even more recognition capital.

What next?

The people in these three cases do all tell a story about their motivation for doing what they do. Most of them seem to attach meaning or symbolic value to their work; a symbolic value that is embedded in an institutional context. The explorative nature of the study at this stage means that no categorization of motives has been carried out. A simple structure is suggested, based on the idea of the tripartite self – social, cognitive and emotional.

Motivating "the self"	Extrinsic motivation – exchange relations	Intrinsic motivation – recognition
Social	"Being a member of…."	Social approval
Cognitive	"A good deal"	Satisfaction
Emotional	"A prize"	Belonging

Although the extrinsic reward often is rather modest, it means a lot for many. It is also a very concrete symbol of the effort, something to show others. By carrying out the work they also participate – maybe without paying any attention – in skills training.

One of the primary assumptions of the relapse prevention theory is that substance use is a result of overlearned maladaptive behavioural patterns, and where drug use is seen as a maladaptive coping mechanism. Therefore, individuals must develop coping skills to resist the temptation (Pelissier, 2006). The necessity of skills training is often obvious. To make the training become motivated by extrinsic rewards could be another matter.

Extrinsic rewards in such settings have been questioned for different reasons, among them:
– Once having started using rewards, you cannot easily go back
– Rewards need in some important sense to be equitable
– If oriented towards rewards, people usually take the shortest path
Of course, it is not possible to return to a situation without rewards; no one will do a day's work or sell the magazine without a profit. It must also be a fair share. And of course, a shorter path (like cheating) than what is expected should not be possible.

Recent policy changes towards work for welfare, active labour market policy, etc., provide a structure with opportunities and a normative frame of reference. This is good for the able and motivated, whereas for others it could be a different story.

The third option, self–development is a more difficult issue. It is not clear-cut what it is and how it should be implemented, but most of the persons in the cases express intrinsic motivation for what they do.

"There is an aspect of intrinsic motivation that sets it quite apart from extrinsic control … It is an aspect that is almost spiritual. It has to do with life itself: It is vitality, dedication, transcendence" (Pelessier 2006:45). It is when you experience "more than ordinary moments of existence", and the experience represents its own justification.

Motivation requires that people see a relationship, a linkage, between be-haviour and outcome – that is, instrumentalities. People must feel competent in producing the outcome. The feeling of competence is in itself also an important aspect of intrinsic motivation. By creating highly controlled interpersonal con-texts, we undermine the natural desire to feel competent. It must be accompanied by the experience of autonomy, ref. Jens Bay (2005)

Looking more deeply into the corner of symbolic interaction in our fourfold table, a kind of process-oriented model could be derived from our discussion:

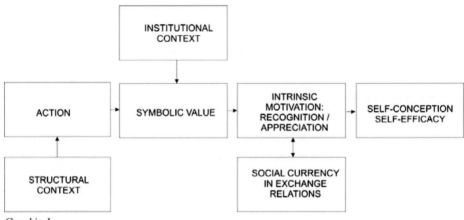

Graphic 1

Changing the self is a matter of changing the self-conception and increasing the sense of self-efficacy. A better self-conception enabled by increasing:
– Social responsiveness
– Social reflexivity
– Social identity – a stronger feeling of togetherness, belonging, etc.
Which all of our cases provide opportunities to handle.

A range of theoretical statements consequently follows. Examples are:
– Improving the self-conception increases the potential for self-efficacy
– Observable by the stated meaning of the chosen action, if it is considered a coping strategy
– A changing self is indicated by statements like: I change myself by seeing my action as coping
– Seeing things in this way is further enhanced by recognition
– "I increase my pool of recognition by investing it in my relations to others"

The follow-up phase of this introductory explorative study will try to shed light on these statements. The idea is to invite the participants to a more reflective dialogue about the meaning of their action and work. The study will be based on the theoretical process model. As we have seen, the model starts with the chosen action and its associated symbolic value.

An article by Vallacher and Wegner (1987) has the title: "What do people think they are doing. Action identification and human behaviour." Action identification theory simply says that your conception of what you do, e.g. how you communicate it, reveals much of your self-conception.

The identification of action and management of social identities are intimately and causally related. When action identities are communicated to others, they could potentially shape the image that others have of the actor. "Chopping wood" or "Helping the old man with wood for burning" is the same action, but reveal two different meanings. "Seeking social approval" is more informative about the actor than is "talking to someone". The theory distinguishes between different levels. Higher levels have greater potential for self-presentation. When do we choose high-level or low-level descriptions? If I am uncertain, I choose low-level. A feeling of competence produces high-level identification. In selecting interaction partners, people with low self-esteem would make their choice based on relationship opportunities, whereas people with high self-esteem make their choice according to self-esteem enhancement opportunities (Rudich et al., 1999)

Self-evaluation tends to be coherent (whether in a good or bad direction), and there is reason to think that evaluative coherence provides the basis for integration in the self system. Vallacher et al. (2002) claims that evaluation is the most global variable in our mental system. Evaluative consistency is widely recognized as providing the basis for organizing social judgments. Mechanisms for making things coherent could be denial, discounting, selective recall, confirmatory bias, defensive attribution and dissonance reduction.

This push for integration promotes internal dynamics, which initiates a self-organizing system, developing regions of coherent self-information/valuation. This shown by Nowak et al. (2000) abstracting from semantic content. It is a mental model of the mind similar to the ecology of a city. This model makes it possible to simulate the self-organizing process as Cellular Automata:

"Specific elements of self-understanding (e.g. goals, values, obsessions) are said to provide platforms for action and self-regulation, and basic properties of self-structure – most notably, global criteria of self-evaluation – are considered central to one's subjective well-being and the quality of one's interpersonal relations. These functions suggest that the self-structure plays a prominent, if not decisive, role in shaping the spontaneous flow of cognitive elements during self-reflective thought and in dictating how the stream of self-reflective thought accommodates incoming information and other factors capable of biasing self-perception in some fashion." (Wallacher et al., 2002:370)

Although my source of inspiration for the essay is Axel Honneth (1995), I have not dug deep into his theory of recognition, offering only some considerations on recognition as an interactional and identity issue, and trying to show that activities that can be considered work carry symbolic value that translates into recognition. Recognition as a source of rights and solidarity, and their possible empirical underpinnings, is yet to be considered.

References

Bandura, A. (1997). *Self-efficacy.* New York: W.H. Freeman and company.

Bay, J. (2005). *Konsekvenspædagogik.* Borgen Kjøbenhavn.

Bîzgan, D.-M., Mâdâlina-Octva, B. (2014). *Dagsverket – a new beginning for drug addicts – observational report.* HiST/AHS Trondheim.

Blumer, H. (1969). *Symbolic Interactionism: Perspective and Method.* Prentice-Hall, Englewood Cliffs N.J.

Bogen, H. (2007). Hadde det ikke vært for jobben, hadde jeg vært drita før kl. 10.00 FaFo-notat 2007–20 Oslo.

Charon, J. M. (2001). *Symbolic Interactionism. An Introduction, An Interpretation, An Integration* (7th ed.) New Jersey: Prentice – Hall.

Deci, E. L. (1995). *Why we do what we do. Understanding Self- Motivation.* New York: Penguin Books.

Dolcos, S. et al. (2012). The Power of a Handshake. Neural Correlates of Evaluative Judgments in Observed Social Interactions. *Journal of Cognitive Neuroscience,* 24 (12) 2292 – 2305.

Epstein, J. M. (2013). *Agent_Zero. Toward Neurocognitive Foundations for Generatvie social Science.* New Jersey: Princeton University Press Princeton.

Fjær, S. (2006). *Dagsverket – lavterskel arbeidstilbud for rusavhengige. Stein Rokkan Senter for flerfaglige samfunnsstudier.* Universitetsforskning Bergen.

Giddens, A. (1991). *Modernity and Self-Identity.* Cambridge UK: Polity Press.

Honneth, A. (1995). *The Struggle for Recognition: The Moral Grammar of Social Conflicts.* Polity Press.

Honneth, A. (2007). *Disrespect: The Normative Foundations of Critical Theory.* Polity Press.

Low, J. (2008). Structure, Agency and Social Reality in Blumerian Symbolic Interactionism: The influence of Georg Simmel. *Symbolic Interaction,* 31 (3), 325 – 343.

Mead, G. H. (1934). *Mind, Self and Society.* Chicago: University of Chicago Press.

Midre, G. (1990). *Bot, bedring eller brød.* Oslo: Universitetsforlaget.

Nowak, A., Rychwalska, A. & Borkowski, W. (2013). *Why simulate. To develop a Mental Model. Journal of Artificial Societies and Social Simulation,* 16 (3), 12.

Nowak, A et al. (2000). Society of Self: The Emergence of Collective Properties in Self-Structure. *Psychological Review,* 107 (1), 39 – 61.

Pelessier, B., & Jones, N (2006). Differences in motivation, coping style, and self-efficacy among incarcerated male and female drug users. *Journal of substance abuse treatment*, 30, 113 – 120.

Rudich, E., Robin, A. & Vallacher, R. (1999). To Belong or to Self-Enhance? Motivational Bases for Choosing Interaction Partners. *Personality and Social Psychology Bulletin*, 25 (11), 1.

Skatvedt, A. & Schou, K. C. (2010). The potential of the commonplace: A sociological study of enmotions, identity and therapeutic change. *Scandinavian Journal of Public Health*, 38, 6, 1389 – 1406.

Schibbye, A.-L. L. (2002). *En dialetisk relasjonsforståelse*. Oslo: Universitetsforlaget.

Steiro, T. J., Andersen, B., Olsvik, L. S., Johansen, P. (2013). Balancing Structure and Learning in an Open Prison. *International Journal of Management, IKnowledge and Learning*, 2 (1), 101–121.

Stinchcombe, A. (1968). Constructing Social Theories. New York: Harcourt, Brace & World Inc.

Sun, R. (2008). *The Cambridge Handbook of Computational Psychology*. Cambridge.

Turner, J. (2011). Extending the Symbolic Interactionist Theory of Interaction Processes: A Conceptual Outline. *Symbolic Interraction*, 34 (3), 330 – 339.

Vallacher, R. R. et al. (2002). The Dynamics of Self-Evaluation. *Personality and Social Psychology Review*, 107 (4), 370 – 379.

Vallacher R. R. & Wegner, D. M. (1987). What Do People Think They're Doing? Action Identification and Human Behavior. *Psychology Review*, 94 (1), 3 – 15.

Vallacher R. R., Wegner, D. M. & Fredrick, J. (1987). The Presentation of Self Through Action Identification. *Social Cognition*, 5, 301 – 322.

Author

Sten, Knut Magne Magister artium (Sociology)
Assistant professor
Sør-Trøndelag University college, Faculty of Health and Social Sciences
Department of Applied Social Science
Research areas: Transactional analysis – the microfoundation of sociology, caring, social science modelling

To be like Copenhagen... Central European city residents' dreams versus reality

Lucjan Miś

Abstract

Krakow is an example of a city that has advanced rapidly in terms of population, economy and social development. The success of the city has caused also some side effects. The article presents an analysis of urban social problems. I am used the results of external comparative studies of big Polish cities. They pointed to problems such as environmental pollution, especially air pollution, crime, alcohol and drug addiction and public transport. The internal study was conducted among a group of city councillors. They pointed to problems such as alcohol and drug addiction, homelessness, chaotic expansion of housing industry, privatization of urban space, poor or inadequate social infrastructure for the youngest and oldest generations. The idea for solving problems is to employ a Copenhagen model of urban development.

Introduction

Cracow is a popular city, it attracts new residents and has a very positive public image, both inside the country and abroad. The success of Cracow is measured by its ability to attract new residents, which was proven by its rise from the third to the second place in the list of the biggest (that is the most populous) cities in Poland. In recent years, the capital of Małopolska has passed Łódź, which throughout almost the whole post-war era had been the second largest city in Poland (after Warsaw).

Cracow is an urban area attracting young people who arrive in large numbers with the aim of finding a job or studying. This ambition often results in finding employment and a flat. Subsequently, Cracow's ability to attract people seems to prevail, as far fewer people leave it to look for a better place to live. On the contrary, newcomers from all parts, yet mostly from the south, of Poland tend to stay in the city for a longer time. Moreover, wealthy people living abroad are willing to buy flats and use them occasionally, that is, they visit the city for some time a few times a year. This ability to attract people also proves that urban problems are not particularly severe for old and new residents of the city. In other words, the current problems are considered temporary and due to the city's expansion.

Cracow experienced a sharp growth for a few periods during the 20th century, namely with the incorporation of Podgórze at the beginning of the century, with the construction and incorporation of Nowa Huta in the mid-20th century, as well as with the construction of housing estates at city's outskirts during the 1970s and 80s (Wood, 2010). Current problems encountered by the city residents have a different character than the ones during the 20th century. They result from an impetuous, uncontrolled development of the city, as a contrast to development that was planned and regulated by the Austrian Partition authorities (with Podgórze having a relatively large autonomy) or by the central government during the so-called state socialism (Nowa Huta).

An external perspective on the city

Data based on independent research confirm the potential and high position of Cracow among other Polish and European cities. "Social Diagnosis 2013", a research team, provided evidence that during the last years Cracow (and the province of Małopolska) had become an outstanding example of the benefits of European and domestic development programmes. Janusz Czapiński (2013) states that throughout the last eight years, the living standard of Małopolska's inhabitants improved significantly compared to other regions. Cracow as a city has risen from the fifth place (2009) to the fourth (2013) as far as living standards are concerned. It is a significant change based on long-term tendencies. One should also stress that this change did not take place in a geographical vacuum, as the metropolis is not a lonely island, isolated from neighbouring municipalities and counties. The rise of the Cracow sub-region from the 33rd place in 2011 to the ninth place in 2013 was the most spectacular development. The rise of the region of Małopolska from the fifth place in 2005 to the first place in 2011 was perhaps less noticed, though also very fast.

The above-mentioned data show beneficial changes in the residents' standard of living and a positive trend during recent years. In such a context, I wish to address some problems of collective life, namely the growth and development of cities as well as population rise – both in the sense of living standards, un-favourable phenomena and social processes (defined by a large number of resi-dents and local elites as "problems"). Mostly, the living conditions in the city are a point of concern on the part of the residents – expressed in conversations, mass media (press, radio, television, the Internet) – the experts (medical doctors, managers, social workers, businessmen) as well as the authorities (the city council, the president's office and the districts).

The residents and the authorities to a large extent agreed as far as the natural environment, mostly air, is concerned. The authorities mobilized to initiate administrative measures that led to a resolution aimed at combatting pollution by changing the way of heating flats. For their part, the citizens used modern information and communication technologies, such as social networks and mobile phones, to fight for better air by promoting public transport and bikes instead of individual car transport.

Research conducted by European and national centres proves that unemployment is the most severe and long-term social problem in the opinion of both Poles and other European citizens. The situation of Cracow seems favourable in comparison with the national and local data. The unemployment rate stands at 5.6%, which is the lowest rate in the whole province (10.2%), and twice as low as the national average (11.9%). Cracow has become one of the largest outsourcing centres in the European Union with branch offices of numerous international corporations.

Due to a large number of university graduates and a high standard in lower education, we deal with the phenomenon of "underemployment", that is, a surplus in education in relation to requirements for offered jobs. A large number of people take up a job when studying, mostly in tourism, gastronomy and ICT. Students' salaries are low, yet they are socially secure, as they include health care, boarding, public transport discounts, etc. In this way, the state co-finances private businesses who employ students as cheap (or sometimes even unpaid) workforce. "Underemployment" is the opposite of "good employment", which provides both a high salary and the possibility of improving one's qualifications and professional development. On the one hand, the potential of university and secondary school graduates is very high, which is conducive to keeping pace with innovative global technology and economy. Still, on the other hand, the jobs offered require a much lower level of education and qualifications than the ones obtained over the years of study at schools and subsequent graduate and postgraduate studies. It results in a sense of frustration and dissatisfaction among people under pressure of obtaining increasingly higher university degrees who are not able to use their knowledge and formal educational qualifications (certificates, diplomas).

The next phenomenon considered a social problem of modern metropolises by both experts and ordinary people is crime. The importance of this issue may again be defined with the help of objectified measures. As far as this phenomenon is concerned, the situation is not as favourable as in the case of unemployment. Compared to other large cities in Upper Silesia, the situation in Cracow is quite good as the crime rate is lower. Over the last years, 44 crimes per thousand of the residents were reported in Cracow, whereas in Katowice, Chorzów or Ruda Śląska the number was much bigger. In addition, Cracow compares favourably with cities like Sopot or Wrocław, in spite of a lower crime rate, especially with regard to serious crime – banditry – being reported in other big cities like Poznań and Warsaw. During the last years, a slight decrease in the number of crimes was recorded compared to the previous years, when it had a slight increase. One should stress that this phenomenon has been monitored by municipal institutions (the police, municipal office departments, social policy observatories) and local media. Examples of particularly dangerous crimes (murders, gang activity) are publicized by the press, television and the Internet and recorded in different statistics and spatial visualizations. Moreover, it not only covers street crime but also some "white collar" crimes (legal proceedings against municipal officials, such as vice-presidents, councillors, department managers, etc., charged with corruption in connection with property and land management) as well as crimes committed by local entrepreneurs.

Alcohol and drug abuse are issues closely related to crime. In Cracow one may observe conflicts between local communities and the owners of shops where alcohol is sold. Alcohol is commonly available and its supply influences the scale of consumption, with over-consumption as a negative consequence. In the city, especially in the streets and public places in the central parts, one may often encounter people in a state of intoxication or people behaving antisocially under the influence of alcohol or drugs. This leads to protests from schoolchildren's parents and residents of housing estates against the granting of additional alcohol licences. The city and local government representatives initiate activities aimed at limiting the negative effects of the mass supply of alcohol or easy access to psychoactive drugs in some circles (secondary school students, students, sports fans). Committees made up of experts and practitioners were established along with long-term programmes aimed at fighting alcohol and other addictions. Consequently, this problem is under administrative control and private residents' initiatives against the expansion of alcohol stores or sales points are on the rise.

In this confrontation, the free market wins as there are more and more possibilities of purchasing alcohol combined with aggressive marketing. An almost unlimited supply of alcohol (alcohol stores open around the clock, on both workdays and holidays), omnipresent marketing (outdoor advertisements, television and the Internet), the tradition of alcohol abuse or acceptance of the presence of intoxicated people in the urban space all contribute to individual addictions, the disintegration of families and public drunkenness.

Having discussed problems mentioned in European and national research as the most troublesome ones for the residents, namely unemployment, crime and addiction, I would like to switch the attention to problems highlighted by local movements in the city. The event in which the Cracow's residents rejected the idea of organizing the 2022 Winter Olympics in a referendum was particularly significant. The observation of social mobilization in this case points to the problem of communication between the authorities and the citizens. For the time being, deliberative democracy seems to be an ideal in the city, although certain positive symptoms of change are noticeable, e.g. referendums or communication and information platforms (Internet-based or on television) which make the opinions of residents heard and plans for urban development available.

Social problems are closely related to the city's development, as was mentioned at the beginning of the article. The influx of new residents, the dynamically developing property market and the construction industry come into conflict with the existing infrastructure. Plenty of areas have been occupied by the house-building industry or services, and consequently the public space (parks, gardens, playgrounds, recreational areas, allotments and other green areas) is shrinking. This has caused negative effects on the natural environment, which was confirmed by European research on the most contaminated cities (Research 1). Thus, the problems of pollution (e.g. air pollution) and negative environmental change (e.g. increase in the average temperature in the most urbanized areas of the city, which is particularly disturbing during the summer months) have become among the most problematic social issues. Grassroot movements have been established to change the situation, for instance by promoting other forms of transport than private cars, like bikes or modern public transportation.

The positive fact is that the city was given a high international rank with respect to the effectiveness of public transportation (Research 2). Demographic changes, the positive image of the city as well as intensified geographical and social mobility pose new challenges for the current system of public transportation and environmental protection. In a sense, Cracow is a victim of its own success; it attracts many people, rich and poor, which results in endless developmental problems related to creating and maintaining institutions and services in the area of social life (e.g. sports stadium, hospitals, schools, the so-called "third places" in public space – cafes, pubs or reading rooms) and welfare (e.g. homeless centres, social assistance centres for the poor and the lonely). The ability to respond to local problems will depend on the skills and industriousness of the "creative class" in the city. Three big waves of intense urbanization, which I symbolically called "podgórska" (Podgórze wave), "nowohucka" (Nowa Huta wave) and "gierkowska" (Gierek wave), did not destroy the urban organism, but throughout the years created a new quality. Similarly, the negative consequences of the current boom (in population growth, construction and education) can be overcome, provided that local politicians are able to implement sustainable and endogenous development.

An internal perspective on the city

In this section, I am going to reflect on transformations in the city and their unintended side effects. The analysis is based on research conducted during the second and the third quarters of 2014 among Cracow districts councillors by the Department of Applied Sociology and Social Work at the Institute of Sociology at the Jagiellonian University. The research in question was initiated by the Municipal Social Assistance Centre (Miejski Ośrodek Pomocy Społecznej). Councillors from six districts were interviewed directly and, after renewing our initial request, we received an opinion from a councillor from one more district. Consequently, the results of the research presented below stem from the opinions of councillors from seven districts (the city is divided into eighteen districts).

This means that the empirical material is not representative of all the districts since councillors from less than half of them took part in the research, reflecting those with the strongest commitment to their communities. Councillors from the remaining districts, in spite of two requests for them to contribute to the research, delivered through the official channel of communication, the municipal office, in May and June, responded to neither[1]. The opinions of councillors from geographically diverse districts are important sources of knowledge of the city's challenges, as they gain their knowledge from direct contacts with the electorate, whose concerns they sometimes convey to municipal offices or the president. Moreover, the councillors most often live in their districts and observe local changes. Their social activity and decisions (in the form of the council resolutions, regulations and plans) influence the direction of urban development.

In the councillors' opinion, the most significant social problems were the following: Alcoholism, as well as new forms of addiction, both because of their consequences for families and neighbours and because they constitute a threat to outsiders, who become exposed to aggression and banditry in public space. Problems connected with alcohol and psychoactive drugs abuse were a concern to the councillors, as they were often asked for help by helpless family members or neighbours.

The problem of homelessness was more significant in certain districts. Alcoholism and homelessness often combine, as a large number of homeless people are permanently addicted to alcohol and not able to make use of services provided by the city, such as dosshouses or stationary centres. Consequently, the homeless stay in public, semi-public and private places, such as busses, trams, bus stops, waiting rooms at stations or staircases. In addition, the city has not solved the problem of

---

[1]   I would like to thank the members of the team for agreeing to let me use their fragmentary studies of the empirical material, and Municipal Social Assistance Centre representatives for their initiative and help with conducting the research.

the homeless as far as access to public conveniences are concerned. The intoxi-cated and the homeless are the most visible in the city. Moreover, according to the councillors, there are problems which are not that easily noticeable, yet they are related to the two issues mentioned above, i.e. negligence of public centres and services for the young and the elderly. Less wealthy young people do not have the opportunity to spend their leisure time among peers in places without alcohol. The elderly are also deprived of the opportunity to maintain social relations in public space. There is a huge commercial offer (pubs, restaurants, parties), though it is only available for affluent people. There is not a similar offer for poor people who do not have enough public space for meetings, and relations that do not depend on alcohol and drugs. The existence of different clubs, attractive places for the young, would be an alternative to alcohol consumption and high-risk behaviour connected with drugs.

In the councillors' districts, residents often complained about the insufficient number of centres and services available for two quite different age groups: Chil-dren under the age of 7 and the elderly. The problem is the lack of places available in day nurseries and kindergartens as well as in day centres for seniors, including the so-called respite care, which takes offer care to *protractedly ill* people.

The councillors were unanimous when it came to the shortfalls in the ur-ban development. The possibility of immediate profits for developers (investors in housing) combined with a low level of social trust in public institutions and the malfunction of courts (issuing building permits, land registers) caused problems with construction and public transport that still persist. Although land develop-ment in vacant urban space takes place in compliance with the law, it appears chaotic and compressed. The housing density is high while roads and pavements remain unchanged, which results in traffic jams and reduction of public space for pedestrians (pavements, passages, alleys). Commuting, diminishing green areas and undeveloped land are all negative consequences of the housing industry ex-pansion. The councillors also point to other negative phenomena in urban spaces, such as a very limited access to public toilets, benches and places of rest (espe-cially outside the city centre), biking and walking paths, recreation grounds for residents of all ages, especially for children and the elderly. In many streets tene-ment houses, particularly their fronts as well as their back premises, staircases and windows, are neglected and broken – left for decades, or even centuries, without renovation or conservation. The fact the buildings are renovated and conserved separately, and not systematically, only *strengthens the impression* of disharmony and disorder. Housing is one of the most common subjects of complaint submit-ted to the councillors. During the interviews with the researchers they raised topics like:

– Frequent antisocial behaviour on the part of people who live in municipal flats and who either refuse to pay the rent or destroy the property.

– A need for new flats for the growing, ageing population of the city, who require special treatment due to their dependence and reliance on external help (institutional and family help).

– Insufficient cooperation between offices responsible for communal flats, privatization of buildings renovated with public money, favouring business establishments (commercial stations) over centres meant to benefit common residents (health centres or transport infrastructure), etc.

In the councillors' opinion. the rapid development of the city is mostly based on the privatization of the urban space, which used to serve public purposes. Countermeasures are not sufficient for keeping the balance between the private capital (building investors for the most part) and local authorities, undermining the possibility of maintaining a sustainable development of the city. Some grassroot activities were highlighted as small success stories. The activities mostly consisted of establishing associations and organizing action aimed at maintaining green areas and cooperating with the existing non-governmental organizations (NGOs). Children, young people and the elderly are the most frequent beneficiaries of such activities. Such actions may take the form of school competitions, assistance to individual residents in particularly difficult situations, scholarships for gifted, yet poor young people, and the social integration of residents of different age groups.

Cracow residents most frequently mobilize in cases of conflicts with the authorities, e.g. in defence of schools or cultural centres *destined for demolition.* Generally, the level of residents' activism is very low (Nóżka, 2014)[2]. Districts councillors judge Cracow citizens in this way due to their low attendance at meetings devoted to local problems or new projects (e.g. participatory budget). They also scrutinize authorities that unsatisfactorily supervise *investment expenditure, are negligent in monitoring and controlling the quality of contractors' work or developers' infrastructure assurances. The most serious charge relates to budgetary cutbacks in the districts and the failure to invest in already planned projects that the residents had been informed about. According to the councillors, housing estates revitalization* and residents' integration programmes as well as local activity programmes coordinated by the Municipal Social Assistance Centre *were the most praiseworthy initiatives. However, fragmentary research shows a negative attitude of residents towards the revitalization initiative, a low level of trust in the district and city authorities as well as a limited feeling of control and influence in relation to social issues (Nóżka, 2014).*

---

[2] I want to thank Marcjanna Nóżka and the members of her research team for the possibility of using the report on the Podgórze revitalization (Nóżka, 2014).

Gentrification versus pauperization

The development of Cracow is an interesting example of changes in a space referred to as the "semi-periphery" by Immanuel Wallerstein. Let us begin with the gentrification of many districts and the growth of prosperity among residents with growing commercial services at their disposal in the areas of health, recreation, leisure and culture. The city has a growing population of young, well-educated people motivated to work. The elderly, on the other hand are still active, helping their families and carrying out voluntary work in non-governmental organizations or the church. Marketing research shows that the city enjoys a good reputation among foreign tourists and investors (Research 3). The positive changes take place simultaneously with the expansion of construction companies and property developers using their funds for projects that ruin the public space with high-density housing. During the last quarter of a century, there was not any innovative and supra-local private architectural investment. Igor Mitoraj's works, donated or sold to the city, Museum of the Home Army, Oscar Schindler's Enamel Factory or MO-CAK (Museum of Contemporary Art) are examples of good, yet publicly funded projects. Private investors tend to be interested in an aggressive transformation of the existing space in order to maximize profits (usually by building different shopping malls or gated housing complexes). As for the construction of buildings that would serve the public interest or represent works of art, they leave it to the authorities and ordinary residents of the city.

On the other hand, the social housing is seriously neglected. The poorest residents in private tenement houses are "purged" by shutting off utilities (water, electricity, gas). Such "economic cleansing" enable the transformation of buildings into much more profitable restaurants, shops or hotels. It happens in a situation of inaccessibility to public housing for the people in need (living on pensions, social benefits or young families). Developers and landowners are able to effectively block development plans and use public resources (water mains, energy network, road infrastructure and sewage system) for their own profits. An objection against such politics resulted in social action opposing the authorities' intentions or negligence (for instance residential development of green areas in the city centre or in attractive spots located at the outskirts of the city), or even the social movement against organizing the 2022 Winter Olympics.

The end

The comparative research presented in the first part of the article indicates the economic and social forces of a big city that determine its success. A dynamic labour market, a low unemployment rate compared to neighbouring urban and rural areas, a growing influx of young, educated people and a positive public image underscore the potential for growth and success in comparison with other metropolitan centres in Poland. The research conducted among the councillors indicates the problems and destruction caused by the expansion of developers and outsourcing companies, destroying the social fabric of the city. The principal urban problem referred to by the councillors was the insufficient number of centres and services for children under the age of 7 and the elderly. The revitalization of some districts led to the influx of residents and tourists but at the same time caused transportation problems, namely the shortage of parking spots, concentration of cars in the public areas, destruction of pavements, squares and roads or the cutting of trees and bushes.

The degradation of urban space causes a reduction of green spots and public space, through the development of gated housing complexes, areas with limited pedestrian access and traffic routes. As a result, the majority of residents find it difficult to get to the places of work and entertainment; they share a crowded space, which causes negative reactions. An attempt to bring the degradation to a halt was made by the young generation who initiated the Cycling Critical Mass and who started to require the authorities to build cycling paths and create a system for bike rental.

The slogan "Copenhagenize" has become a watchword of the young generation that is highly critical of cars as the basic means of transportation in the city. Young people dream of a people-friendly city, created with an ambition to reconcile the requirements of globalization with post-materialistic values, pursuit of profit and social goals (maintaining neighbourly bonds, community building, decrease in the number of gated housing complexes, the reduction of segregation between the rich and the poor).

The empirical research mentioned above leads to a conclusion indicating the hybridization of changes. A dynamic development based on free market forces brings about an increase in the prices of properties, urban density, privatization and consequently the reduction of areas once used by the residents. Free property, commerce and the services market resemble the pattern described by Richard Florida in his conception of the creative class. Free market created new jobs (shopping malls, recreation places, fitness clubs, gyms, cinemas or theatres) and it helped the revitalization of neglected districts (Kazimierz or the old Podgórze). In this sense, we may talk about dynamic growth and an increase in the quality of life of the residents who possess financial resources that enable them to use new facilities (buying a flat, entertainment centres season tickets or shopping in malls). The attractiveness of the city has also come as a result of planned activities by the urban authorities. They took advantage of "good practices" and led to the implementation of such investments as a footbridge above the river Wisła, the city stadium, Cracow Arena (a sports and show hall), ICE *Congress Centre and the building of the opera. The projects were mostly financed by the European Union budget and some of them were built as public-private partnership projects.*

By a hybrid model of change I mean the coexistence and mutual interaction of processes of dynamic growth and planned activities in response to new challenges. Among them, I would like to highlight the construction of a large sports centre for young people in a neglected district of the city which became an alternative for previous antisocial patterns of spending free time. The authorities also supported programmes for selected demographic and social categories: The elderly (financed or co-financed from abroad, e.g. Switzerland), women (Norway), people addicted to psychoactive drugs or socially impaired people (the poor and the unemployed).

Finally, we should mention grassroot activities, in the form of protests, demonstrations and self- of different social groups. An exceptional example of such activities was the protest against ACTA, a movement of young people, enthusiastic about modern information and communication technologies, who organized themselves in order to defend free access to them. Other social action included protests by tenants defence movements or in favour of investment in incinerators, garbage dumps or occupational workshops for mentally ill people. The councillors also noted so-called grassroot action taken within a kindergarten, a school, a street or a non-governmental organization working for the benefit of socially impaired people.

In other words, dynamic growth, planned problem solving and the residents' objection against the failure to respond to their needs coexisted and interacted. In a democratic perspective, reflected in election results, the previous forms of governing the city on the basis of free market mechanisms and social planning proved effective. The previous presidential and city council election in 2014 strengthened the status quo, the voters extended their term of office for the next four years. Grassroot initiatives, struggles in the streets and on the Internet were new social phenomena. Those spontaneous protests and demonstrations aimed at influencing decisions concerning the living conditions in the city were unexpected and unconventional attempts to create new forms of socialization, citizenship and renewing the political process.

References

Czapiński, J. (2013). Jakość życia w Polsce – wygrani i przegrani. In: Czapiński, J., Panek T. (eds.) Diagnoza społeczna 2013. Warunki życia i jakość życia Polaków, Warszawa: *Contemporary Economics. Quarterly of University of Finance and Management. Special Issue*, vol. 7, september 2013.

Florida, R.L. (2010). *Narodziny klasy kreatywnej: oraz jej wpływ na przeobrażenia w charakterze pracy, wypoczynku, społeczeństwa i życia codziennego*. Warszawa: Narodowe Centrum Kultury.

Kaszyński, H. (2014). *Problemy mieszkańców Krakowa zarysowane przez radnych dzielnicowych. Refleksja badawcza*. Instytut Socjologii Uniwersytetu Jagiellońskiego, Miejski Ośrodek Pomocy Społecznej w Krakowie, niepublikowany maszynopis.

Krakowski przewoźnik z EuroCertyfikatem. (2011). Retrieved from: http://www.mpk.kr akow.pl/pl/aktualnosci/news,2688,krakowski-przewoznik-z-eurocertyfikatem.html (25.02.2015)

Nóżka, M. (2014). *Oczekiwania lokalnej społeczności wobec rewitalizacji starego Podgórza i okolic. Raport z badań*, Kraków, Instytut Socjologii Uniwersytetu Jagiellońskiego, niepublikowany maszynopis.

Ochrona powietrza przed zanieczyszczeniami. Informacja o wynikach kontroli. LKR-4101–007–00/2014. 2014. Retrieved from: http://www.nik.gov.pl/plik/id,7764,vp,9 732.pdf (25.02.2015).

Rothman, J. (2001). Approaches to community intervention. *Strategies of community intervention*, nr 6.

Top 150 City Destinations: London Leads the Way – Analyst Insight from Euromonitor International. Retrieved from: https://www.google.com/fusiontables/DataSour ce?docid=1kQcs_NbIPr_nsc0ETXBpGlDKkRNq3UhmBGTwm0g{#}rows:id=1 (25.02.2015).

Wallerstein, I. (2007). *Analiza systemów-światów. Wprowadzenie*, Warszawa: Wydawnictwo Akademickie DIALOG.

Wood, N. D. (2010). *Becoming Metropolitan. Urban Selfhood and the Making of Modern Cracow*, Northern Illinois: University Press.

Author

Lucjan Miś, Ph.D.
Professor of the Jagiellonian University
Jagiellonian University, Kraków
Faculty of Philosophy
Institute of Sociology
Section of Applied Sociology and Social Work
Research areas: sociology of social problems, unemployment, social policy, solution focused approach, Video Home Training

Framing the problem and challenges of dropouts in Croatia: Invisible people around us but not us

Danijel Baturina, Marijana Majdak, Gordana Berc

Abstract

This paper is focused on high school students dropp-out in Croatia. The domestic and foreign sources for students' drop-out in Croatia show different rates for the same period of time even at national level (from 3,4% to 6%). The non-systematic methodology of monitoring is criticised and some suggestions for more efficient and transparent cooperation between schools and the ministry of education are made. Some research studies dealing with high school drop-out in Croatia are presented as well as their results, with conclusions and suggestions for further research challenges in this area. The main focus of this paper is on strategies and policy documents that recognize drop-out as a social problem and give a clear context for institutions and policy makers. Also, prevention programs and programs for re-integration are described and discussed as one of the policy measures that should be provided at national level.

Introduction

This paper deals with the students who drop out[1] from the system of secondary education in the Croatian context. Drop out is a phenomenon that has many different definitions. One of definitions is that drop out might represent students'

---

[1]   Review of domestic and foreign literature shows that the term early school leaving is most widely used. In this paper the term dropping out is used. Although in our literature some authors avoid it because it is considered somewhat stigmatizing, we believe that in our context it is suitable. Also, there are certain stigmatizing connotations, but we believe that the experience of dropping out from secondary education is dramatically stigmatizing for the future life chances of individuals (and their families) who find themselves in this situation. Likewise, we believe that the chosen term can encourage scientific and general public in Croatian context to recognize drop-out students as a vulnerable group and construct this area as serious social problem with relevant, multi-dimensional, negative implications for the individual.

drop-out from education or specific training programs before completing certain levels of education and acquiring certificates (Puljiz & Živčić, 2009). Dropping out from the system of secondary education could also be defined as a decision of the student to withdraw from continuing his education, by which he would attain the minimum qualifications for entry into the world of work (Bouillet & Uzelac, 2007). Dropp out is termination of education of students who are enrolled in secondary education, which they do not complete, and so do not obtain qualifications (Rumberger, 2011). In the most general sense, people who have dropped out of school are the ones that do not gain the education that would enable them to be competitive in the labour market (Finn, 1989; Milas & Ferić, 2009) and those that are aged 18 to 24 years, who did not continue any form of education or training after they interrupt their high school education (Eurostat, 2013).

Young people who are at risk of dropping out of secondary education represent a specific vulnerable group because they are at risk of social exclusion and entry into the trap of poverty. They become especially vulnerable social groups (O'Neill Dillon, Liem & Gore, 2003, Bridgeland, DiIulio & Morison, 2006). Specifically, dropping out jeopardizes the welfare of the individual, because it leads to low labour competitiveness in an increasingly demanding labour market, higher risk of insecure employment and long-term unemployment, and consequently social exclusion (Milas, Ferić & Šakic, 2010; Strugar, 2011). In addition, as a result of incomplete secondary education and difficulties in finding jobs an individual can be faced with various problems in daily functioning due to long-term personal dissatisfaction that can lead to a variety of internalizing and externalizing problems that can impact on relationships within the family and in the wider world (Radin, 2002, Blažeka, 2002).

Dropping out from secondary education in our context so far has not been sufficiently recognized and researched, although it leads to many disadvantages for the individual and society. Therefore, in this paper we want to analyse and position the problem of young people who drop out of high school according to several possible prisms for perceiving problems in the Croatian context.

The paper is structured in couple of thematic areas. In the first part of the paper we will present the data about dropping out in statistics and research so far, with comments about methodology in reviewing each source. We will provide a critical review of the methodology in an attempt to determine the real numbers of young people who drop out of secondary education. The second part will focus on scientific research about dropping out produced so far in which different aspects of the problem have been investigated. After reviewing the research we will draw integrative conclusion about what has been researched so far but also about what is uncharted, and what are areas for future research. Status of the drop out issues in strategic and policy documents will be the content of the third part of the paper which will analyze documents that deal with drop out bearing in mind the context, the stakeholders, the content directly focused on the area, and possible measures. A further part of this paper will address prevention and reintegration of young people who drop out or are at risk of dropping out by analysing the programs we have now, and questioning what are their main effects, who are the stakeholders involved, and what does the state, civil society, private sector do in that area. Also we will identify areas of weakness and spaces for development of new programs and measures. The conclusion will address the main findings in the light of the importance of education for upward mobility, and rethink possibilities for modernization of Croatian social policy by inclusion and wider acknowledgment of the drop out problem, especially as a part of social investment perspective.

Data for high school drop-out students in Croatia

The available data for the students who dropped-out from high school in Croatia shows different results that mostly depend on the source that measured and published the data. For example, the European Commission (EC) recorded 3,7% drop-out-students in 2009 in Croatia, which was the lowest percentage in the 33 EU countries. Regarding this result the EC pointed to the lack of reliability of available data and the sample size. A few years before another European source (GHK, 2005) stated that in 2003 in Croatia there were 8.4% of students who were early school-leavers (Jugović & Doolan, 2013). On the other hand, Eurostat recorded the following data for drop-out students in Croatia the period from 2009 to 2012: 4.2% in 2012, 4.1% in 2011, 3.7% in 2010 and 3.9% in 2009 for students who did not complete secondary school (Eurostat, 2013).

Domestic sources also do not show uniform rates of high-school dropp-out in Croatia. For example, according to Croatian Government data for the period from 1998 to 2008 the drop-out-rate was 11% to 7% (Matković, 2010). So, this data shows that the students' transition through secondary school levels is from 89.7% to 92% with a downward trend, which means that the percentage of students who do not finish high school increased in the observed period. This result corresponds to those published by Ferić, Milas and Rihtar (2010) that used Statistical Yearbook (2001) data which show that 12% of students in each annual cohort do not finish high school.

In addition, the study from 2008 that was supported by the UNDP and the Croatian Ministry of health and social welfare and conducted as a result of the Joint Memorandum on Social Inclusion of the Republic of Croatia (JIM) sponsored by European Commission and Croatian Government showed interesting results (Matković, 2009). The study included 2429 young people who finished or left high school education 2003 – 2008, which is a representative sample because it presents 1% of this population in Croatia for that period of time. The results show that there was 6% drop-out at different levels of high school education (3-year vocational schools, 4-year vocational schools, gymnasiums). The biggest percentage of drop-outs was recorded for vocational schools – 5% for both programs.

Another national study (Strugar, 2011) was conducted in one Croatian county to measure drop-out students in 15 high schools (5441 students) from 2006/07 to 2008/09. Results show that in each generation the percentage of drop-outs was 2,4 % that is 260 students. When these results are analysed at school level they show that in vocational schools with 450–500 students the percentage of drop-out students rises to 25,5 and 28,8% (Strugar, 2011).

In addition, the study that was conducted in the city of Zagreb in 33 high schools showed that the drop-out rate goes from 4,8% to 6,4% in a period from 2006/2007–2010/2011 (Berc, Majdak & Bežovan, 2015). Results refer to 300 to 450 students in each cohort who dropped-out in the observed period in Zagreb. The highest percentage of drop-outs is recorded in 3-year vocational schools (16,2% is the highest percentage in the observed period for these schools) and the lowest in gymnasiums (2,9% was the highest percentage in the observed period for these schools).

In comparison with some other European countries the data for 2010 – 2012 show (Eurostat, 2013) that some countries have significantly higher rates of drop-out than Croatia, such as Spain (28,4%-24,9%) and Portugal (28,7–20,8%). So, we could say that regarding the European Commission recommendation the rate of high school students drop-out in Croatia should not be seen as a problem because is below 10%[2], but there are other questions that still should be asked. First, it should be noted that Croatia has no systematic records of drop-outs, nor has this problem been addressed. So the first question is whether the rate of 4% or 6% is realistic indicator of drop-outs in Croatia. Second, the unified and systematic methodology of monitoring drop-out should be applied in the educational system in order to obtain an accurate rate of high-school drop-out at national level. Also, there is a need to recognize a structure of drop-outs not only by gender and age, but by family status, social-economic status, nationality, health status, behaviour and law issues, location (rural or urban area), motivation for school program and other factors that could increase the risk of drop-out. And third, there is a lack of coordination between schools and the ministry of education that should be addressed to provide relevant data about school drop-out and to create a prevention strategy. In addition, it would be necessary to systematically monitor the causes of drop-out among students, at individual, family and local level as well as more

---

[2]   Regarding European commission recommendation (Europe 2020) the rate of dropping-out in each country of the EU should be below 10% until 2020 (European Commission, 2011).

attention paid to monitoring the choices that these students make after they left school before the diploma degree (exp. if they continued some other education or training, search for a job, started with family life, have children ...). The basic idea for this active policy would be to provide more efficient measures for social inclusion of this vulnerable population and to prevent serious consequences (such as delinquency, addiction, low chances in the labour market, low life standards and life quality).

Research on dropping-out in Croatia

In Croatia dropping out is a relatively new research area. There are some authors who made attempts in this area and got some results which will briefly be mentioned here.

Milas and Ferić, in 2009 found that duration of compulsory schooling is not significantly correlated with the rate of early school dropout.

A year later (in 2010) some studies of drop out appeared. Ferić, Milas and Šakić (2010), continuing research from 2009. got the results that differences in social position for young people with secondary school and without it are significant. Matković (2010) in his research found that low level of parental education and low household income increased the risk of early school leaving.

Ferić, Milas and Rihtar (2010) found that the most common reasons for dropping out are poor school performance, lack of motivation and interest for school, disciplinary problems and poor family financial situation.

In 2011. Strugar found a connection between attending vocational school, poor socio-economical status of family and low educational level of parents and number of reasons to leave school. He got a kind of "profile of Croatian drop out students" by which these students are mostly male students, coming from poor and single parent families with low educational level.

Jugović and Dolan, in 2013 have made comments about Croatian studies which mainly tend to focus on the characteristics of the individual and family in explaining drop out, rather than on the school system and wider society characteristics.

While the above mentioned research is quantitative, some have recognized the value and necessity of qualitative researches in this area. Recently there have been two qualitative studies of drop-out in Croatia. Both focused on professionals in secondary schools and their experience and knowledge of students who drop out.

One of the studies was conducted by authors Berc, Bežovan and Majdak (2015) and the other one by the non profit organisation PRAGMA (2011/12).

These two studies started from similar questions and gave some broader data about drop outs.

The findings:

1. Personal characteristics of drop out students: mostly boys, negative social picture, ambivalent relationship with peers in school, often have some behavioural problems (delinquent behaviour, drug dependence, discipline, aggressive behaviour and truancy) and some specific intellectual characteristics; low school attainment (as a main risk for dropping out), low educational motivation, repeating class problem, low participation in school activities, withdrawn behaviour, depressive, with low self-esteem and self-respect.
2. Values, needs and free time of drop out students: freedom, free time, happiness, friendship, life without worries, entertainment, family members support, success. Free time of drop out students is not structured.
3. Main risk factors for dropping out: negative and low school grades, avoiding school, inacceptable behaviour.
4. Socio-demographic and economic status of drop out student: single families, parents with lower educational status, average and low economic status, socially vulnerable families, parental divorce, abuse, drug and alcohol dependence, unemployment or workaholic parents, parents do not participate in school care, and they do not recognize child needs, abilities and motivation.
5. Future of drop out students: research confirmed that the future of students who drop out is likely to be difficult. They have problems with finding jobs while those who find a job work mostly in the private sector or on seasonal jobs.

On the basis of these findings we can see that students who drop out mostly come from disadvantaged families and there are many factors which influence their dropping out of the school system. Still, we do not know enough about this phenomenon.

The findings need to be considered in future professional work, planning of prevention strategies as well as of future research planning.

As we can see, there is a need and a potential for drop out research in Croatia. Some elements to be considered in future researches are: research in different parts of Croatia, research with drop out students, their parents, school peers, and longitudinal and qualitative research.

Finally, findings of these studies are important for adjusting policy documents and strategies for preventing drop outs in Croatia which will be covered in the next part of the paper.

Dropout in strategic and policy documents

Dropping out from the system of secondary education is set at the level of EU policy as a strategic priority. The European Commission advocates ending initiated education, especially secondary school, in order to ensure the competitiveness of youth in the labour market and their economic independence. The document Europe 2020 – A European strategy for smart, sustainable and inclusive growth[3] highlights the problem of early school leaving/dropping out[4] and it states recommendations for member countries for the reduction of early school leaving/drop out from 15% to 10%. The document Europe 2020 emphasizes that the national EU member states should: ensure efficient investment in education and training system at all levels (from pre-school to tertiary), fix educational outcomes, touching on each segment (pre-school, primary, secondary, tertiary) within an integrated approach, encompassing key competences, in order to reduce drop out. Also in other contexts we can see an orientation toward action in the field of dropping out problem. The European Social Fund[5] advocates the use of preventive and complementary measures to enhance the contribution of vocational education and training in combating drop out, in the secondary and tertiary level (Eurofound, 2012). Latest recommendations of the Commission on investment in children in order to break the circle of poverty are strongly advocating prevention, intervention and additional measures for dropouts.[6] This is reiterated by the European Parliament Pact on social investment (European Parliament, 2012), which emphasizes the importance of this area for future development of the member countries and recommended them, as well as The Commission, to take all possible measures concerning the improvement of the education system at all levels, especially emphasizing the improvement in secondary education.

Although at EU level the problem of dropout is emphasized, our strategies and documents for educational and social policy question do not give it priority. The problem of students who drop out of secondary education first came onto the policy agenda in the process of developing The Joint Inclusion Memorandum –

---

[3] http://www.mingo.hr/public/documents/eu_hr.pdf

[4] The European Commission has previously commented on this issue in the document: European Commission (2011) Reducing early school leaving. Commission Staff Working Paper. Accompanying document to the Proposal for a Council Recommendation on policies to reduce early school leaving. [SEC (2011) 96], 26 January 2011th The stated document highlighted how each Member State should set as the priority in measures to reduce the number of students who drop out education system.

[5] http://ec.europa.eu/esf/search.jsp?pager.offset=10&langId=en&mainKeywords=drop-out, visited 8. 04.2013.

[6] Official Journal oft he European Union, 2.3.2013.

JIM,[7] which, the Croatian Government adopted in 2007.[8] This document and its implementation have indicated that reform of the education system is one of the key preconditions for reducing poverty and social exclusion. It was argued that the educational structure for younger age groups is much better compared to the overall population, but it still needs to improve in the following key areas: increased coverage for children in pre-school education, by increasing the numbers of children and youth who successfully complete programs, and analysis of the causes and prevention of school dropout. The overall goal is to broaden the scope of secondary and higher education (through the expansion of compulsory education, monitoring and prevention of school dropout, and promoting the completion of various forms of education. But, despite clearly set targets regarding drop out activities, implementation is not well documented.[9] Moreover, it is worth mentioning the National Programme for the introduction of compulsory secondary education published in the Official Gazette 71/2007 by which Ministry of Science, Education and Sports proposed to make secondary education mandatory[10] and thus reduce the then high rate of 30%[11] early dropout (Milas & Ferić, 2009).

We can follow development of rhetoric and concrete actions on strategic documents through two strategies for development of education. We can observe what status dropping out issues have received in the documents that are considered crucial to focusing educational policy in Croatia. Characteristics of the documents are presented in the table below.

In 2005, the Croatian Ministry of science, education and sport has started an ambitious reform of the education system, based on the document "Plan for development of Education system 2005th to 2010th," which emphasizes the need to increase the education level of early school-leavers. The second document is a freshly adopted strategy for development of education, science and technology, which was enacted in 2014.

---

[7]   http://ec.europa.eu/employment_social/social_inclusion/docs/2007/JIM-croatia_en.pdf, visited 15. 10 .2013

[8]   Before that issues of dropouts were mentioned in the context of a plan for the development of education 2005–2010 in which we discuss below. However in development of JIM dropout issues are first time discussed in relevant way. In part, this is due to the influence of the EU and cognitive Europeanization in the preparation and adoption of this document.

[9]   In a report on the implementation of the Joint Memorandum on Social Inclusion of the Republic of Croatia, which have fallowed in the years after the adoption of JIM it is not concretely stated what Is done in this area.

[10]   Although it was proposed, that did not happen. Even more former minister announced that this would be part f the new strategy for Development of education, science and technology, but that minister was released of duty and this plan once again failed.

[11]   This document lists 30% as information dropping out from secondary education. About problems of dropout measurement more is mentioned in the section of the paper that discusses this specific issue.

Table 1: Dropouts from the education system in the strategies of educational development

	Plan for development of Education system 2005–2010 (Ministry of science, education and sport, 2005)	Strategy for Development of education, science and technology (Croatian Government, 2014)
Goals	– need to increase the education level of early school-leavers – increase the rate of enrolment in secondary schools, – increase the population of students who have graduated, – reduce the number of young people who drop out of high school[1]	– ensure systems for early identification of risk school dropout, – develop and introduce records and monitoring, to develop mechanisms for early interventions – ensure that procedures are are in place for the students who dropped out of the system so they can successfully complete their education[2]
Reasons for dropping out	– not specified	– not specified
Target groups	– special educational needs pupils	– not specified, pupils with risks of dropping out

Measures	– provide counselling – remedial classes – customizable programs – learning in practice	– development of early warning system about risk of leaving school – development systems for records and research about reasons of dropping out – develop and introduce support for students at risk – develop compensatory mechanisms and flexible curricula for acquiring relevant qualifications for students returning in education – redefine the system of pedagogical measures

[1] The document pointed out that although there are estimates on how many children and young people who enrol do not complete primary and secondary education, the Central Bureau of Statistics does not systematically process the data and there is no official information on completion ratio and dropout. Authors (Berc, Bežovan Majdak, 2015) conclude that the stated document had incomplete and wrong information about such a large number of students who are not enrolled in secondary school, and those who do not complete secondary education

[2] As you can notice measures and goals overlap in sense. Measures are just little more elaborated goals that are generally stated. Also , of course, measures are specified in terms of jurisdiction for measure: jurisdiction for implementation, deadlines, and indicators of implementation

Both strategies fail to state the reasons for drop-out among students which clearly suggests a serious lack of analysis and empirical research which could inform such analysis. Specific groups that are particularly at risk of dropping out are not mentioned which also suggest a lack of analysis and specific data related to dropouts. Both strategies use general, very imprecise technical language such as vulnerable groups, or groups at risk.[12]

Despite concrete plans we are not aware of data or reports by which achievement of development goals mentioned strategy 2005–2010 can be verified. The new strategy mentions stakeholders responsible for monitoring the measures, but

[12] Some other documents (Report on the implementation of the Joint Memorandum on Social Inclusion of the Republic of Croatian (JIM) in 2012) mention the Roma as a group in special risk of dropping out.

not the way in which implementation could be tracked and, especially important ways in which impact of the measures would be evaluated.

The measures are not specifically designed, but generally set, which also suggests that there is a lack of compelling insight into dropout and ways in which the situation can be improved. It is important to note that although in the new strategy dropout issues are more specifically stated there is a significant difference between the working version and final version of the document. It is a question of demagogy against real strategic orientation. Issues of drop-out were just mentioned in the initial working version of the document and the approach was broadened after the process of public consultations.[13] There is no systemic strategy about the issues, especially at policy level. Activities and measures were added after the comments of stakeholders who are involved in the problem area.[14] This is certainly one indication that of drop-out is still not perceived as a socially relevant problem which has significant consequences and should find its place within comprehensive strategies.

The lack of systematic measures to deal with the prevention and integration of those individuals who dropped out of the education system is part of a neglected education policy. A radical approach to address dropout demands structural changes in several policy areas, including poverty, labour market structures, and gender inequality, but this is not mentioned in policy documents not only in Croatia but in SEE region as a whole (Jugović & Doolan, 2012:373) Analysis demonstrates the problem of determining the number of students who drop out of secondary education, and we do not have systems designed for monitoring that population after dropping out (Berc, Majdak & Bežovan, 2015) Obviously, this is a multidisciplinary field where due to lack of cooperation and professional capacities of all stakeholders, but especially political will and lack of awareness in government structures, we still do not have drop-out framed and seen systemically in strategic documents.

Prevention programs and programs for re-integration: subjects and measures

Generally speaking approaches to prevention of high school dropping out are divided into two categories (Tyler & Löfström, 2009). The first category includes interventions oriented to individual students or groups of students who are iden-

---

[13]   As it can be seen differences in the working version of the document from September 2013 and adopted versions of the document in 2014.

[14]   One part refers to the remarks of the author's of this paper in the public debate on the draft document with pointing out the shortcomings of inadequate representation of this area in the strategy

tified as a risk group, and it provides preventive programs in schools and communities. The second category consists of interventions that have a broader goal and includes a wider target group of students "at risk" to meet students' needs and school interests and to reduce the drop-out rate. This category includes suggestions and actions for school reform models based on current data and the broader context of this vulnerable group. The programs in both categories are focused on increasing the number of students who regularly attend classes, increase student engagement, build self-confidence and help students to cope with the challenges and problems which tend to increase risk of dropping out (Tyler & Löfström, 2009).

Neither of these strategic categories are recognized in the Croatian educational system as priorities.

Prevention actions that are present in our schools are based on interventions in the classrooms and usually include the following: individual and group work with a student, cooperation with parents, intervention in peer groups, teachers' training for managing student behaviour and cooperation with a centre for social welfare which provides intervention in the family (focus on social and economic issue of the family, family relationships and parenting competence, health issues, etc.) (Strugar, 2011).

In order to provide drop-out preventive programs the schools in the formal educational system are still faced with a few main obstacles: a) the size of classes is too big to allow an individual approach to the students, b) lack of professional staff in the school that would take care of specific situations and work with students and their families using specific methods, c) lack of cooperation between school and other important institutions (centres for social welfare, medical institutions) and non government organizations, d) lack of measures that teachers and schools could apply to protect students and their families (Baturina, Berc & Majdak, 2014). In order to reduce the risks of drop-out we need to provide preventive activities that could help students and their parents to overcome impacts of risks like: behavioural difficulties and disorders, peer violence, addictions, insufficient learning skills, specific aspects of family disfunctioning (violence, addiction, illness), lack of parental skills and others. Also, target groups in these programs should be students exposed to poverty, neglect, social isolation, students who live in institutions (without parental care) as well as male students and students that come from minority groups (European commission, 2013). Many preventive programs are provided by non-governmental organisations in Croatia and they are mainly focused on these risks at local and national level (more than 200 of them). But targeted activities to reduce the risks of drop-out are neither available nor implemented in the National strategy for prevention programs.

It is worth mentioning that some experiences, from Germany and Ireland show

how the problem of students dropping out of the school system is taken seriously and prevention measures for dropping out are incorporated in policy and supported by the Ministry of education and culture. Some of the measures are: individual support to students with different problems, support to children of immigrants, seeking sponsorship for poor children, motivation for education, support to children with choice of school and profession. In Ludenscheid (Nordrhein-Westfalen) there is a special school called "School for peace" for students with problems in education (with support to children and parents). In Dublin (Ireland) there is a project "Equal chances for all students in schools" which consists of early interventions in the age range 3 to 18 for children in disadvantaged families and settings. All these programs already have paid dividends.

Recently in Zagreb the theme of drop out among students became popular and there are Institutions (Faculty of Law Department of Social Work) and Non-profitable organisation (PRAGMA[15]) that are starting to do research and preventive work on this theme.

It is recognized that preventive work should be based on professional education for teachers, social workers, also incorporation of social work in schools, and on knowledge about risk and protective factors from an early age. Experience shows that team work in schools and local settings as well as creating a positive atmosphere in schools can be good prevention for drop-out. Also, there is a need for social work in schools which would include work with the student's family and cooperation between school and social welfare centres.

The non-profit organisation PRAGMA is offering some services to drop out children and youth and their families through: counselling, mentorship for youth, counselling for parents, workshops and lectures. Some of the areas they cover are: advice to parents if they suspect their child wants to leave school, help to children who avoid school, help with school motivation, and help with free time structure and other matters.

These programs are good but not accessible for all children, youth and families who are in need. There is a serious need for development of preventive programs for drop out students at formal (state) and informal (non-profit organisation) level, which should be based on research results.

Conclusion: Drop-outs far from the eyes far from the heart – which direction to forward

Analysis of the Croatian context showed multidimensional limitations in constructing drop-out as a social problem.

---

[15] PRAGMA is a non-profit organisation which performs preventive and treatment programs for children, youth and families at risk.

There is a shortage of systemic methodology for measuring drop-out rates. This results in uneven and inaccurate data. One of the first goals in the fight against drop-out would be to harmonize methodology, to have clear guidelines and procedures for measuring drop-out rates, and also stating who is responsible for obtaining the data for official records, which would be the starting point for further research and framing programs and measures. However, it is important to keep track of what is happening to students after dropping out and of those students who used the opportunity to continue education after drop-out by finishing secondary education through alternative models of education. In the strategic documents there is a lack of recognition and validation of dropout. It is therefore necessary within educational and social policies to develop systematic strategies, informed by concrete data, and input from all relevant stakeholders, for prevention of drop-out and development of measures for helping students that have already dropped out. The system of prevention and assistance programs is completely undeveloped when we look at all aspects of national social policy, civil society and private initiative. Initiatives and programs that are aimed at this group are almost unknown.

The Ministry of education should be a relevant agent for monitoring, analyzing and publishing data about drop-out students as well as creating a national prevention policy for coping with this phenomenon and to design re-integration strategies for the majority of drop-out students who did not continue their education in other schools or training settings.

The area is significantly under researched. Only a few sporadic studies have been carried out. There is not much reliable data. Studies up to now were quantitative and investigated mostly the profile of dropouts and reasons for dropping out at individual or family level. But there is a chronic lack of qualitative research and studies that deal with the nature of the school system and its role in drop-out. There is a need to undertake action and longitudinal research to obtain a deeper understanding of the complexity of the issue and use these results for improvement of current or developing new strategies programs and measures.

All the above-mentioned findings about drop out in Croatia are inadequate to support the emergence of this group as a social problem that would imply some form of intervention. Among the wider public, this group is also not recognized as a group at particular risk which would be worth public engagement. In order to recognize this problem, it is important to inform the general public[16] about the

---

[16]   Based on one research on drop-outs that was supported by local authorities (the city of Zagreb) in last two years one round time was organized, two interviews are published in the newspapers, and three interviews are done on national television and radio. These are just few initiatives that are done but more publicity is still very needed to give a voice of these vulnerable and invisible group in our population and to recognize the drop-out as not only a student's and family's fail

nature and seriousness of the problem and make this issue visible enough to gain the broad support of the professional and general public.

In this sense, it would be necessary to provide a thorough analysis of the current situation so that activities could be planned and implemented in a timely manner. As the issues of drop-out are associated with academic and social problems, prevention strategies need to be flexible and guided by individual needs. This is certainly an opportunity to modernize Croatian social policy to include new social risks and groups that are at risk that so far have been neglected. Investing in secondary education dropouts, and developing policies and programs aimed at them should be seen as human capital development through the prism of a social investment paradigm (Morel, Palier & Palme, 2012). Such investments can achieve visible effect and have positive return in labour market and economic policies that would further contribute to the improvement of the life chances of individuals and advance social cohesion in society.

References

Baturina, D., Berc, G. & Majdak, M. (2014). Invisible problem – a real risk: students dropping out of high school. *Revija za socijalnu politiku*, 21(1), 43–67.

Berc, G., Majdak, M. & Bežovan, G. (2015) The perspective of professional associates of high school drop-out students as a new social problem. *Revija za socijalnu politiku*, 24 (1). *(excepted for publishing)*.

Blažeka, S. (2002).*Psycho-social potentials of graduates (of war affectedparts of the Croatian) for successfully coping with life's challenges.* Faculty of Philosophy, University of Zagreb. Department of Sociology. Master theses.

Bridgeland, J. M., DiIulio, J.J., & Morison, K.B. (2006). *The Silent Epidemic Perspectives of High School Dropouts.* A report by Civic Enterprises in association with Peter D. Hart Research Associates for the Bill & Melinda Gates Foundation. Rerieved from http://www.temescalassociates.com/documents/resources/transition/The%20Silent%20E pidemic%20Perspectives%20of%20High%20School%20Dropouts.pdf

Bouillet, D. & Uzelac, S. (2007). *Basics of social pedagogy.* Zagreb, (Croatia): Školska knjiga.

Croatian Government (2010) Report on the Implementation of the Joint Inclusion Memorandum (JIM) of the Republic of Croatia in 2010. Retrieved from http://www.mspm.hr/djelokrug_aktivnosti/medunarodna_suradnja_i_eu_poslovi/e u_poslovi/jim_zajednicki_memorandum_o_socijalnom_ukljucivanju_rh/joint_mem orandum_on_social_inclusion_of_the_republic_of_croatia

Croatian Government (2014). Strategy of Education, Science and Technology. Retrieved from http://blogs.vvg.hr/kvaliteta/files/2014/07/Nacrt-prijedloga-strategije-o brazovanja-znanosti-i-tehnologije.pdf

---

but as a social problem as well.

Croatian Ministry of science, education and sport (2005). Development Plan for the Education System 2005.-2010. Retrieved from http://www.national-observatory.org/doc s/85--05a_WB_Programme_for_education.pdf

Eurostat (2013). Glosary: Early leaver from education and training Retrieved from http://epp.eurostat.ec.europa.eu/statistics_explained/index.php/Glossary:Early_school_leaver

Eurofound (2012).*NEETs* – Young people not in employment, education or training: Characteristics, costs and policy responses in Europe,Publications Office of the European Union, Luxembourg. European Foundation for the Improvement of Living and Working Conditions. Retrieved from http://eurofound.europa.eu/sites/default/files/ef_files /pubdocs/2012/54/en/1/EF1254EN.pdf/

European Commision (2010) Europe 2020 – A strategy for smart, sustainable and inclusive growth. Retrieved from http://ec.europa.eu/eu2020/pdf/COMPLET%20EN %20BARROSO%20%20%20007%20-%20Europe%202020%20-%20EN%20versio n.pdf

European Commission (2011). Reducing early school leaving. Commission Staff Working Paper. Accompanying document to the Proposal for a Council Recommendation on policies to reduce early school leaving. [SEC(2011)96], Retrieved from https://www.spd.dcu.ie/site/edc/documents/ESLfinalpublishedstudy-execsum.pdf

European Commission (2013). *Progress in talking early school leavers and raising higher education attainment – but males are increasingly left behind*. Retrived from http: //europa.eu/rapid/press-release_IP-13--324_en.html

European Parliament (2012). Report on Social Investment Pact-as a response to the crisis(2012/2003(INI)), Committee on Employment and Social Affairs. Retrieved from http://www.europarl.europa.eu/oeil/popups/printfichedocumentation.pd f?id=600640&lang=en

Ferić, I., Milas, G. & Rihtar, S. (2010). The reasons and determinants of early school leaving. *Društvena istraživanja*, 19(4–5), 621–642.

Finn, J.D. (1989). Withdrawing From School. *Review of Educational Research Summer*, 59 (2), 117–142.

GHK (2005) *Study on Access to Education andTraining, Basic Skills and Early School Leavers: Final Report*, DG EAC 38/04 (Brussels, DG EAC) (http://ec.europa.eu/edu cation/pdf/doc284_en.pdf)

Jugović, I. & Doolan, K. (2013). Is There Anything Specific about Early School Leaving in Southeast Europe? A Review of Research and Policy. *European Journal of Education*, 48(3), 363–377.

Matković, T. (2009). Youth between education and employment: Is it worth getting educated? Zagreb: United Nations Development Programme (UNDP). Retrieved from http://www.undp.hr/upload/file/231/115824/FILENAME/Nakon_skole_web.pdf

Matković, T. (2010). Parent education, economic status and early school leaving in Croatia: trends over the past decade. *Društvena istraživanja*, 19(4–5), 643–667.

Milas, G. & Ferić I. (2009). Does extended Compulsory Education give an influence on Reducing the Dropout Rates? *Društvena istraživanja*, 18 (4/5), 649–671.

Milas, G., Ferić I., & Šakić, V. (2010). Condemned to social exclusion? The living conditions and quality of life of young people without completed high school. *Društvena Istraživanja*, 19(4–5), 669–689.

Morel N., Palier B. & Palme, J. (2012). Social investment: a paradigm in search of a new economic model and political mobilisation. In N. Morel, B. Palier, J. Palme (Eds.). *Towards a social investment welfare state? Ideas, policies and challenges* (p.p. 353–377). Bristol, USA: The Policy Press.

O'Neill Dillon, C., Liem, J. H. & Gore, S. (2003) Navigating disrupted transitions: Getting back on track after dropping-out of high school. *American Journal of Orthopsychiatry*, 73 (4), 429–440.

Support for young people, parents and professionals – preventing early school leaving. (2014). (Eds.) N. Marković, Zagreb, (Croatia): Grafokor.

Puljiz, V. & Živčić, M. (2009). *Međunarodne organizacije o obrazovanju odraslih*. Zagreb, Croatia: Agencija za obrazovanje odraslih.

Radin, F. (2002). Value hierarchy and structure. In F. Radin, V. Ilišin, B. Baranović, H. Štimac Radin, & D. Marinović Jerolimov (Eds.). *Young people on the eve of the third millennium* (pp. 47–77). Zagreb, Croatia: Institute for Social Research and the National Institute for the Protection of Family, Maternity and Youth.

Rumberger, R. W. (2011). *Droping out – Why students drop out of high school and what can be done about it*. Harvard University Press.

Strugar, V. (2011). *Closed door to the future – early leaving of secondary school*. Bjelovar, Croatia: HAZU 1861–2011.

Tyler, J. H. & Lofstrom, M. (2009). Finishing High School: Alternative Pathways and Dropout Recovery: The Future of Children. *America's High Schools 19*(1),77–103.

Author

Danijel Baturina
Position: Junior researcher/assistant
University of Zagreb, Faculty of Law
Department of Social Work
Research areas: social policy third sector and civil society, social innovations, social entrepreneurship, new social risks

Marijana Majdak, Ph.D.
Assistant professor
University of Zagreb, Faculty of Law
Department of Social Work
Research areas: children and youth with behavioural problems, youth in conflict with the law, social work with perpetrators of criminal acts, interpersonal communication, supervision

Gordana Berc, Ph. D.
Assistant professor
University of Zagreb, Faculty of Law
Department of Social Work
Research areas: families at risks, school social work, dropping-out, prevention, counselling and therapy

Better Schooling for Children in Residential Care

Lasse Skogvold Isaksen

Abstract

Children in residential care often lack basic learning skills, but traditional so-cial pedagogics of the kind practiced in residential institutions have not addressed this issue. Basic learning skills (reading, writing, and math) are not only essen-tial for inclusion in knowledge society, but also essential for inclusion in school. The article describes strategies that can enhance productive collaboration between schools and residential institutions, aimed at enhancing children's basic academic skills and inclusion in the schooling environment.

Introduction

The article draws on our experience in the project "Milieu Therapy in Knowledge Society". Three residential care institutions in Norway are participating, the pri-mary objective being to enhance inclusion in school for children in residential care by encouraging *proficiency in basic skills*. The development phase in the project focused on a description of current practice inside the care institutions concerning schooling. We wanted to set up new objectives and define a new social pedagogi-cal practice.

Success in school is one of the main indicators for social inclusion in child-hood (Frønes, 2007, 2010; Frønes & Strømme, 2010; Phipps & Curtis, 2001). Inclusion, not only attendance in school, is vital if children are to participate and take part in core activities in school. Children in residential care often lack the prerequisite basic skills that are required to be included in school and they often have a personal school history of poor attendance and inadequate support (Con-nelly & Furnivall, 2013; Francis, 2008; Gjertsen, 2007, 2013; Townsend, 2011). Inclusion in school for children in residential care is not only important for out-come or well-becoming, but is a key factor in children's present social inclusion and well-being (Franz, 2004; Gjertsen, 2007).

The project has shown that one of the most substantial stress factors for children in public care is adjustment or lack of adjustment to school. Some studies have indicated that school is an even a more significant stress factor for children while in residential care before entering residential homes (Franz, 2004). *Milieu Therapy in Knowledge Society* focuses on inclusion in school as an essential element in preventing present social exclusion and as a significant factor for well-being. Outcome or well-becoming can be a positive side effect, but our main concern attention is present inclusion in school for children who are often in emotional crisis.

There is a broad political consensus in Norway that as few children as possible should live in residential homes and that those who have to live there should be there for a short period – up to one year. Residential care in Norway is a temporary and often an emergency-driven placement of children in the age- range 13 to 18 years, often seen as a last resort. Residential care is designed to provide emotional support during a highly stressful context of transition (Kvaran & Holm, 2012). Most of the children involved are in acute emotional crisis and schooling traditionally has been seen as an added stress factor that can be avoided by lowering expectations in respect of schooling and playing down the importance of school. Our project challenges this thinking in residential care homes by seeing school as a cornerstone for present social inclusion and well-being in childhood.

Context

The main function of mass-schooling in knowledge-society is to secure children's development of basic cultural skills such as reading, math, English and writing, not as a goal in itself, but as basic tools for *learning* (Tenorth, 1994, 2004). The back-to-basic approach, with a narrow focus on basic skills is often misunderstood as an ideology borrowed from new public management and so rejected as neo-liberal ideology, but the approach reflects the fundamental function of mass-schooling in knowledge society – *learning to learn*. The skills are not goals in themselves, but rather requirements for inclusion in all social systems (Luhmann, 1997; Luhmann & Schorr, 1979; Tenorth, 1994, 2004). Acquisition and development of these basic skills is a lifelong process and not only a starting point that at some stage is complete.

Formerly schools could transport most students out of the system and into the labor market. In knowledge-society, however, schools become the only gateway to inclusion. Knowledge-based society creates higher barrier for inclusion in the labor market and the strong inclusion dynamic in the industrial labor market no longer functions as a gateway for inclusion to young people who have failed in school (Frønes, 2010; Frønes & Strømme, 2010). The logical differentiation inside school in industrial-society between students that would directly enter the blue-collar labor market, and students that would continue in vocational education or prepare for higher education, cannot be maintained in knowledge-based society. Schooling is no longer selecting students for different positions in society, but selecting for inclusion or exclusion. Schooling is the engine of marginalization in knowledge-based society. In industrial society the children that failed in school, but maintained a normal social and emotional development, were welcome in labor-intensive industrial production – teachers could more or less leave the kids alone.

A close correlation, compared to other countries, between social economic background and school performance in the unified school system in Norway has been confirmed in international student achievements test studies from 2001 up to the most recent study in 2013 (Lie & Programme for International Student Assessment, 2001; Olsen & Kjærnsli, 2013). One of the main arguments behind the unified school system is to create a school system that secures equal opportunities for all, despite family background. The weak school-effect in Norway gives most parents a great responsibility for securing children's academic progress. Child welfare service families often lack the capacity to provide necessary support to their children. As a consequence the majority of CWS children in Norway have by the end of lower-secondary school (10th grade) not developed the necessary basic skills to continue education in high school and so drop out of the system (Backe-Hansen, 2014; Clausen, Kristofersen, & Barnevern i Norge, 2008; Falch & Nyhus, 2009; Valset, 2014).

Children that have received residential care seem to benefit least from the unified school system and are the group of students in Norway with the lowest final grades in lower-secondary school .(Valset, 2014). Final grades in lower-secondary school are a strong predictor for drop-out in higher secondary school (Falch & Nyhus, 2009). Accordingly, most children in residential homes do not have the basic skills that are required to be able to complete higher secondary school and are very likely to drop out of the education system.

Two longitudinal studies in Norway (Backe-Hansen, 2014; Clausen et al., 2008) deal with outcomes for Child Welfare Service children. The results have been compared with international research (Vinnerljung, Öman, & Gunnarson, 2005). One of the overall findings is low attainment in the education system.

Present practice in residential care institutions

A starting point for the project was the present situation in three residential care institutions The development group concluded that the institutions:

1. Lacked systems to monitor academic progress.

(a) Did not have any defined academic objectives for children during their stay.

(b) The institutions' concern was confined to attendance in school and their responsibility seemed to stop at the school entrance.

Systems to monitor academic progress

Institutions were satisfied with their collaboration with the local schools that the children attended, but cooperation between schools and institutions was mostly limited to the children's attendance and their behavior in the classroom. Meetings between schools and residential homes did not deal with questions regarding academic development or lack of such. When academic development or subject matter were not discussed we can assume that the social pedagogues from the institutions did not convey any academic ambitions on behalf of the child. The short- term duration of stay in residential homes might act as an explanation for this lack of focus on academic progress.

Nor was the academic level of the particular child an issue in staff meetings. They did not have collective knowledge of the academic level or learning challenges for the particular child. Lack of knowledge about the child also inhibited any collective approach to academic issues.

Lack of academic objectives for the children during their stay

Child welfare services do not set up aims for academic progress that residential homes might pursue. Expectations were limited to attending school and to adjustment to the school situation. Academic development is seen as the schools' affair and not as an aim related to the stay in residential home. None of the institutions had development of academic skills as an element in their plan documents.

Attendance in school and institutional responsibility seems to stop at the school entrance

Schooling was the schools' business. The main task for the social pedagogues was to motivate children to attend school. To follow up schooling was understood as making sure that children did their homework, went to school and did not engage in any anti-social behavior in school. The professional collective did not discussed academic development or level of the children in the regular staff meetings.

Even if the residential homes had activities that drew on academic skills there was no precision about how daily activities in the institutions might enhance such skills.

New objectives for residential care

The main aim in the project is to enhance inclusion in school by enhancing core competence for participation in learning activities. Two objectives were defined:

1. Children should experience development of basic skills during their stay in the residential home.
2. Institutions should be responsible for academic development of their children.

Children should experience development of basic skills during their stay in the residential home

This aim is what most parents expect from schooling. It should be conveyed to children when they enter a residential home, as part of the objective for their stay. It is also an objective that one can to some extent monitor and evaluate.

The institution is responsible for the academic development of its children

Instead of moving responsibility around, the residential homes have decided to assume responsibility regarding the academic development of the children. Academic development is defined as an objective in the milieu therapeutic practice.

Academic development is a collective responsibility in residential homes aligned with objectives related to socio-emotional support. Inclusion in school is both emotional support and inclusion in school.

New Practice

Three pathways were outlined to establish a new practice in the residential homes:

1. Implementing instructional tools in the institutions that target the development of basic skills.
2. Implementing new routines to monitor academic development.
3. Implementing and identifying milieu therapy that nurtures development of basic skills.

Implementing instructional tool in the institutions that target the development of basic skills

All the children that enter residential homes are tested in math and reading. The schools conduct the test and inform the institutions about the level and challenges for each child. The test provides for collective knowledge to everyone caring for the child, both in school and institutions, and at the same time identifies a starting point for development. It also give the institutions a tool to monitor progress in school.

Schools and institutions use a well-known literacy program. The program mandates the schools and the institutions to collaborate around enhancing reading skills for the single child. The teachers and the social pedagogues in the residential home have participated in a professional development course in order to be able to use the instructional programs.

Implementing new routines to monitor academic development

The schools and the residential homes hold four meetings during the school year to define academic objectives, and to monitor and evaluate progress. The meeting are exclusively devoted to the academic development of the child. An evaluation scheme is developed and used to structure the content and agenda in the four meetings.

Implementing and identifying milieu therapy that nurtures development of basic skills

The residential homes identify practice and daily activities that can act as developmental tasks to foster basic skills. The aim is to evolve a residential "culture" that involves basic skills. The institutions have a range of activities to scaffold academic development. Social pedagogues facilitate learning situations in daily life inside the homes that support learning objectives for the child. In staff meetings, academic progress for each child is discussed and knowledge about challenges and progress are shared.

Discussion

Children living in residential homes have generally had a life history and an instructional quality that did not give them the necessary support to go through a normal development of basic cultural skills. The low final grades from lower secondary school confirm this assumption (Valset, 2014). The strong correlation between family background and school performance in Norway might suggest that the ambitions and expectations of the parents are crucial for the teacher's personal objectives for the single children. When academic development is lacking as an issue in the meeting between schools and residential homes the external pressure on schools to secure development is absent. Failure in school is explained on an individual level instead of questioning the quality of instruction.

Residential homes are a window of opportunity to compensate for lost opportunities and to foster a positive academic development that helps children to experience inclusion in school, but the role of academic development as a factor for inclusion in school seems to be underestimated in milieu therapeutic work in residential homes. School is viewed as important, but the institutions do not have any strategies to work collectively and systematically to enhance inclusion and support academic development. Residential homes have not established systems that make it possible to formulate collective ambitions for children's academic development and they are not able to convey expectation of progress toward the schools. To get the institutions to act as parents requires new tools and routines that enable the whole staff to share information and objectives around the single child. It is up to 25 staff members who will have to act as functional parents.

Schools do not necessarily secure academic development, regarding the high correlation between family background and school performance in Norway, so parents have to do the job themselves. Residential homes have to convey expectations and ambitions on the behalf of the children to teachers and schools and to be able to monitor progress and confront schools with lack of progress. Children in residential homes are not at present represented by institutions acting as substitute parents, but rather constrained by an institutional culture that protects them from school expectations. This traditional mind-set also gives the school an easier task, for example in respect of securing attendance.

New objectives for residential homes challenge the traditional division of responsibility between social pedagogues and teachers. At the same time as social pedagogues are intervening in defining learning objectives for the child, the teachers are also able to demand support from the residential homes for the values and objectives in school. It is a clear objective to collaborate to put forward expectations and ambitions for the children's academic development. Social pedagogics can be ineffectual and passive in relation to mass schooling in knowledge society when they do not focus on the prerequisite skills for social inclusion

All pedagogics or work with children in knowledge-based society, also social pedagogics, has to nurture the development of basic skills, and professionals have to have to possess competence to foster the development of these skills – this competence seems to be lacking among professionals in residential homes. Social pedagogues in knowledge-based society cannot restrict their practice to social and emotional development and leave schooling as somebody else's business. Social pedagogues has to possess and be able to create a milieu therapy that helps children to develop their basic cultural skills.

Different agendas among schoolteachers and social pedagogues in residential homes may have created a long lasting tension between the professions. General pedagogics was associated with teaching and learning, and social pedagogic targeted the development of the whole human being – often grounded in humanistic values. Schooling has been an additional arena for exclusion for children from marginalized families, and still is. Reform pedagogics involved an anti-schooling bias. The back-to-basic approach was seen as narrow. Social pedagogues encounter in residential homes children who have failed in school. They see the school as an additional burden in a stressed life situation.

One of the core assignments for the field of social pedagogics is to secure inclusion and prevent exclusion. In knowledge-based society, the marginalization dynamic is changing and traditional social pedagogical practice is challenged. This practice has tended to give the child responsibility for deficits at the individual level. This state of affairs not only leads to considerable moral and economic burdens for individuals and for society, but also supports and prolongs dysfunction in a child welfare and educational apparatus that is not fit for purpose.

References

Backe-Hansen, E. (2014). *Barnevern i Norge 1990–2010: en longitudinell studie*. Oslo: Norsk institutt for forskning om oppvekst, velferd og aldring.

Clausen, S.-E., Kristofersen, L. B., & Barnevern i Norge. (2008). *Barnevernsklienter i Norge 1990–2005: en longitudinell studie*. Oslo: Norsk institutt for forskning om oppvekst, velferd og aldring.

Connelly, G., & Furnivall, J. (2013). Addressing low attainment of children in public care: The Scottish experience. *European Journal of Social Work, 16*(1), 88–104.

Falch, T., & Nyhus, O. H. (2009). *Frafall fra videregående opplæring og arbeidsmarkedstilknytning for unge voksne SØF-rapport 07/09* (pp. IV, 42 s.).

Francis, J. (2008). Could Do Better! *Residential child care: Prospects and challenges, 47*, 19.

Franz, B. S. (2004). Predictors of behavioural and emotional problems of children placed in children's homes in Croatia. *Child & family social work, 9*(3), 265–271. doi: 10.1111/j.1365–2206.2004.00324.x

Frønes, I. (2007). Theorizing indicators. *Social Indicators Research, 83*(1), 5–23. doi: 10.1007/s11205–006–9061–7

Frønes, I. (2010). *Kunnskapssamfunn, sosialisering og sårbarhet*.

Frønes, I., & Strømme, H. (2010). *Risiko og marginalisering: norske barns levekår i kunnskapssamfunnet*. Oslo: Gyldendal akademisk.

Gjertsen, P.-Å. (2007). *Forebyggende barnevern: samarbeid for barnets beste*. Bergen: Fagbokforl.

Gjertsen, P.-Å. (2013). *Når skolen svikter*.

Kvaran, I., & Holm, J. (2012). *Barnevernsfaglig miljøterapi*. Kristiansand: Cappelen Damm Høyskoleforl.

Lie, S., & Programme for International Student Assessment. (2001). *Godt rustet for framtida?: norske 15-åringers kompetanse i lesing og realfag i et internasjonalt perspektiv*. [Oslo]: Institutt for lærerutdanning og skoleutvikling, Universitetet i Oslo.

Luhmann, N. (1997). Globalization or world society: how to conceive of modern society? *International Review of Sociology, 7*(1), 67–79.

Luhmann, N., & Schorr, K.-E. (1979). *Reflexionsprobleme im Erziehungssystem*. Stuttgart: Klett-Cotta.

Olsen, R. V., & Kjærnsli, M. (2013). *Fortsatt en vei å gå: norske elevers kompetanse i matematikk, naturfag og lesing i PISA 2012*. Oslo: Universitetsforl.

Phipps, S., & Curtis, L. (2001). The Social Exclusion of Children in North America. Halifax, Nova Scotia: Dalhousie University.

Tenorth, H.-E. (1994). *Alle alles zu lehren Möglichkeiten und Perspektiven allgemeiner Bildung*. Darmstadt: Wissenschaftliche Buchgesellschaft.

Tenorth, H.-E. (2004). Bildungsstandards und Kerncurriculum. *Zeitschrift für Pädagogik*(5), 650–661.

Townsend, M. L. (2011). Are we making the grade? The education of children and young people in out-of-home care.

Valset, K. (2014). Ungdom utsatt for omsorgssvikt – hvordan presterer de på skolen? In E. Backe-Hansen (Ed.), *Barnevern i Norge 1990–2010: en longitudinell studie* (Vol. 9, pp. 129–156). Oslo: NOVA Rapport.

Vinnerljung, B., Öman, M., & Gunnarson, T. (2005). Educational attainments of former child welfare clients – a Swedish national cohort study. *International Journal of Social Welfare, 14*(4), 265–276. doi: 10.1111/j.1369–6866.2005.00369.x

Author

Assistant Professor Lasse Skogvold Isaksen
Sør-Trøndelag University College
Faculty of Health and Social Science
Department of Applied Social Science
Research areas: Education policy, social pedagogic and schooling for children in residential care

User-Participation in Services for Homeless

Peter Szynka

Abstract

Today Homeless Services Germany try to give service users more chances to participate in improving the services and to make them more user-friendly and more adequate to their needs. Though there are important philosophical, political and ethical reasons to do so, participation fails regularly. It is because most of the time we find a more traditional understanding of social help in the homeless services and it is because there are different commitments of the key-persons to their social milieus. Nevertheless, we are able to identify useful methods of participation. Furthermore, we have tools to measure the quality of participation. This contribution closes with some actual examples of participation and give recommendations, how to support participation in homeless services.

Homeless Services as a Part of a Middle-Class Partizipation System

The history of homeless services in Germany shows, that they are part of the welfare system and as such part of a system of redistribution. The German Social Model with privileged corporatist welfare o organizations came out of the civic engagement of more or less wealthy citizens. They saw that a lot of people lost their roots at the beginning of the industrial revolution. The hardship of the developing proletariat was touching their compassion. They could not bring together this reality with their religious values or political ideas.

Especially religious welfare organizations and self-help-organizations in the worker's movement tried to ease the destitution of the masses. These facilities have been at the core of the Germen welfare tradition up to the present.

Therefore we still find within the social services for homeless people today mostly middle-class oriented and patriarchal attitudes towards homeless men and women. Social workers and Homeless people come from different social milieus. Social workers participate in social development by activities in Universities,

Unions and professional Associations and within the networks of the welfare organizations at local, regional, national and even at the European level. The service
users don't. The challenge for more user-participation therefore is the question
how to include the users into processes of improvement of facilities for homeless.
We could see them as users, consumers or experts. We could also see them as
representatives of groups of users, actors in networks and as organizers of victims
in an environment of dramatic competition.

What do we think about homeless people, and how do homeless people see themselves?

The earliest examinations of the homeless phenomenon stated that homeless people especially, when they move from one location to another are somehow crimi-
nals, at least suspicious and have to be observed critically. Early criminalists made
very far going observations. For instance they collected words of a so called secret language for special dictionaries. This should help to discover criminal acts
in advance (Luther, 1528; Avé-Lallemant, 1914). In Germany it was against the
laws to move without a home and without a goal up to the 1970th. It was seen as
a disruption of the public order.

During the 1920th and 1930th a lot of homeless were on the streets looking for
food and for work. The Bayrische Wanderdienst (somehow: Bavarian Service for
Migrant Workers) tried to introduce the "ordered wandering". Back to the roots
of nature and free wandering in a clean air was valued since the young people's
movement at the turn of the 19th to 20th century. This movement was a reaction to
industrial revolution in itself. Free wandering was to be regulated now. Everybody
should have a goal. This goal was to be documented by public authorities or labor
offices. Who was met without these papers on the streets could arrested and lead to
workhouses. The ways lead from workhouse to workhouse and from labor office
to labor office, from one homeless service to the next. These facilities were the
institutional predecessors of homeless services in Germany.

The criminalization of mobility led directly to the persecution and extermina-
tion of homeless people during German Nazi times.

At the same time in the USA sociologists of the Chicago School worked on
a groundbreaking study on migrant workers. Nels Anderson wrote his book on
the American Hobo which was an outstanding declaration of honor for every
homeless man and woman at that time (Anderson, 1923). The social affiliation of
homeless people to a criminal milieu was not essential for Anderson but the mem-
bership of the hobo to the working class. Andersons Mentor, sociologist Robert
E. Park, described the difference between human beings and the animals (Park,
1925). Men are free to set their goals by themselves and to pursue their goals and

their happiness. After long years of participatory observations and a lot of ethnographic interviews Nels Anderson described three types of humans on the streets. He distinguished between "hobos", "tramps" and "bums": The hobo "wanders and works", the tramps "wanders and dreams", the Bum "wanders and drinks". The number of Hobos was very high especially during the years of railway construction.

Following Andersons analysis, the hobos, who mixed themselves up with the tramps and the bums were part of the working class. According to Anderson, they were also some kind of avant-garde of the working class, because they took jobs which were not secure, which were dangerous, which were unhealthy and paid bad. Doing so, they showed to the working class where most of them will be, when they are not able to organize and to fight for collective working class rights and standards. They had a political mind.

On the other hand, they were dreaming of a better world. They were part of the bohéme, the dreaming artist, creative artists, writers, songwriters. A part of Chicago was called Hobohemia. In Hobohemia were a lot of chances to participate. There was the hobo college, there were self-help organizations, there were clubs, missionaries and above all: the art of public and political speech was trained in public spaces and in the parks (Anderson, 1923; Bruns, 1987).

Partizipation as Core Business of Social Work

In Germany history, most of the traditional methods of homeless services could be described as educational and character-building. The goal was to improve the individual by religious and moral education. Misbehaving should be corrected in special settlements, sometimes far out of the cities and urban communities.

This lasted until the 1970, when a change of paradigm occurred in Germany. Vagrancy was no longer seen as criminal behavior. Step by step the homeless services were oriented to the improvement of the material and juridical situation of their clients. Participation was put on the lists of the important goals of social work. It was Falk Roscher, who in the 1980's demanded enhancement of the "chances to realize citizens rights" and the "chances to realize political rights" in his commentaries to the German social laws for homeless people.

Probably it is in contrast to the regulations of other European countries, that the German social law defines the target group especially because of their lack of participation. The law defines, that there are people, whose special circumstances and difficulties hinder their participation in community and society. Therefore the goal of social work is to care for participation of the clients and to ease, lower, or eliminate the difficulties which hinder participation. The juridical goal of social work with homeless people therefore is participation.

Another juridical term which belongs to participation is cooperation. Clients should cooperate as best as they can. But there has taken place a reversion to the ideology of law and order, "character"-building and of forced labor: The German labor-reform of 2005 has established a duty to cooperate. These duties should be defined in written contracts. The administrations got the right to impose sanctions if these contracts were not fulfilled. These attempts to enforce participation are contrary to the idea of voluntary participation. In many cases this administrative attempts of forced participation lead to a never ending homelessness, an unwillingness to tolerate bureaucratic procedures, and a loss of confidence in social work, and so hinder "real" participation.

How can we organize Participation?

Homeless-Services are, as we saw above, are part of a structure, which became real because of political participation of middle class people. This political participation is still working and takes part in the political world.

In this structure, professional and clients rather work "for each other" or "beside each other" than "with each other". The chances of political participation are not equally distributed. There is much space for constructive cooperation.

Clients of homeless-services participate most of the time only with the help of their social-workers. Only during the most recent years, this participation-for-and-by-others became fractured. Speaking for others became suspect especially when professionals spoke for their clients. There is more credibility, when the clients – experts about their own situation – speak for themselves.

Especially disabled people have built self-organizations and have coined slogans like "Nothing about us without us!". The critical public has developed a new feeling for the authenticity of life stories and about individual or social problems. Only the clients themselves can guarantee the authenticity of their life stories and can say what helps and what does not. It is the special experience of the clients which helps us to understand the genesis of problems and the route to their solution. Therefore we have to respect the clients as experts of their own situation, to listen and to improve their ability to talk about their lives and to take back control.

The interests are clear: the professionals need the experience of the clients and the clients need the experience of the professionals to be heard.

Regarding participation professional services have to include attempts to transform personal experience into political expertise and action. Most effective and successful are those clients, who have solved a main part of their problems and who are ready to explain their situation to the public. These are those who can explain their failings, their experience with bureaucratic and counterproductive regulations, their experience with social-workers, their vulnerability and their ways of surviving. Therefore the ability to speak and the courage to be a part of a greater community are essential. This is difficult, but not impossible.

Therefore political experience is necessary. For me, community organizing seems to be the best practice in the field of participation. This participative practice has its roots in the American citizen's rights movement, and in Germany it is taught to social workers during their training.

Within phases of intense listening, clients find that their individual problems are in many cases not single and individual but common and shared. Therefore we can define public problems out of shared experience.

How to evaluate Participation?

Once we want to improve participation a lot of methods and procedures come into our minds. The range is from "kitchen-table-meetings" to "happy afternoon", "planning for real" and from "action research" to "listening processes" in facilities and neighborhoods. A way to measure which kind of participation within a defined period of time happened is my "User-Involvement-Table" (Szynka, 2010). The example shows a more traditional and top-down designed organization development process and a bottom-up-designed Community Organizing process. It shows that the methods of Community Organizing reach relatively large numbers of people, which could be involved in development processes. In this way, wishes, interests, problems and solutions could be communicated from the base to decision makers.

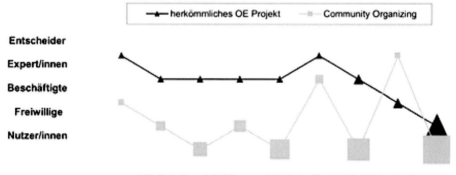

Häufigkeit und Größe von Arbeitstreffen im Projektverlauf

There are also methods to measure the quality of participation. The quality could be differentiated and described in scales. The classic among these measuring procedures is the "Ladder of Participation" developed in city-planning processes of the 1970th by Sherry Arnstein in the US (Arnstein, 1969). Arnstein's scale includes 8 steps. It identifies also attempts to manipulate Citizens. Events of only "so called" participation we find on the lower steps and "real" participation we find on step eight. The methods of Community Organizing seem to have the potential to reach high quality in the Arnstein Scale.

The Way Ahead

In German Homeless Services participation has a strong juridical base because the terms "Participation in Community Life" and "Cooperation" are used in the law. Social work practice seems to have developed useful tools to strengthen participation also with groups, who are not used to be involved in decision making processes. We have procedures which make voluntary participation possible. To the un- and contra productive procedures which hinder participation or make it impossible, I referred to above. What are examples of good practice in Germany today?

The demand for more user participation gets support from all sides. But only few successful examples become known. The bigger biannual Congresses of conventions of the German Umbrella Organization provide regularly space for this theme. They offer places and participation-fees for users and ex-users of services. They offer papers and invite users not only to listen but also to speak for themselves. More and more Welfare organizations put participation on the program.

Several outstanding examples of participation of homeless people are discussed in interested circles.

One has taken place in Ursulaheim in the City of Offenburg in southern Germany. Ursulaheim is a facility of German Caritas which has provided Shelter, Counselling and Work for homeless men for many years. The service users are involved in all aspects of their facility and are systematically confronted with all kinds of problems in their neighborhood. Meanwhile some users and ex-users are trained activists who founded the regional branch of the National Anti-Poverty-League. As such they confront politicians and key person with problems of housing and social services and demand sustainable solutions.

Another example is the "Bundesbetroffeneninitiative wohnungsloser Menschen e.V." (National Initiative of Homeless People in Germany) founded in the city of Cologne. This group sends experts to the umbrella organizations of homeless facilities.

Then there is the Armutsnetzwerk e.V. (Poverty-Network e.V.), founded in the city of Sulingen. This group runs a website with thousands of clicks every day. It shows a list of homeless services in Germany and Europe and it gives space to discuss problems in the internet. Activists of this group are delegates in the European Antipoverty Network (EAPN) which is involved in developing European strategies to help homeless people.

 Then there is the Homeless-University in Berlin, which trains the capacities and resources of homeless people. It brought to mind the learning interests of homeless man, where political theory and philosophy was in the first rank. The Homeless-University brings together Scientist, Artists and homeless people.

In numerous Art projects, homeless people and artists work together and organize events.

Therefore this list cannot be complete. But nevertheless this does not mean that there is enough participation. All projects suffer from a chronic lack of money. If homeless people want to meet, they need money to communicate with each other and they need money to travel. Foundations near to welfare organizations slowly begin to realize this problem and to support attempts at self-organization. Once we find activists and they can be trained, they should be supported for several years.

But not only material support is necessary. The everyday life of activists can turn into an unpaid fulltime job very quickly. Welfare organizations and charitable foundations are kindly asked to provide more money for participation. Social Workers are kindly asked to learn and practice methods of participation.

References

Anderson, N. (1923). *The Hobo. The Sociology of the Homeless Man. A Study prepared for the Chicago Council of Social Agencies under the Direction of the Committee on Homeless Men.* Chicago, London.

Arnstein, Sherry R.(1969). A Ladder of Citizen Participation. *Journal of the American Planning Association*, 35: 4, 216 — 224

Ave-Lallemant, F. C. B. (1914). *Das deutsche Gaunertum in seiner sozialpolitischen, literari- schen und linguistischen Ausbildung zu seinem heutigen Bestande.* Wiesbaden.

Bruns, R. A. (1987). *The Damnest Radical. The Life and World of Ben Reidman, Chicago's Celebrated Social Reformer, Hobo King, and Whorehouse Physician.* Urbana/Chicago.

Dietz, A. & Gillich, S. (Hrsg.) (2013). *Barmherzigkeit drängt auf Gerechtigkeit. Anwaltschaft, Parteilichkeit und Lobbyarbeit als Herausforderung für Soziale Arbeit und Verbände.* Leipzig.

foco e.V./Stiftung Mitarbeit (Hrsg.) (2014). *Handbuch Community Organizing. Theorie und Praxis in Deutschland.* Bonn.

Lauritzen, L.(Hrsg.) (1972). *Mehr Demokratie im Städtebau.* Hannover.

Luther, M. (1528). *Von der falschen Bettler Büberei.* Gesamtausgabe.

LPK-BSHG (1989 ff.). *Lehr- und Praxiskommentar zum BSHG; ab 2005: Lehr und Praxiskommentar zum SGB XII.* Baden-Baden: Nomos.

Szynka, P. (2010). Wertschöpfung durch Beteiligung. *Sozialwirtschaft* 2/2010, S. 21–23.

Internetlinks

1. http://www.armutsnetzwerk.de/
2. http://www.berber-info.de
3. http://www.homelesspeople.eu/014)
4. http://www.berlinpiloten.com/sites/default/files/maik-eimertenbrink-broschuere-obdachlosenuni-2011.pdf
5. www.kunst-trotzt-armut.de
6. www.armut-das-ist-doch-keine-kunst.de

Author

Peter Szynka (Dr. phil, Social Scientist) works for Diakonia, one of the big German welfare umbrella organizations. The areas of interest are Services for Homeless People, Community Organizing (Saul D. Alinsky), the Relevance of Sociology for Social Work (Max Weber).

"Because I deserve it": Self-assured welfare claimant action amongst socially marginalized young adults (18–23) as an intake to current tendencies in the newer Norwegian welfare state.

Anne Juberg

Abstract

Changes in post institutional, consumerist society may particularly affect young adults (18–25) in a marginalized position. The newer welfare state counts on a self-reliance among its citizens that young adults with lifestyle problems may find problematic to realize, not least at in the housing market. Nevertheless, their desires with regard to proper housing may not differ much from the remaining population and their claims for such a standard may be self-assured in a way that could affect the balance between individual and collective concerns in the newer welfare state.

The paper discusses selected elements from an empirical material on homeless, but not roofless young adults with substance problems. The self-assured way in which the young adults advanced their welfare claim is its primary focus. The discussion takes place in the light of the pervasive influence of consumerism on current mindsets and welfare systems, and the dislocations in the relationship between civil and social rights that this could entail. The paper also discusses whether self-assured claimant behavior among young adults represents elements of oppression or liberation in the newer welfare state.

Paper

The overall focus of this paper is on the relation between welfare claimant action amongst young homeless adults with substance problems and those ideological currents in the newer Norwegian welfare state that potentially affect marginalized populations. My interest in this issue was evoked when doing a case study with colleagues during 6 months in 2011–212 on the housing needs of young adults

(18–23) in Trondheim, Norway who were using substances in problematic ways and who had a more limited access to safe and proper housing than other same-age youth (Juberg, Kiik & Johansen, 2012). An article that presents and more broadly discusses those results in a perspective of social inequality is in progress (Juberg & Kiik, 2015).

The case we examined was a social work program in which the young adults were participants. The aim of the program was both prevention of problem aggravation and rehabilitation. Most of the young adult participants were "homeless although not roofless". The managers of the program viewed lack of safe and proper housing as participants' major challenge. Among other things, being in lack of proper housing significantly reduced their chance of rehabilitation and access to employment or education. A wide range of research literature on social housing describes young adulthood as a critical phase with regard to the risk of permanent homelessness (Thompson, Barczyk, Gomez, Dreyer, & Popham, 2010; Natalier & Johnson, 2012; Quilgars, 2012). The study aimed at providing a detailed picture of the barriers that hindered young adults in the program in entering the house market.

However, the finding in the described material that particularly evoked my research interest was the tendency among participants to feel entitled to safe and proper housing in a very self- evident and self-assured way. They were certainly in their full right to do so, as housing appears as a global human right and is a gateway to global social citizenship (Davy & Pelissery, 2013). Yet housing has never been considered a welfare good in Norway to the same extent as children's allowance, education benefit, sick-leave benefits etc. (Hellevik, 2005). By speaking of it as such, they tended to run counter to certain underlying discourses in Norwegian society concerning deservedness (Juberg & Kiik, op.cit.). Moreover, even if they were young and had not yet contributed much to the national wealth, they did tolerate neither the most marginalizing housing solution nor mediocre housing standards. Despite being of young age, they wanted a housing situation like "anybody else": *"It is obvious . . . It has to be an ordinary dwelling. At least 40 square meters and a bedroom"*.

When claiming their housing needs the program participants tended to draw on salient contemporary discourses. One of them derived from commercial advertising, in which expressions like *"Because I deserve it"*, *"I'm worth it"* etc. are frequently occurring. A young girl participant, for instance, who previously had stayed in a shelter with older problem substance users, communicated in an interview that when she with help from the social work program could move into a stylish flat had exclaimed, *"I deserve this"*!

Yet that participant also put existential dimensions to her positive housing experience:

"I was offered a safe place to stay, a place where I could just be by myself. It rendered me a dignity I had thought of as lost"

The following statement rather seems to reflect the symbolic capital of predominant value in contemporary Norwegian society, such as affluence, cleanliness and being morally immaculate (Danielsen, 1998): *"Living in a place in which the same room serves both as sitting – room, kitchen and bedroom isn't hygienic (...) it is simply not bearable"*.

Anecdotal parts of our material add to these impressions. For instance, the social workers in the program mentioned program participants who had got annoyed if there was no access to Internet in the dwellings they had got from the local housing allocation service. According to the social workers, the young adults tended to view the lack of internet access as *"the greatest assault of all"*.

My tentative conclusion after a theory-driven re-analysis of the study report (Juberg et al., 2012) was that the young people in question generally seemed to perceive themselves as deservers, not losers, at least in respect of housing. This thematic is also touched on in the above-mentioned article (Juberg & Kiik, op.cit), but we do not discuss it thoroughly there.

The study report also refers to discussions from focus groups in which social workers and other welfare service providers of different kinds participated. All of them agreed that safe and proper housing was necessary in order to prevent worsening of problems and to enhance the chance of full participation in normal society. More interesting with regard to theme of this paper, however, were some discussions in the focus group that revolved around the degree to which the standard claims of the young people were reasonable with regard to age and position in society. In the re-analysis, I identified two positions in relation to this: The first implied a view of unsatisfactory housing conditions as normal in young adulthood: A comment from one of our focus groups that seems to reflect this is *"When I was young, I would not mind living in a closet"*.

This position seems to be in line with some critique of the universal welfare state, as an all-pervasive *"rule-setter, service provider and a safety net"* (see Benington & More, 2011). In a neoliberal perspective on welfare, dependency on services without any intention or obligation of paying back to society must be avoided (Djupvik & Eikås, 2010). The mentioned position also involved ascription of propensities like extravagance, lack of realism, and lack of capacity for delayed gratification to the young claimants: *"They want theapartment right away"*.

The second position implied a view of the young adults as in their full right as citizens of the consumerist welfare state to claim a housing standard they perceived as normal. The following utterance from a service provider in one of our focus groups, for instance, has clear reference to newer poverty definitions: *"This* (lacking a flat of "usual" standard)*is in a way today's version of poverty- not* (being able)*to participate on those* (certain?)*venues* (...). *Before, poverty was about being hungry ... having nothing to eat."*

According to some newer poverty definitions, people are poor when they lack *"the diets, amenities, standards and services "*a lack that hinder them in*"playing customary roles, entering customary relationships and following customary behaviour"* (Townsend, 1993:36). Other newer definitions are more concrete and rely on a consensus in the general population around which goods could count as necessities. Poverty in that perspective is *"an enforced lack of socially perceived necessities"* (Mack & Lansely, 1985:39)

Both definitions imply that exclusion from customary lifestyle choices, if the individual in question genuinely desires them, could threaten citizenship. Jensen & Pfau-Effinger (2005) define citizenship as the capability to shape life in line with own interest, yet the concept is in constant change.

The specific aim of this paper is to explore and discuss "self-assured" welfare claimant action from different angles. Since the empirical material that evoked my interest for this issue after all has its limitations, I primarily view the cited utterances as something that "could be" and approach the thematic merely theoretically. I have based myself on literature from academic social work and welfare research and on Honneth's and others' perspectives on human and social rights.

The question that govern the exploration is whether such action is likely, reasonable or unrealistic in the newer welfare state with regard to social inclusion and maintenance of citizenship.

Firstly, I discuss this in the light of the two positions I identified in the described material in relation to transformations in the universal welfare states in general, with a specific sidelong glance at the Norwegian welfare state of today. The positions I identified seem representative of a salient tension in discourse on welfare, namely the tension between individual and collective concerns, rights and obligations. Secondly, I try to view "self-assured" welfare claimant action on the background of contemporary currents in societal development with a specific emphasis on consumerism. Those two themes tend to merge, however.

I have structured the paper into three main sections. One is on the impact of consumerism in the newer welfare state, the second is the section that most directly deals with the above-mentioned tension, and the last section looks at self-assured welfare claimant action as adaptation or resistance. In the end, I briefly discuss the implications of my tentative conclusions for marginalized youth.

Retrieving literature for the paper

Since I intended to write a paper that was primarily theoretical, I never made that review of literature with the intention of getting a full-fledged systematic overview of literature on the topic. Rather, I wanted material that could provide analytical depth to the phenomenon in focus.

I employed two generic digital article bases for that purpose: Google scholar and Oria. In addition, I made literature searches both in central journals like International journal of social welfare, British Journal of Social work, Nordic Social Work Research etc. I employed "welfare claimants" "welfare benefit claims", "claimants" etc. as keywords.

Search words from housing and consumption research like "housing quality" and "housing standards", "housing preferences", "housing satisfaction" etc., were also employed, mostly in combination with "young", "youth", "young adult", etc. along with the combination "consumer and housing". I also made some searches with the above search words in combination with "substance". The usefulness of these searches varied. Most of the articles retrieved by means of the above-mentioned search words were on workfare and general welfare state development and not welfare claimant action.

Interestingly, few of the articles that I succeeded in tracing dealt with welfare claimant or house seeker agency, and none were directly addressing "self-assured agency". Towards the end of the paper, I discuss possible implications of the way in which I retrieved literature for validity and reliability.

Welfare claimant behavior in a consumerist perspective

To determine whether we live in line with an "ism" or in a "post- something" society is generally difficult (Sjöström, 2006). Historical periodicity could lead to fallacies on more levels (Foucault, 2003). Consequently, one must also deal with the issue whether human action reflects discernable historical conditions with care. All the same, several theorists claim that we at the present time live in consumer society (see Baudrillard, 1998; etc.).

"Consumer society" in the sense Zygmunt Bauman (1998; 2005) has described it, is a society in which consumption influences life in a far more existential manner than did consumption in industrialist society. According to Bauman (1998), there is reason in consumer society to ask the following question: *Could we at all live without consuming anything?*

The references to dignity in the statements I presented in the introductory section seem fit the link that Bauman has established between existential life dimensions and the potentiality for immediate satisfaction that is involved in consumption. The young adults in our material referred to "stylish" surroundings as an indication of recognition. When living under stylish or at least "proper" conditions they got a sense of dignity that was either new or regained.

Another of Bauman's major points is that the life satisfaction implied in consumption is preliminary in its character and apt at nurturing the urge to consume in a repetitive pattern. This shapes the ground for a fluid self, apt at taking advantage of the many commodities and lifestyles that exist under consumerism (see for instance Giddens, 1991). Those young people in consumer society who really succeed in enhancing their life chances must adapt to prevailing circumstances in consumption-oriented, flexible ways (Fergusson, 2000).

Since universal welfare and consumerism are allies (Eriksen & Weigård, 1993), self -assured wishes among welfare claimants are not surprising. Welfare is dependent on consumption and most people have access to necessary consumer goods and consumer goods of a more symbolic value. As pointed to by Honneth (1995; 2006) the prerequisite for the historically strong emphasis on egalitarian ideas has been the historical development towards general access to property, which paved the way for a more general principle of social equality (Honneth, 1995). Recognition, citizenship and successful self-realization in consumer society certainly does not only relate to the autonomy granted by those rights that make access to consumption possible. Capacity to cultivate neoliberal ideas like self-reliance, activation, and recognition of own capacities also is a fruit of it. This is a pervasive force according to Bauman (op.cit.). If people in consumer societies do not have immediate access to such potentialities, they are anyhow likely to have exactly the same consumption desires as people who are better off and have better life chances. Bauman even underlines that this closeness to better life chances for the poor; seems to be seen as a threat by the more advantaged population.

Newer social housing strategies also reflect the impact of consumer society. A focus on typical consumerist aspects like "preference" and "choice" is, for instance, a principle underpinning the "Housing First" movement (Tsemberis, 2004). Moreover, realized housing preferences significantly influence quality of life of both for the mentally ill and problem substance users (Hauge, 2009). Yet research results are somewhat inconclusive on this point. Some suggest that homeless people are more oriented towards what they perceive as pathways out of homelessness than what they perceive as appropriate housing standard (see for instance Daiski, 2008). Most research about this seems to be on persistently homeless people. It therefore could be that young homeless adults emphasize style and housing quality differently.

Anyhow, as noted by both Fergusson and his critiques (Garrett, 2004) the above-described ideal of self – reliance and flexibility that prevails in consumer society is an elitist ideal after all.

The volatility implied in consumerism and the marketization of the welfare state, understood as the tendency to solve problems by means of reduction and re-structuring in the public sector (Eriksen & Weigård, 1993) seem to go hand in glove. This alliance may negatively influence chances in the house market among marginalized young adults as well as their chance of self-realization in other domains. For instance, Eriksen & Weigård (op.cit.) suggest that the consumer, whether of goods or of services under such conditions might become an isolated individual who fits the need in markets for flexibility (op.cit.). Such isolation may even compromise citizenship for marginalized people. In the housing sector, marketization in terms of down-sale of public property etc. also affects access to housing for people who are not sufficiently self-reliant in the market (Quilgars, 2012).

Much literature on welfare development and social housing issues that has its origins in critical theory has paid much attention to the insidious aspects of consumerism. In this light, self-assured welfare claimant action in the population of young adults that I here am focusing on is not necessarily likely, although reasonable.

For instance, the risk implied in consumerism of becoming what Bauman (1998) has called a "faulty consumer" ranges among the dark aspects of consumerism.

"Style failure" among young people may entail loss of status and social exclusion (Croghan, Griffin, Hunter & Phoenix, 2006). "Non-consumers"; meaning people who either desire nothing or more or less permanently lack energy to realize themselves through consumption, constitute a new group of outcasts (Brinkmann, 2008). Non-consumers even run the risk to be eliminated from commercial townscapes (Jones & Foust, 2008).

Besides, failure to fulfil the consumerist demand of keeping a balance between enjoyment and control may be viewed a source of pathology development. Pure hedonism was never the "intention" of consumption (Baudrillard, 1998). The protestant ethic, which shaped the basis for the consumerist stage of capitalism also implies an imperative to curb consumption excess (Measham op.cit; Brinkman, op.cit.). It follows from this that the consuming, style-oriented individual must be able to bear the burdens of the liberty involved in consumerism (Measham, 2006). Self-assuredness about what one deserves seems ambiguous in this perspective. It may uphold dignity but could always engender doubt in the immediate environment about one's capacity to keep the balance between enjoyment and excess.

Such doubt seems particularly likely in relation to young people's alcohol, drug or digital media use. Many marginalized youths are, on their side, not immediately ready to advance their consumption desires and their capacity for self-reliance in socially adequate ways (Whitbeck, 2009).

The relationship between individual and collective concerns in consumer society

We may view consumption and citizenship as opposites. Whereas the overall concern of the consumer has been *"What is good for me?"* the overall concern of the citizen has been *"What is good for society?"* (Horner & Hutton 2011). Disregard of self-assured welfare claims as "unrealistic" may reflect this dichotomy.

Yet, the dichotomizing of individual and collective seems to build on false premises about contemporary society. As noted above, without arrangements that ensure the interest of the entire collective the market would not exist (Eriksen & Weigård, 1993). Overall, since even individualism involves rights and responsibilities (Webb, 2006) individualist and communitarian ideas in consumer society may complement rather than oppose each other (Jordan, 2010).

Along with the growth in legal rights for everybody, which above all was promoted during the growth of city-states and the merchant bourgeoisie, all individuals to an increasing extent are entitled to a minimum of social standards and to realize participation at approximately the same level as others (Honneth, 2006). Modern societies not only recognize people for their independence, but also make them subjects of shared concern. In order to demonstrate this mutuality, Honneth (1995) draws on attachment theory, above all represented by the theories of Bowlby and Stern, in which individuation and socialization are described as intertwined processes.

Certainly, the issue of *"What is good for me"* is a central issue in contemporary society. The predilection for self-reliance in consumerist society may explain this.

Yet, we cannot regard expressions of self- worth from young adult welfare claimants only in relation to "pure" consumerist ideals. A sense of being a deserver of welfare services and welfare goods is as likely in the conventional welfare state as in the newer and more market-oriented welfare state. For instance, an egalitarian rights- focus has been a major characteristic of the Norwegian pre-workfare welfare state until the last decade (see Vetlesen & Henriksen, 2003 etc.), although possible negative consequences of enhancing consumption capacity for the poorest also have been considered in Norwegian welfare policy (Hvinden, 2001).

In any case, legal recognition in terms of civil rights today are detached from social status (op.cit.). Moreover, citizenship is less dependent on employment and gender that was the case in industrial society (Jensen & Pfau-Effinger, 2005).

Only when society grants rights to individuals, independent of status, is he or she able to view rights of all kinds in an objectivized light, according to Honneth (op.cit.). The egalitarian aspect of western democracies has even reached a point in which the individual when claiming rights must *not* refer to a collective in order to gain respect. It is sufficient to refer to oneself and a "feeling of self-worth" or deservedness. This appears as a major premise both for universal citizenship and for the universal welfare state. On this background self-assured welfare claimant action from individuals who for the time being do not contribute to the common good is a product of the very idea behind the welfare state itself, rather than an unscrupulous desire to revel in luxury by means of taxpayer's money. Opposed to Marshall's (2006) viewpoint that social rights, in terms of education and economic security, are of another character than civil and political rights and merely serve as an *alternative* to citizenship, Honneth is stating is that social rights intertwine with civil rights and the political right to participation associated with citizenship. Paradoxical as it may seem at first sight from a consumerist point of view, ideas of solidarity thus could constitute the basis for self-assuredness in welfare claimant action.

However, the question is whether Honneth's perspective on the link between a sense of self-worth and recognition from society is valid in the newer welfare states. The acknowledgement is growing that post- industrialist, consumerist welfare states cannot afford to provide the same opportunities to all (Jordan, 1998). Some welfare regimes have even transformed social rights into support provided on condition (Shaver, 2002).

Some of the rationale behind the newer workfare-oriented Norwegian welfare organization (NAV) and probably other Nordic welfare regimes seems to be to weaken the self-evidence of the above-mentioned link between self-worth and recognition from the collective. This does not necessarily occur in order to combat egalitarian principles per se, but to reduce the passivity that the old regime could entail. This neo-liberal shift from passivity and dependency to self-sufficiency and the self-reliant individual has been one of the most marked shifts in the Norwegian history of welfare (Hernes, Heum & Haavorsen, 2010). From a neoliberal perspective on welfare, it would be appropriate to ask with what right young people, whose capacity to contribute to the common wealth is temporarily reduced, claim their rights without any sidelong glance to responsibilities towards the collective. The above -cited statement that living in one room is "unbearable" or "unhygienic" is, at least in such a perspective somewhat "unrealistic".

Yet, we can not exclude that a will to achieve housing conditions of the same standard as "anybody else" actually represents an attempt at fulfilling exactly those demands that prevail in the workfare version of the Norwegian welfare state. Housing is inevitably a gateway to participation also in that field, and claims for safer and more appropriate housing could be a strategy to achieve that aim. Hernes et al., (op.cit.) suggest that the more independent one appears in contemporary society, the more the collective is willing to help. Young adult and marginalized welfare claimants might have captured that premise. Sandberg (2009), for instance, has shown how the most marginalized and stigmatized youth in Norway today, namely young lone asylum seekers may gain respect in encounters with welfare providers, by drawing on the responsibility and respectability required in up-to-date welfare discourse.

Overall, the empirical basis for the notion that young people generally are unambiguously selfish, opportunistic or passive receivers of services tends to lack solid empirical basis. A certain imbalance between rights and responsibilities in favor of responsibilities seems to have manifested itself in younger generations. A study from the UK (Lister, Smith, Middleton & Cox, 2003), for instance, indicates that communitarian rather than liberal or civic-republican citizenship paradigms tend to prevail among youths. One of the conclusions from the cited study is that the youths perceive articulation of rights as more demanding than articulation of responsibilities. Relevant research literature on welfare claimant action in particular tends to strengthen the impression that a relation- to- self as a "loser" is more likely among people who live in consumer society than is a relation- to- self as a deserver (see for instance Rønning, 2005). This may apply even more to young people. Young people who are poor in the sense of low degree of employment, low housing standards and low scores on scales that measure "future happiness" generally demonstrate low future expectations (Aaboen Sletten, 2011).

Even youths involved in risk-taking activity, like illicit substance use, tend to give supremacy to collective concerns in terms of identifying and comparing self with the most predominant lifestyles in the larger society (Juberg, 2011). Peretti – Watel (2003) developed a theoretical framework inspired by cultural criminology and communitarian ideas in order to improve understanding of meaning- making around minor deviance from moral and legal codes today. An empirical material was basis for this framework. Peretti-Watel suggests that young cannabis users tend to take responsibility for risky health behavior in order to neutralize their own guilt and to avoid being accused of abusing taxpayers' money.

The critique of the universal welfare state could also apply to critique towards welfare regimes based on New Public Management models. Some argue that there are regimes that in quite undifferentiated ways have elevated the service user without putting equal emphasis on responsibilities, though on other grounds than the conventional welfare state (Benington & More, 2011). Public services according to those authors, who represent Public Value theory, still have obligations in terms of being responsive to needs in the population, but the citizen as a taxpayer is as important for continued welfare as the consumer citizen who relates to the welfare system as a servant and pays less attention to the common wealth and welfare.

This seems important to keep in mind also when trying to answer the question of whether self- assured welfare claimant action is reasonable or "unrealistic" in newer welfare states. If not overwhelmingly apparent, there might be a potentiality here for acknowledging marginalized welfare claimants as contributors to the common value if admitted fundamental preconditions. Erikson & Vogt (2013) suggest that concepts like *"consumerist citizenship"* fit newer welfare user roles. Personal responsibility shapes the basis for the concept, but it also represents increased consciousness about the importance of social citizenship for welfare.

Accordingly, polarizations between rights and obligations, deservers and non-deservers are hardly fruitful other than for analytic purposes.

Welfare claimant behavior in the perspective of social inequality and oppression

So far, the thematic of the paper has revolved around the concerns between which marginalized young adult welfare claimants must balance in order to avoid that their audiences regard them as "far out" in relation to citizenship in consumer society. This section addresses the likeliness that young marginalized adults raise their voice in a self-assured way within the frames of the newer welfare state. The concept of "consumerist citizenship" and its implication may might merely exist as a potentiality. It is not given that the sense of self-worth that democratization processes according to Honneth, so far have nurtured actually affect welfare claimants at the present time. Earlier sections of this paper have provided some examples of the tendencies that threaten the citizenship of young adults who are homeless.

Those examples of inequality in the Norwegian welfare state put young adult marginalized welfare claimants in an ambiguous situation. On the one hand, society expects them to stand up for themselves in order to unburden the system. A certain willingness to horizontalize former hegemonic relationships exist in newer democracies (Honneth 1995). The welfare systems of today may certainly allow for this to a greater extent that was the case in paternalist welfare regimes. Partnership between social services providers and receivers could certainly counteract some of the negative effects that marketization of welfare states have brought about (Moe, Tronvoll & Gjeitnes, 2014).

Yet, the notion of the creative and self-expressive subject, who participates in dynamic dialogue, also has its limitations (Born & Jensen, 2010). Some argue that social work practices tend to be as much hegemonic as non-hegemonic even today (Carey & Foster, 2013) and that empowerment as a phenomenon has a so far un-realized emancipatory potential (Hyslop, 2012). In encounters between service providers and receivers, suspicion has largely taken over for the feelings of solidarity that prevailed in the conventional Norwegian welfare state (Hernes, Heum & Haavorsen, 2010).

In a climate as described above self – assured welfare claimant action among the most marginalized does not appear as very likely, although the necessity to encourage homeless people to become welfare claimants is acknowleged in some literature (Carr & Hunter, 2008).

From a perspective of symbolic power, Bourdieu (1992:52) describes people in oppressed situations as "speechless", "tongue-tied" or at "a loss for words". Bauman (1998) as well as Bourdieu (1998) point to how a misrecognized tacit contract based on continued power imbalance may predominate the consumers' mind-sets and actions. Injustice remains unquestioned by those who are affected by it. Consumers may certainly experience patterns of consumption as free will (Bauman, op.cit.). Yet, according to Foucault's power concept, freedom in consumer society is ambivalent to the extent that individuals do not only realize themselves but also govern themselves (Reith, 2004). People may thus put constraints on themselves that undermines the individual freedom implied in the versions of citizenship that prevail in consumer society.

According to Honneth (1995), a feeling of respect is the prerequisite for an experience of disrespect. A "positive- relation- to- self" is dependent as much on love as recognition, but also on the rights that political authorities grant to the individual independent of feelings and social status. People who lack love and recognition thus miss a vital fundament for operating in self-assured ways towards welfare authorities. Yet, Honneth describes the link between recognition and rights as a conceptual rather than an empirical relationship. He thereby seems to accept the critique raised against him that his analysis of a positive link between misrecognition, the experience of shame and eventual sense of moral outrage is doubtful at vital points (see Houston, 2015).

One could tentatively conclude on this background that self-assured action among marginalized welfare service receivers, to the extent that it occurs, in its utmost consequence could be an expression of subjugation to power hegemonies rather than opposition to them. Misrecognition of social inequality may nurture advancing of claims that by more advantaged audiences may appear as both ridiculous and far-fetched.

To the extent that active citizenship and active participation among marginalized people in welfare societies occurs, literature about it is primarily focusing on grass-root social development, consciousness raising, and social action work among "hard-core" marginalized youth populations (Karabanow, 2004). "Insurgent citizenship" in the sense that marginalized groups contest state welfare arrangements by establishing alternative dwellings and alternative economies (Davy & Pellissery, 2013) could be viewed as a part of this, although it seems relatively marginal in a Nordic context.

However, *indirect* forms of agency could represent a tendency that at least in its effects challenges repression in welfare regimes. The phenomenon of coach surfing could serve as an example. According to Eberle, Kraus & Serge (2009) we have to do with coach surfing as a solution to homelessness when the holder of the household (and the coach) in question is a friend or family member under 25 years of age. Many sources mention the potentiality that coach surfing represents for many youths in order to avoid the most humiliating encounters with welfare systems. Yet, more offensive welfare claimant action could also be involved. Some argue that coach surfing expresses a dynamic of "the new homelessness" (Minnery & Greenhalgh, 2007) which, at least when compared to available alternatives, includes both surprising and innovative elements. The extent to which the tenants are satisfied or dissatisfied with the arrangement also counts as a criterion, according to Eberle et al. We thus could subsume coach surfing under the broader concept "stigma management" (Ogden & Avades, 2011).

Stigma management is a very indirect way of tackling oppression both in the housing area and in other life domains, but it still appears as a reflexive or even critical position towards negative culturally dominant categorization (Juhlia, 2004). The cited author has demonstrated how shelter inhabitants by means of "talking back" on their stigmatized identities manage to shape a distance to stigmatized others.

A more promising perspective on the scarcity of literature around offensive welfare claimant action is that such action may well exist without being sufficiently noticed. Scholars are inevitably but often unconsciously part of a socio-cultural universe that is significantly different from the universe of the people they are studying also with regard to positions in the status hierarchy (Bourdieu, 2004). Therefore, they may also ignore emancipatory projects. Besides, hegemonic power in terms of discipline domination may influence what we focus on. Conventional psychological and medical approaches to homelessness have displayed a tendency to overemphasize victimization at the cost of young peoples' capacity for entrepreneurship (Osgood, Foster, Flanagan & Ruth, 2005). Certainly, hegemonic power is involved also in this, but the frameworks of both Bourdieu and Foucault implicitly base themselves on power concepts that are not necessarily negative for people at risk of losing their citizenship (see for instance Bourdieu, 1990).

In order both to discover and encourage self- assured welfare claimant action Leonard's (1997) suggestion that we need to re-think welfare seems appropriate.

The post-modern individual is according to Leonard more double-faced than is assumed in conventional theory on justice and emancipation.

Conclusion

The specific aim of this paper was, to try to understand "self-assured" welfare claimant action in light of the complex and shifting relationship between collective and individual concerns in the newer Norwegian welfare state and in the light of consumerism as an influential tendency in contemporary society. I wanted to find an answer to whether self-assured welfare claimant when it comes to young adults who cannot immediately contribute to the common wealth is likely, reasonable or far-fetched.

I have only partially achieved those aims. There is little empirical evidence that self- assured welfare claims are widespread among marginalized young adults, but because most research on welfare development, social work and social housing generally seems to have had focus on structure rather than agency, it may have overlooked the phenomenon here at issue. However, to the extent that self-assured welfare claimant exists, the literature I have employed to elicit the phenomenon clearly underscores the importance of being conscious about the ambiguities implied in recent welfare development. This seems to be a ground premise for meeting young adult welfare claimants in professionally and ethically appropriate ways. The sense of deservedness that some young adults have, despite the unstable fundament for their citizenship, has its apparent historical roots. Yet, there are also forces that undermine it.

A weakness of the paper is that I retrieved the literature that it bases itself on in relatively arbitrary ways. A more systematic review could have brought about other conclusions. Yet, the terminology that is related to the current thematic represents a problem. For instance, titles of publications often do not display their content in appropriate ways. Yet, if I could have accounted for the literature searches in a more appropriate way, I could with more strength have discussed the reasons why self-assuredness and feelings of self-worth as part of marginalized people's welfare claimant repertoire are relatively absent from relevant literature.

A possible strength of the paper is that it might contribute to putting more focus on welfare claimant action in future research.

References

Aaboen Sletten, M. (2011). How 14–16-year-old Norwegians in poor families look at their future. *Young* 19(2), 181–218.

Baudrillard, J. (1998). *The consumer society: Myths and structures*. London, Thousand Oaks, New Delhi: Sage publications.

Bauman, Z. (1998). *Globaliseringen og dens menneskelige konsekvenser*. Oslo: Vidarforlaget AS.

Bauman, Z. (2005). *Work, consumerism and the new poor*. New York: Open University press.

Benington, J. & Moore, M. H. (2011). Public value in complex and changing times. In J. Benington and M. H. Moore (Eds.). *Public value theory & practice* (pp. 1–20). Basingstoke (UK), New York: Palgrave Macmillan.

Brinkmann, S. (2008). Changing psychologies in the transition from industrial society to consumer society. *History of the human sciences*, 21(2), 85–110.

Bourdieu, P. (1990). *In other Words: Essays towards a reflexive sociology*. Stanford, California: Stanford University press.

Bourdieu, P. (1992). *Language and symbolic power*. Cambridge (UK) Malden, MA (USA): Polity press.

Bourdieu, P. (1998). *Practical Reason – On the theory of action*. Cambridge, Oxford (UK): Blackwell Publishers ltd.

Bourdieu, P. (2004). *Science of Science and Reflexivity*. Chicago: The university of Chicago press and Polity press

Born, A. W. & Jensen, P. H. (2010). Dialogued-based activation – a new "dispositif"? *International journal of sociology and social policy* 30(5/6), 326 – 336.

Carey, M., & Foster, V. (2013). Social work, ideology, discourse and the limits of post-hegemony. *Journal of social work*, 13(3), 248–266.

Carr, H. & Hunter, C. (2008). Managing vulnerability: homelessness law and the interplay of the social, the political and the technical. *Journal of social welfare and family law*, 30(4), 293–307.

Croghan, R., Griffin, C., Hunter, J. & Phoenix, A. (2006). Style failure: Consumption, identity and social exclusion. *Journal of Youth Studies*, 9(4), 463 – 478.

Daiski, I. (2008). Perspectives of homeless people on their housing needs and approaches to ensure success. *The International journal of interdisciplinary social sciences*, 36(6), 53–61.

Danielsen, A. (1998). Kulturell kapital i Norge. *Sosiologisk tidsskrift*, 6(1–2), 75–106.

Davy, B., & Pelissery, S. (2013). International journal of social Welfare, 22(S1), 68–84.

Djupvik, A. R. & Eikås, M. (2010). *Organisert velferd: Organisasjonskunnskap for helse – og sosialarbeidarar*. Oslo: Samlaget

Eberle, M., Kraus, D., & Serge, L. (2009). *Results of the pilot study to estimate the size of the hidden homeless population in Metro Vancouver*. Vancouver: Mustel research group market POWER Research Inc.

Eriksen, O. & Weigård, J. (1993). Fra statsborger til kunde: Kan relasjonen mellom innbyggerne og det offentlige reformuleres på grunnlag av nye roller. In O. Eriksen (Ed.). *Den offentlige dimensjon: Verdier og styring i offentlig sektor* (pp. 133–167). Tromsø, Bergen (Norway): ISV/ Universitetet i Tromsø /LOS-senteret.

Eriksson, K. & Vogt, H. (2013). On self-service democracy: Configurations of individualizing governance and self-directed citizenship. *European journal of social theory*, 16(2), 153–173.

Evans, M. E. (2001). Britain: Moving towards a work and opportunity-focused welfare state? *International journal of social welfare*, 10(4), 260–266.

Fergusson, R. (2004). Discourses of exclusion: Reconceptualising participation amongst young people. *Journal of social policy*, 33(2), 289–320.

Foucault, M. (2003). *The essential Foucault: selection from the essential works of Foucault1954–1984*. New York: New Press

Garrett, P. M. (2004). More Trouble with Harry: A Rejoinder in the 'Life Politics' Debate. *The British journal of social work* 34(4), 557–589.

Giddens, A. (1991). *Modernity and self-identity: self and society in the late modern age.* Cambridge (UK): Polity press.

Hauge, A. L. & Støa, E. (2009). "Here you get a little extra push": The meaning of architectural quality in housing for the formerly homeless – a case study of Veiskillet in Trondheim, Norway. *Nordic journal of architectural research*, 21(1),18–31.

Hellevik, T. (2005). Ungdom, etablering og ulike velferdsregimer. *Tidsskrift for ungdomsforskning*, 5(1), 89–110.

Hernes, T., Heum, I. & Haavorsen, P. (2010). *Arbeidsinkludering: Om det nye politikk-og praksisfeltet i velferds- Norge*. Oslo: Gyldendal Akademisk

Honneth, A. (1995). Patterns of intersubjective recognition: Love, rights and solidarity. Chap 7. In A. Honneth (Ed.). *The Struggle for Recognition. The moral grammar of social conflicts*. Cambridge: Polity press.

Honneth, A. (2006). *Kamp om anerkendelse: Sociale konfllikters moralske grammatik*. København: Hans Reitzels forlag.

Horner, L. & Hutton, W. (2011). Public value, deliberate democracy and the role of public managers. In J. Benington & M. H. Moore (Eds.). *Public Value* (pp. 112–126). Basingstoke (UK), New York: Palgrave Macmillan

Houston, S. (2015). Empowering the 'shamed' self: Recognition and critical social work. *Journal of social work*. January 13, 2015, doi: 10.1177/1468017314566789.

Hvinden, B. (2001). *Fattigdom og tiltak mot fattigdom i Norge: Diskusjonsnotat skrevet på oppdrag fra Sosialdepartementet* Desember 2001. Oslo: Sosialdepartementet.

Ilan, J. (2011). Reclaiming Respectability? The Class-cultural Dynamics of Crime, Community and Governance in Inner-city Dublin. *Urban Studies*, 48(6),1137–1155.

Jensen, P. H. & Pfau- Effinger, B. (2005). "Active" citizenship: the new face of welfare. In J. Goul Andersen, A.M. Guillemard & P. H. Jensen (Eds.). *Changing face of welfare: Consequences and outcomes from a citizenship perspective* (pp. 1–14). Bristol (UK): Policy Press.

Jones, R. G. J. & Foust, C. R. (2008). Staging and enforcing consumerism in the city: The performance of othering on the 16th Street Mall. Liminalities: *A Journal of Performance Studies*, 4(1), 1–28.

Jordan, B. (1998). *New Politics of Welfare: Social Justice in a Global Context*. UK: SAGE Publications Ltd.

Juberg, A. (2011). Exploring tentative lives: Reflexive social work with adolescents who stay in the space between respectability and disrespect with regard to substance use and law abidance. *Journal of Comparative Social Work*, (1), 1–19.

Juberg, A., Kiik, R. & Johansen, PE. (2012). "Alt henger på boligen – vi får ikke gjort noe uten den". Sosialfaglige utfordringer blant ungdom(16–23) i *Trondheim som har rus-*

vansker og boligbehov. Trondheim, HUSK Midt-Norge, NTNU- Institutt for sosialt arbeid og helsevitenskap, NTNU Samfunnsforskning AS.

Juberg, A. & Kiik, R. (2015). *Good enough for "them?" Housing challenges among young adult problem substance users in the contemporary Norwegian welfare state.* A Bauman – inspired approach. Article in progress.

Juhlia, K. (2004). Talking back to stigmatized identities: Negotiation of culturally dominant categorizations in interviews with shelter residents. *Qualitative social work*, (3), 259–275.

Karabanow, J. (2004). Making organizations work: Exploring characteristics of anti-oppressive organizational structures in street youth shelters. *Journal of social work*, 4(1), 47–60.

Kvist, J., Fritzell, J., Hvinden, B. & Kangas, O. (2012). *Changing social equality: the Nordic welfare model in the 21st century.* Bristol: Policy Press.

Leonard, P. (1997). *Postmodern welfare: Reconstructing an emancipatory project.* Sage publications.

Lister, R., Smith, N., Middleton, S., & Cox, L. (2003). Young people talk about citizenship: Empirical perspectives on theoretical and political debates. *Citizenship studies*, 7(2), 235–253.

Mack, J. & Lansley, S. (1985). *Poor Britain.* London: Georg Allen & Unwin.

Marshall, T. (2006). Citizenship and social class. In C. Pierson & F. G. Castles (Eds.). *The Welfare state reader* (pp. 30–40), Cambridge: Policy Press.

Measham, F. (2006). The new policy mix: Alcohol, harm, minimization, and determined drunkenness in contemporary society. *International journal of drug policy*, 17(4), 258–268.

McNaughton, C. (2006). Agency, structure and biography: Charting transitions through homelessness in late modernity. *Auto/Biography*, 14, 134–152.

Minnery, J. & Greenhalgh, E. (2007). Approaches to homelessness policy in Europe, the United States, and Australia. *Journal of social issues*, 63(3), 641–655.

Moe, A., Tronvoll, IM. & Gjeitnes, K. (2014). A reflective approach in practice research. *Nordic social work research*, 4(1), 14–25.

Natalier, K. & Johnson, G. (2012). Housing pathways of young people who have left out-of-home state care. *Housing, Theory and Society*, 29(1), 75–91.

Ogden, J., & Avades, T. (2011). Being homeless and the use and nonuse of services: a qualitative study. *Journal of Community Psychology*, 39(4), 499–505.

Osgood, D. W., Foster, E.M., Flanagan, C & Ruth, G.R. (2005). Introduction: Why focus on the transition to adulthood for vulnerable persons? In D. W. Osgood, E. M. Foster, C. Flanagan & G. R. Ruth (Eds.). *On your own without a net. The transition to adulthood for vulnerable persons* (pp. 1–26), Chicago: University of Chicago press.

Peretti-Watel, P. (2003). Neutralization theory and the denial of risk: some evidence from cannabis use among French adolescents. *British Journal of Sociology*, 54(1), 21–42.

Quilgars, D. (2012). Homeless people: Youth in the United Kingdom. In D. Quilgars, S. Johnsen & N. Pleace (Eds.) *International encyclopedia of housing and home* (156–160) York (UK): Elsvier Ltd.

Reith, G. (2004). Consumption and its discontents: Addiction, identity and the problems of freedom. *British journal of sociology*, 55(2), 283–300.

Rønning, R. (2005). Den institusjonelle ydmykingen. *Nordisk sosialt arbeid*, (2),111–120.
Sandberg, S. (2009). A Narrative Search for Respect. *Deviant Behavior*, 30(6), 487–510.
Shaver, S. (2002). Australian welfare reform: From citizenship to supervision. *Social policy & administration*, 36(4), 331–345.
Sjöström, S. (2006). Post-samhället, dess zombier och nya sociala problem. *Nordisk sosialt arbeid* (4), 282–292.
Thompson, S. J., Barczyk, A., Gomez, R., Dreyer, L. & Popham, Amelia. (2010). Homeless, street-involved emerging adults: Attitudes toward substance use. *Journal of adolescent research*, 25(2), 231–257.
Townsend, P. (1993). *The international analysis of poverty*. London & New York: Harvester Wheatsheaf.
Tsemberis, S., et al. (2004). Housing First, consumer choice, and harm reduction for homeless individuals with a dual diagnosis. *American journal of public health and the nations' health*, 94(4), 651–656.
Ulfrstad, L.M. (2011). *Velferd og bolig. Om boligsosialt (sam-)arbeid*. Trondheim: Kommuneforlaget.
Vetlesen, A. J. & Henriksen, J.-O. (2003). *Moralens sjanser i markedets tidsalder: om kulturelle forutsetninger for moral*. Oslo: Gyldendal Akademisk.
Webb, S. A. (2006). *Social work in a risk society: Social and political perspectives*. Basingstoke (UK): Palgrave Macmillan.
Whitbeck, L. B. (2009). No one knows what happens to those kids: Interrupted adolescence and emerging adulthood. In L. B. Whitbeck (Ed.). *Mental health and emerging adultood among homeless young people* (3–17), New York: Psychology Press.

Author

Anne Juberg, associate professor
Faculty of Health Education and Social Work at Soer Troendelag University College, Trondheim, Norway. The Social work department
Research areas: Qualitative research within social work: Social inequality, transition to adulthood, social housing, substance use etc.

How to include marginalized youth in local community development? – Evaluation of a leisure time project in Trondheim

Geir Hyrve and Ragnhild Collin-Hansen

Abstract

Local and national political guidelines in Norway stress that the child welfare services should manifest themselves as a positive resource, which assists young people in distressed situations. The aim is to develop inclusive services with a focus on the welfare of children. The school system has changed and the authorities are concerned about the dropout rate. In the article, we discuss how to use the leisure arena as an alternative and complementary venue for the development of children and youths.

By participating in a motor sport project the youths develop an identity linked to cars and motor sports. This has positive repercussions for the status and self-esteem of the participants. In addition, it enables them to develop other types of skills, such as social, disciplinary and action-oriented skills. The project aims at motivating the participants to acquire new knowledge. There is a strong focus on relational aspects, as well as positive activities and experiences that promote development and well-being for the youths. Sufficient time and space for the children is provided by accessible and confident adult figures, contributing substantially to the experience of being seen, heard and recognized in their daily life.

The Public Sector in Norway

In the recent years, the child welfare services in Norway have been subject to attention from the media and public authorities regarding organization and the content of the services.

The 2013 state budget allocated resources to secure children and youths that are involved in cases where intervention is considered (Barne-, likestillings- og inkluderingsdepartementet, 2013). The government emphasizes that a priority of the child welfare policy is to provide suitable high-quality measures in accordance with legal requirements to secure good growing up and living conditions to vulnerable children and youths. Therefore, it is necessary to develop skills and knowledge within the municipal child welfare services in general and to apply new methods in multicultural child welfare work in particular. It is also important to develop measures targeting youths with serious behavioral problems as well as children with parents who are mentally ill and/or who abuse drugs or alcohol.

It is accepted that children and youths should enjoy the same rights and opportunities for personal development regardless of geographical location and of their parents' financial situation, ethnicity and education. To maintain services, which are capable of identifying children in the risk zone, it is crucial to counteract poverty and social exclusion among children. It is also necessary to assess local development work in order to improve the quality. The reviewing process will also illuminate what measures prove effective for different youths within the child welfare services. Given our awareness of the great varieties in living conditions for children and youths in Norway it becomes important to discover how support measures could help children and youths to achieve better lives.

Our knowledge from research on children in the child welfare services indicates that these children experience significantly poorer conditions in a number of areas compared to the average population (Clausen & Kristofersen, 2008; Fauske et al., 2009). Poor living conditions and welfare problems are among the reasons why children and youths have received assistance from the child welfare services.

Education remains the major tool to empower people and to increase the economic, social, and personal well-being of all citizens in a pluralistic society. The mission for every school should be to educate children and youths to become *knowledgeable, responsible, socially skilled, healthy, caring and contributing citizens.* But in many countries large portions of the young population never complete school and drop out. This has a deep and wide-ranging impact on the countries' long-term economic outlook. In Norway, formal qualifications have become more or less required for permanent employment and participation in present-day society.

The drop-out rates in upper secondary education has been a concern for the authorities. The government's white paper no. 16 (2006–2007) on early intervention for lifelong learning stated:

Everyone must have the same possibility of developing themselves and their abilities. A society characterized by community and equal worth provides the best setting for individuals to pursue their own life projects. Societies with small economic and social differences are also among the most productive in an economic sense. Education systems are affected by changes in other areas of society and actors at all levels of the education system must use their know-how to develop a proactive approach to developments in society. When social inequality increases, efforts to combat the differences must be intensified in the education system. (p. 1)

The white paper addressed social differences in participation and learning and presented the government's policy for how the educational system can make a greater contribution to social equality. To fight the drop out phenomenon in upper secondary education the major challenges was identified as:

The main challenge in upper secondary education is getting as many pupils as possible to complete their schooling with a certificate of upper secondary education, a craft certificate or a journeyman's certificate. Without a certificate from the upper secondary school, the probability of poverty or marginalization later in life increases dramatically. Weak learning in the primary and lower secondary school appears to have great significance for the probability of dropping out of upper secondary school. Choices, learning and drop-out rates in the upper secondary school are linked with lower level grades, which vary according to the pupils' family background. Pupils with poor basic skills from primary and lower secondary school find it very difficult to acquire knowledge that is presented in writing or in a theoretical form. The introduction of Reform 94 brought to light the problems young people face in later education and in the labor market if they have not acquired adequate skills in primary and lower secondary school. The current labor market demands competence in the form of basic skills. This is reflected in the organization of and requirements regarding technical and vocational education in Reform 94 and in the Knowledge Promotion program. (p. 8)

Local and national political guidelines stress that the child welfare services should manifest themselves as a positive resource that assists young people in distressed situations. The aim is to develop inclusive services with a focus on the welfare of children. In this article, we discuss how to include dropouts from school in local community development. The article focuses on how alternative educational options can contribute to give youths a better and more meaningful learning arena. The second area we find central in the work of including youth in the community, is leisure activities.

Background – The Nordic model

To explain the society in which young people today grow up in Norway, we will make a short outline what is usually referred to as the Nordic model.

The Scandinavian welfare model is based upon a *pot-luck-party principle*. Every citizen is expected to contribute to the funding of services through taxes while benefiting according to their needs. The intention of the Welfare State idea is to achieve a general coverage of all situations of need. Market-based arrangements are available for those who can afford them. Every citizen is expected to contribute through participation in education and employment. Hence, family politics – which has seemed successful – is based upon measures to help young adults to combine family life and work. Children growing up are exposed to expectations towards education and work, which is clearly reflected in the school system.

Today's Education System in Norway

The Norwegian school system is mainly public, with a marginal, though increasing private supplement. In 2013, about 5 per cent of the children attended private schools.

Every child is entitled to thirteen years of education. Ten years of primary school and lower secondary schooling is compulsory. Since 1994, everyone subsequently has the right to upper secondary schooling for at least three years, in academic or vocational training, on which some are required to spend up to five years. Those who wish and who have the required qualifications can acquire a higher education. Following the 2006 Competence Reform, adults now have the right to complete their primary and secondary education, and employees have the right to leaves of absence in order to do this.

Recent developments in the schools system

Over the last 30 years, the school system has gone through numerous reforms.

The 1990 reform era was initiated by then-minister of education, Gudmund Hernes, as the ministry the Labor party government streamlined the education system for life-long learning. Hernes as a committee leader had stated that the challenge for Norwegian politics of knowledge is that the country does not get enough competence out of the population's talents (Ministry of Culture, 1988, p. 8). Reform 94, which introduced the right to three years of upper secondary education for everyone, was followed by Reform 96, which adjusted the school start for children from seven to six years.

The 2006 Competence Reform restructured the goals and content of the basic education (Report no. 30 to the Storting). The initiative was taken by the center-right government, and was justified by poor achievements by Norwegian schoolchildren in international comparative studies, PISA, TIMMs, etc. The goals and the measures of the Competence Reform were unanimously supported by the red-green (center-left) government which entered office in 2005.

The objectives and quality framework for education and training are described in The National Curriculum for the Competence Reform. It applies to all levels of primary and secondary education and training based on five basic skills of the subject curricula: The ability to read, to express oneself orally, to express oneself literally, to develop numeracy, and to use digital tools. The basic skills should be integrated in a way that is adapted to each subject through thirteen years of education.

Upper secondary education and training has twelve programs, including three academic and nine vocational programs.

How do young people comply with the expectations?

As pointed out above, there is a strong expectation that all young people should use their right to education. The great majority, nearly 100 per cent of pupils completing the 10th grade, applies for admission and around 96 per cent advance to upper secondary school. However, a great number does not complete upper secondary education. In 2007, only about 75 per cent of the pupils have passed the exam within five years (White paper no. 44, 2008–2009, p. 14). During the latest years, in average 70 percent of pupils have fulfilled academic or vocational training five years after they started (Ministry of Education and Research, 2013).

The completion rate is particularly low in vocational training programs. This is linked, for example, to the fact that there are a larger number of pupils with poorer grades and a great deal of absence from lower secondary school in these courses. This must in turn be seen in the light of the pupils' family background. Moreover, it appears that the quality of technical and vocational education varies.

However, it is also important to remember that in addition to school, leisure activities may represent an alternative and complementary arena for children and youth's development. A central theme in Vygotsky's writing relates to what he calls the *zone of proximal development (ZPD)*. Children grow and can be supported in their growth towards the next stage of development through the guidance of resourceful adults and more skilled peers who can help them to identify and develop their skills in particular areas (Smith, 2009).

The child welfare services are institutions that officially are supposed to improve the lives of young people.

The story of Lade Motor – a leisure-time project

Lade Motor was initiated by a group of volunteers at a lower secondary school in Trondheim in 2004. The initiative was meant to be an alternative learning environment where theoretical education was replaced by practical disciplines. This resulted in an emphasis on leisure activities carried out in Trondheim. Leisure activities were established in the districts and The Children's Resource Centre

(RBU)[1] was created as an offer to young people above 10 years with great composite problems.

The initiative is currently divided into two parts:

1. Daytime leisure activity for schoolchildren. The pupils are recruited whenever the school headmaster contacts the relevant team at The Children's Resource Centre (RBU). Together they decide whether the pupil should be admitted. The pupils spend one or two days at Lade and the rest of the week in their ordinary class. The project has the capacity to receive 16 pupils.
2. Evening leisure activity, two days a week (Monday and Wednesday). In addition, there are weekend sessions during the summer in connection with motor sport events. The administrative section of the child and family welfare services are responsible for establishing the contact between the youths and RBU's projects.

The target group of the initiative is children and youths who have been involved with the child welfare services in Trondheim and who are in the process of dropping out from school and/or are overwhelmingly or entirely excluded from contact with positive social environments. The users need alternative arenas of learning in order to achieve a positive personal development. The objective is to help create a positive link between school, spare-time and the established social environments as well as to prevent an unfortunate development involving abuse of alcohol/drugs and crime. Another objective has been to promote integration through the participation of boys and girls as well as young people of multicultural backgrounds.

The aim of the initiative on the part of RBU has been to assist children and youths in handling their lives in a better way. A key element of Lade Motor's project has been to develop personal relations. As one of the admission criteria is a lack of contact with positive social environments among the youths, it becomes all the more important to create an environment involving positive adult role models. Through the activities, relations between adults and youths are established and the youths develop new attitudes as a result of their socialization. By participating in the environment, the youths develop an identity linked to cars and motor sport. This has positive repercussions for the status and self-esteem of the participants. In addition, it enables them to develop other types of skills, such as social, disciplinary and action-oriented skills. The project aims at motivating the participants to acquire new knowledge.

The project represents an alternative to children and youths between 10 and 18 years who struggle to adapt to the ordinary school. In the evaluation, a key

---

[1]   The Children's Resource Centre (RBU) is a part of Trondheim Municipality's "resource bank". RBU as a unit covers the entire town and is responsible for children and youths who undergo a serious crisis

issue has been to assess the significance of Lade Motor in generating change and development among children and youths who participate.

A number of adults of both genders, a number of them above the age of 50, on a voluntary basis participate in the leisure time activity. As role models, they generate enthusiasm about the project and actively take part in the activities. Private companies also contribute by backing the project financially. This enables both development and participation in drag racing activities. Cooperation has also been established with the Amcar[2] club in Trondheim, which takes part in the project and offers assistance in car tuning. The board of the Amcar club in Trondheim has voted to support the project at Lade. It has been agreed to let youths with an interest in motor sports continue their spare-time work in the Amcar club after having passed *the age limit* at Lade Motor. In order to participate in drag racing, one must belong to a club and the Amcar clubs represent such an alternative.

The aim is to help the youths develop new attitudes as a result of socialization. By participating in this community, they develop a new identity linked to cars and motor sports. In turn, this has a positive effect on the status and self-esteem of the participants. As an additional effect, social, disciplinary and action-oriented skills are developed. The project also aims at motivating the participants to acquire new knowledge. The primary goals of Lade Motor's project are subsequently:

1. To offer children and youths who are in danger of dropping out from school an alternative educational option, which along with a follow-up in school should contribute in offering the young people a better and more meaningful school week.
2. To establish a set of activities where young people without a belonging to positive social milieus and with a vulnerability to crime, alcohol, drugs, etc., get a chance to spend time with adults, while working towards new objectives with things that interest them. It is possible for everyone to qualify for drag racing, which requires practical and theoretical training.
3. To ensure that ten of the youths involved in the project are recruited as members of the Amcar club within 3 years.
4. To develop the project in cooperation with The Children's Resource Centre (RBU) via The Day School, The Cultural Section of Trondheim Municipality and The Centre for Adult Education.

The evaluation of the project has focused on objectives 2 and 3.

---

[2]   Amcar is an abbreviation for American cars

Evaluation design

The aim of the evaluation is to discover what results the project has yielded. In this evaluation, we have primarily focused on the project itself and its consequences for the participating youths. We have emphasized what short-term and long-term effects the initiative has had on the youths taking part in an organized leisure activity like Lade Motor.

In the evaluation, we have carried out interviews with various parties involved in Lade Motor in order to be able to describe the project. The research design is based on an inductive approach in which we have sought to arrive at some general conclusions about the effect of the project on its participants based on our collected material. The approach is based on Pattons (2008) *Utilization-focused evaluation.* The aim is to get an understanding of what meaning the project may have for marginalized children and youths linked to the child welfare services. We have sought to highlight the stories and the experience of being a part of a drag racing community, from the perspective of the youths as well as the adults. In addition, we have stressed the significance of the project in preventing young people from resorting to drugs, alcohol and crime.

Participants in Lade Motor's leisure activity

Lade Motor has a strong emphasis on transformation, development and learning. In order to put the work at Lade Motor into context it is important to consider the number of children and youths recruited to the project. The aim is to integrate the participants into society with the help of the project. Integration and the *struggle* for normalization have a long history. The debates about integration are ideological, as they concern the attempt to bring people together. It could be viewed as one of society's objectives to socialize children and youths into *normal citizens.*

Altogether 46 participants have taken part in Lade Motor's leisure activity from its beginning in 2005 and until 2009. The child welfare authorities are responsible for recruiting participants and funding the project. Mainly boys have participated in the project. 39 boys (85%) and 7 girls (15%) have joined the organized initiative. The boys represent a clear majority.

One of the objectives has been to integrate children with multicultural backgrounds. Relatively few children with multicultural backgrounds have so far participated (approximately 10%).

All participants have previous been in touch with the child welfare services and most of them have been subject to a review by The Child and Youth Mental Health Service (BUP). It is interesting to note that the number of participants who have been reviewed by BUP seems to increase every year. This does not necessarily mean that changes have occurred among the participants, but could also be due to an escalation plan of BUP, which has made it possible to review a larger number of youths.

The children and youths who were offered to participate in the leisure activity have all experienced problems at school and in their spare time. 70% of the participants pursue alternative educational programs in their local school or day school. In addition, the youths say they just have limited contact with positive social environments.

The children and youths who participate in the project also have a genuine interest in cars and motor sports. Not everyone had such an interest initially, but this is crucial if the youths are to fully appreciate the activities. As became evident during the interviews, the participants had extensive knowledge of cars and car tuning. Their knowledge of drag racing and its rules were detailed and elaborate.

The youths describe their childhood as problematic. Both at home and at school, they have experienced situations that are harmful to children. The normal pattern reflected a childhood marked by social isolation and bullying. It would be justified to seriously question the educational situation for many of the participants. They describe their school day as extremely challenging. At several lower secondary schools in Trondheim, we find subcultures in which the abuse of alcohol and drugs is subject to glorification. The social pressure to join such environments is also present.

As the children have previously been involved with the child welfare authorities, Lade Motor does not represent the first attempt to offer them an out-of-school activity. They consider the previous measures to have had little impact on their personal development. These included contact with support persons, sports like basketball, etc., and new methods like MST. It seems like these measures were not able to respond to the interests of the youths.

Car tuning and drag racing represent something else than being socialized into a group. The significance of drag racing lies in the fact that the youths must be understood based on their life history, requirements, motivations and objectives. Further, it is crucial how the project is organized and in what context the activities take place.

Activities like car tuning and drag racing have an intrinsic value. Accordingly, the project represents both a means to integrate the participants into society and an objective in its own right. From previous surveys, we know that motor sports are highly popular among youths. A NOVA survey (Bakken, 1998) shows that particularly vulnerable youths rate motor sports as one of their favorite activities.

Using motor sports while working with youths is not a new phenomenon. Minken (2005) has described the motor sport initiative 2&4 in several articles and textbooks. We also know that many of these projects after a while are phased out. An explanation may be the failure to realize the more complex connections and the inclination to view motor sport as a positive spare-time activity in itself, regardless of individual or contextual factors.

Another theoretical viewpoint and practice that is typical of Lade Motor is that the main concern is the present and the future, not the past. There is little focus on the problematic histories of the participants. A common interest for motor sport is shared between the participants, the employees and the volunteers. It creates a form of community and an emphasis on the activities that transcends the differences in the past and the present. This distinguishes this project from a number of other initiatives within the child welfare services. Children and youths are able to start from scratch and acquire new skills as time goes by.

A natural community

Lade Motor represents a natural collective in which participants, employees and volunteers make up a community with a focus on motor sports. This collective body has its own norms, values and sense of reality, and the participants are connected through their dreams, talents and interests.

We will later discuss the key norms and values, though the admiration for and dreams associated with American cars is something the participants have in common. The stress on the present and future of the target group is reasonable from both a therapeutic and pedagogic viewpoint. In the community at Lade Motor, one is able to meet like-minded people who have the same genuine interest in motor sport. This is clearly reflected in the use of symbols. The fact that everyone wears the same boiler suits works to reinforce the common identity of the group. In addition, the boiler suits are sponsored by private companies, which reflects the connection to the outside world. The symbolism could in fact be worth a separate study. It is very interesting to note that the participants wear the coat of arms of the city of Trondheim during the drag racing competitions.

In the interviews, we asked both the youths and parents about their way into the project. Both groups seemed uncertain about how participants were recruited to the project. Some of the youths think that BUP funds the project, while others believe the parents or the technical aids center supports it. In some cases, assistant teachers from school were credited for their recruitment. The youths we interviewed did not seem too interested in how they had ended up in the project in the first place. The project itself was their main concern. The youths express great happiness about being a part of Lade Motor. It is qualitatively different from the other initiatives of the child welfare authorities they have experienced.

It appears that Lade Motor is able to satisfy the youths' demands for meaningful activities. The same applies to the parents who participate during evening sessions and competitions. The youths enjoy *making use of their hands* to achieve something. They appreciate the opportunity to meet others with a shared interest in motor sport. According to one of the youths: *"If it* had *not been for this project I would have suffered a breakdown "*.

We may well view Lade Motor as an alternative arena for learning, which enables the participants to experience mastery. The ability to create something, to solve practical and theoretical tasks leads to self-esteem. A number of the participants describe a meaningless school day, which nevertheless may develop in a positive direction with the help of the project. The participants have obtained upper secondary school text books related to motor sport, which they enjoy reading. They also consume English language literature on the topic. It is interesting to observe this, given what we know about their experience from the ordinary school system. It is fair to claim that Lade Motor contributes to motivating the participants for further learning, which goes beyond what they pick up during competitions, courses and evening sessions at Lade Motor.

Motor sports

To participate in drag racing competitions you need to acquire a license. This includes both a theory course and racing tests. There are different versions of drag racers with different engine sizes and effects. For instance, only the biggest drag racers have methanol-fueled engines, which are more efficient than petrol engines. In other words, both practical and theoretical skills are required to become a good drag racing driver. You also have to pass formal tests to become a driver. One of the participants put it like this: *"Learn the rules of the game. Then you get addicted to the sport"*.

Above we have described Lade Motor as a natural community. The key values and norms are acquired through participation in the activities. For instance, justice is an important value for the participants. The competition needs to take place according to the agreed rules, which the participants need to obey. In all sports, justice is a key value that is strongly appreciated by the participants.

The participants themselves rate the racing as the most important element in the project, though the social interaction is also emphasized. This includes the evening sessions at Lade and the trips in connection with competitions. The racing represents the prize for all the work carried out during the winter. For many participants, the dream of motor sport is the main motivation behind their participation. This demands an effort on the part of the adult leaders and volunteers to learn motor sport if they wish to be credible participants.

Knowledge and knowing will take shape according to what aspect of knowing is seen as important in å given context. This influences our understanding of high quality. Among other things, we have in this evaluation highlighted process-based learning and good follow-up routines. As the dream of motor sports is the key motivation for the participants, the adults need to possess skills and knowledge in the area. This is what gives you credibility and the ability to confront problems, endure hardship and handle conflicts, disciplinary requirements and long-term processes. It could be said that skills within motor sport contribute to the legitimate position of employees and volunteers within the community.

The dream of drag racing seems to be alive among all the participants who we interviewed. As we see it, drag racing shares the uniqueness, dynamics and ethics that are typical of all sports; it demands training and a continuous attempt to challenge one's own boundaries. There are clear similarities to other sports that are distinguished by competition. Some of the sport's dynamics is evident in the sense of belonging to the drag racing community, locally and internationally. Lade Motor has links to a number of local organizations as well as to clubs outside Trondheim. In such a setting, fair play and acceptance of the rules of the game make up part of the sport ethics. In addition, Lade Motor is famous within the Scandinavian drag racing community. This means that Lade Motor is met with respect and inclusiveness during competitions. Generally, there is little abuse of alcohol and drugs in this environment, as the sport demands concentration. Subsequently, it is no need to discuss such problems during competitions.

Above we have described Lade Motor as a natural community. The team spirit becomes even more pronounced during competitive events. Here, people merge into a unified group of participants from both Norway and Sweden.

Training is required if you want to succeed in sport. It is interesting to observe that many participants who are reported to be suffering from concentration problems do not have similar problems in this environment. Drag racing demands concentration in order to succeed. This sport is unique in the sense that it requires the participants to carry out a number of procedures before the start of the race. Even if the participants are friends during such events, they turn into competitors as soon as the race is underway.

The youths and their experience

In interviews with current and former participants, the social environment is described as positive and safe. For many participants, it represents a sanctuary where they can be successful. At 6 pm on Monday and Wednesday evenings, young people queue up outside the doors at Lade Motor. In the interviews, some said that one would have to enjoy the time during competitions and evening sessions before passing the 18 years age limit. When describing the project, enjoyment was the word most frequently mentioned by the participants.

The leisure activity has managed to include the parents in a positive way. Even when the children are ill and unable to participate, the parents tend to show up for the evening sessions. Many of the parents interviewed tell us that they have been able to meet their children in new ways during such evenings, and to join in a common activity has reinforced the relations between them. The meetings become an enriching experience for both parties who are able to view each other in new and different ways. The joint participation in motor sports produces a new understanding of the other party. The sociologist R. Enerstvedt (1982) has described how we can weave our lives into those of other people with the help of our activities. In the activities at Lade Motor children and parents are *interwoven* into a new understanding of each other.

There is also good reason to stress that Lade Motor is concerned with the present and future. Participation in this leisure activity does not cause stigmatization as it is highly respected among youths in general and in particular among those interested in motor sports, and this is one explanation why the youths enjoy being part of the project.

For many participants, the leisure activity represents a useful supplement to their school day in the sense that their learning in the project enhances their performance at school. This applies to both those who attend the day school and those who pursue a more regular educational path. Several youths claim to have developed their social and communicative skills through their participation in the leisure activity. They say it is easier to discuss things when working together. By taking part in the activities, one is able to get in touch with one's inner psychological world, according to Enerstvedt (op.cit). Many participants indicate the same, though they express it in different words.

Motor sport as an activity seems to work well as a joint effort that promotes community and communication between the various participants. Whether other activities can produce the same effect, is uncertain. This probably depends on the activity's status and inherent possibilities for inclusion and cooperation.

Learning and development also become easier when based on clear objectives. Participation in competitive events enables people to pursue clearly defined objectives. In addition, drag racing is an exciting activity, which gives young people an experience that is both interesting and favourable for their social status.

Adult role models

The community is characterized by the heavy presence of adult participants. We may well call this a *tight-knit community* that makes sure people are followed up. The adults are described as *great guys*. Even if the majority of them are males, female participants are also observed during the various activities. They joke a lot and pay a great deal of attention to the young participants. Particularly valued are the two leading participants who have been decisive in establishing an inclusive community.

Lade Motor has a clear leader who everyone respects. In addition, the youths emphasize the social aspect during the evening sessions at Lade and the competitive events, which another adult participant is responsible. The shared effort of the two adults in many ways initiated the project in the first place. One organizes car tuning sessions and races while the other is responsible for social events. The well-being of both youths and adults is an important ambition and during the evenings at Lade waffles and hamburgers are prepared for the participants. The trips to the competitions are more than just racing, as the social aspect is crucial in bringing people together.

Not all adults have been able to interact positively with the youths, but such problems have been effectively handled. Many participants initially tend to view adult males with skepticism as their negative experiences affect the way they interpret other people. However, at Lade Motor they have learned how to trust others. The adult volunteers contribute heavily by bringing their own cars to the premises. As they work on them, the youths can observe, ask questions and learn from their fellow participants.

The cooperation between youths and adults is something that is highly valued by both parties. Earlier, we have pointed to the fact that several of the participants have reached a mature age. Some participants even belong to the grandparent generation. Perhaps they view interaction with youths from a more relaxed and realistic perspective?

The fact that so many adults take part in the leisure activity and that so many people meet to participate in the same activity makes it possible to exert strong social control. Lade Motor has a clear social structure, which ensures that everyone is aware of what is demanded of them. Some of the youths may find the adults too strict, but at the same time, they realize that a clear structure is required to make the project work. For instance, all equipment has regular places and needs to be put back where it belongs after use. This ensures predictability and makes activities like racing and car tuning easier to carry out.

As mentioned, peer pressure to abuse alcohol and drugs is an experience that many youths have encountered in their daily lives. At Lade Motor, there are few signs of such tendencies. The close follow-up routines ensure that the participants are socialized into different values. The racing itself also contribute to give abuse of alcohol and drugs a bad name. As one participant puts it: *"Dull people are dull drivers"*.

Within the community, clear rules against the abuse of alcohol and drugs have developed, and these are maintained by social control. According to one youth: *"The activities save people from dope, smoke and things like that"*.

Discipline is required to maintain a rigid structure. Both during competitions and the evening sessions at Lade we are struck by how disciplined the youths behave. In motor sport, discipline is important as it emphasizes:
– The security during races (and tuning sessions)
– The learning, which becomes impossible under chaotic circumstances. One needs to be able to find the tools in their regular places
– The performance of the participants

As all similar initiatives, Lade Motor has to a large extent been shaped by voluntary enthusiasts. The quality of the project is clearly related to the extraordinary effort of leaders to develop the activity. They appear as role models within their respective fields. For instance, they always turn up and make an effort when required. In one instance, when an engine went dead the evening before a race, a leader spent the whole night fixing the engine so that two participants could take part in a race they had been looking forward to all through the winter. This kind of attitude leads to respect and contributes to a positive culture. It is also material for stories told to newcomers by the established participants.

The significance of the activity

The smallest unit is subsequently the dyads, which are set up in a deliberate way. Two of the youths fix, maintain and take turns driving during competitions. The second group is made up of the participants in the project. We have described them as a natural community bound together by a shared interest in the activities at Lade Motor. The activities shape the participants and the inner psychological reality becomes linked to the outer world. Figuratively speaking, we could say that a bridge appears between the inner and outer realities through the activities. The two worlds are unified with the help of motor sport.

One of the criteria for admitting the youths to the project is that they have had very limited contact with positive social environments. The question is if Lade Motor contributes to the forging of bonds that also may affect the spare-time habits of the participants. Mostly, this does not seem to be the case. The youths say they have little contact with each other outside the project. Any contact takes place through other channels like SMS, the Internet, Facebook and MSN.

Generally, the parents are very positive towards the youths' participation in the project. When we ask the youths how their closest relatives assess the initiative, this is how we could sum up the answers:
– Mum is dead scared
– Dad is proud and supports me

– My siblings find it cool
– My school mates do not understand what it is or are envious
We should point out that drag racing enjoys a high status among youths. It contributes to raising the awareness of the participants and gives them a feeling of mastery.

One of the unique achievements of Lade Motor is that one has been able to pave the way for cooperation between the municipality and private companies. In the motor sport community, Lade Motor enjoys a strong backing for its work and private companies have been willing to sponsor the initiative. The companies have facilitated the participation of Lade Motor in competitions and made dragsters available for the youths.

Conclusion

To include and integrate marginalized youth in society has been the official policy in Norway for many years. The school represents perhaps the most important arena to include children and young people in society. Formal qualifications have become more or less necessary for permanent employment and participation in society. School dropout represents a significant problem for society due to its consequences. However, other venues are central to integrate young people. In this article, we have seen how the leisure arena may be used for this purpose.

Lade Motor is run by voluntary enthusiasts and adults who are skilled and understand the necessity of such a leisure activity. It represents a *tight-knit* environment that is able to follow up the participants on an individual basis. Still, the way such follow-up measures are implemented is far from irrelevant. The adults are the carriers of cultural values and norms. In a community like Lade Motor an understanding of interaction with children and youths is crucial for the ability to get socialized into the community.

Above we have emphasized that justice is among the key values of this community. Justice is important, though it is also true that some need a bit more training than others do. Equality and equal status are tricky concepts that may get confused. To strike the right balance between equality and equal status in a just manner always represents a challenge.

We have referred to Lade Motor as an arena of socialization. Lade Motor has become an alternative place of learning that partially compensates for the lack of schooling among the participants. For many of the participants, the traditional school does not represent a relevant activity. By participating in leisure time activity, young people get opportunities to learn and grow in an area that interests them. This also means that they acquire the knowledge and skills necessary to cope with everyday life.

Lade Motor marks a break with the diagnostic culture often found in the welfare support services. Lade Motor has a focus on the present and the future and represents a new opportunity for the participants. The decisive factor is not what diagnosis the children and youths have as they arrive. The free-time activity represents the possibility of a fresh start for the participants. In our mind, this is one of the success factors behind the project. However, when interacting with the welfare services one is unconsciously drawn into a world where they define the reality. Welfare support often requires a diagnosis; how should Lade Motor relate to this? Diagnoses may be useful for the planning of new measures, but they may also cause an exaggerated focus on the past.

Preventive work may be tricky as one is only able to document the effects after some years. In this case, changes in the behavior of the participating youths were reported by the youths themselves as well as by parents, project employees and municipal staff involved in the project. But are the results just temporary? We have tried to answer this by interviewing former participants. They also tell a story about an integrating community that has meant a lot for their personal development besides other support measures they have experienced. Even after quitting the project, they tend to drop by to greet their old friends.

As in other similar projects, it is difficult to underrate the personal contributions to the leisure activity. Its success is due to both talented professionals and the effort from volunteers, which has been both determined and useful. In some ways, Lade Motor has developed into a sort of *community* with strong bonds between the participants. There is a strong focus on relational aspects, as well as positive activities and experiences that promote development and well-being among the youths. Sufficient time and space for each child is made possible by accessible and confident adult figures, contributing substantially to the experience of being seen, heard and recognized in their daily lives.

The interviews reveal moving stories about the significance of the project. One word that keeps appearing is the understanding of Lade Motor as a *rescue package* for the youths' personal development. In spite of drag racing being a costly sport, the rewards reaped by the participants and society will be far greater. By participating in the motor sport project, the youths develop an identity linked to cars and motor sport. This has positive repercussions for the status and self-esteem of the participants. In addition, it enables them to develop other types of skills, such as social, disciplinary and action-oriented skills. The project aims at motivating the participants to acquire new practical knowledge, which is exemplified and learned. There is an obvious link between this practical knowledge and the theoretical learning of the school system. Lade Motor is a good example of how youths obtain knowledge through observation and practice. Knowledge and learning has always been central to society, but what has changed is the way the knowledge about such processes has been given an expression. Knowing about the forms of knowing based on practice is central to include marginalized youth in society (Jensen, 2012).

References

Bakken, A. (1998). *Ungdomstid i storbyen*. Oslo: NOVA.
Barne-, likestillings- og inkluderingsdepartementet (2000). *Barnevernet i Norge. Til-standsvurderinger, nye perspektiver og forslag til reformer. NOU 2000:12*. Oslo: Staten forvaltningstjeneste.
Barne-, likestillings- og inkluderingsdepartementet (2009). *Satsing på barn og ungdom. Regjeringens mål og innsatsområder i statsbudsjettet 2009*. Oslo: Barne-, likestillings- og inkluderingsdepartementet.
Barne-, likestillings- og inkluderingsdepartementet (2013). St. Prop. 1. Statsbudsjettet
Clausen, S.-E. & Kristofersen, L. E. (2008). *Barnevernsklienter i Norge 1990–2005*. Oslo: NOVA.
Enerstvedt, R. T. (1982). *Menneske som virksomhet*. Oslo, Tiden
Eriksen, H. S. (2012). The changing role of knowledge in the knowledge economy: concepts of knowledge and knowledge management. In Knut Ingar Western (red). *Foundation of the knowledge economy – innovation, learning and clusters*. Chelterham: Edward Elgar.
Fauske, H., Lichtwarck, W., Marthinsen, E., Willumsen, E., Clifford, G. & Kojan, B. H. (2009). *Barnevernet på ny kurs? Det nye Barnevernet – et forsknings- og utviklingsprosjekt i barnevernet*. Sluttrapport fase 1. Nordlandsforskning NF-rapport nr. 8/2009. Bodø: Universitetet I Nordland.
Jensen, H. S. (2012). The changing role of knowledge in the knowledge economy: concepts of knowledge and knowledge managemennt. In K. I. Westeren (Ed.), *Foundations of the knowledge economy: innovation, learning and clusters*. Cheltenham, UK: Elgar
Kulturdepartementet (9. February 1989). *Med viten og vilje,* NOU 1988:28. Oslo: Kulturdepartementet.
Kunnskapsdepartementet (15. March 2013). *Meld St. 20 (2012–2013): Melding til Stortinget. På rett vei. Kvalitet og mangfold i fellesskolen*. Oslo: Kunnskapsdepartementet.
Kunnskapsdepartementet (2. April 2004). *St. meld. nr. 30 (2003–2004) Kultur for læring*. Oslo: Kunnskapsdepartementet.
Kvello, Ø. (2007). *Utredning av atferdsvansker, omsorgssvikt og mishandling*. Oslo: Universitetsforlaget.
Minken, A. (2005). "Motor- ikke hva, men hvem hvordan og hvorfor". In Reidar Säfvenbom (red) *Fritid og aktivietter*. Oslo, Universitetsforlaget.
Patton, M. Q. (2008). *Utilization – Focused Evaluation*. Thousand Oaks: Sage.
Smith, M. (2009). *Re-thinking residential child care: Positive perspectives*. Bristol: The Policy Press.

White paper no. 44(2008–2009) The Education Line: (https://www.regjeringen.no/en/do kumenter/report-no.-44-to-the-storting-2008--2009/id565231/)

Authors

Geir Hyrve
Associate Professor
Sør-Trøndelag University College, Faculty of Health and Social Sciences
Department of Applied Social Science
Research areas: Evaluations, Public administration, Residential child care, Family group conferences

Ragnhild Collin-Hansen
Associate Professor
Social Education and Child Welfare Work Programme, Faculty of Health Education, Sør-Trøndelag University College
Research areas: Legislation on Childrens' rights, and how they are enforced, the right to education, to care and to health and social services

The Children's Interview – From resistance to partnership

Sofie Dahlø Husby

Abstract

The qualitative interview within child research is especially challenging with regard to inequalities of power between researcher and child. The dialogue can easily descend into resistance and conflict. This study presents a case where this resistance and power struggle between researcher and child creates a turning point in how child interviews are conducted. The researcher and the child struggle over what place the activity of video gaming should have in the interviews. When the researcher gives the child the right to determine how and when video games should be integrated into the interaction, the resistance ends, and the dialogue is instead marked by cooperation and equality. In the following article, the researcher raises the question of how activities and aids can be used to give the child more influence and can give the child a space in which to formulate his thoughts. The author ends with a short reflection over the various requirements children have to shape their communications, and that their own initiatives to activities and play are worthwhile and should taken seriously.

Introduction

The qualitative child interview is increasingly used in social science research on children. Jensen (2012) has reviewed the suitability of the interview method when used with children in difficult life circumstances. Her conclusions are that the interview should be given a prominent position in these studies. Her fear is that research and professional practice will both be too much coloured by adult perspectives if children's voices are muted.

Power and Resistance in Qualitative Interviews with Children as Informants

Qualitative research interviews share many similarities with ordinary conversations between people, but are nevertheless quite different from everyday conversation. The interview method is, according to Kvale (1997) a specific form of conversation where the interviewee is given the opportunity to formulate their own opinions through dialogue with the interviewer. In contrast with ordinary or everyday conversation, we are dealing with an academic conversation. The interviewer is responsible for posing the questions and the power relations are asymmetrical. Kvale (2014) discusses the understanding of the qualitative research interview in an article concerning ways in which conflict may contribute to knowledge. He points out the danger that research interviews may become repressive and manipulative. He also point out that in the 1980s, when qualitative research interview became common within the social sciences, they were considered a dialogical form of research. The qualitative interview was viewed as a democratic, liberating form of social research. The dialogical understanding of the qualitative interview suggests reciprocity and equal worth. He suggests, however, that referring to an interview as a dialogue is misleading. He outlines the dynamics of power in the research interview through a discussion of how the interview-as-dialogue differs from dialogues between equal partners. The interviewer defines the interview situation, decides when it should be conducted, what the topic should be as well as asking the questions. The interview is hence no dialogue in the sense of the parties seeking mutual understanding. Kvale (2014) claims instead that the interview is a one-way dialogue. The interviewer queries while the other responds, so this is not a mutual exchange of questions and answers. The interview is far from what one might call a spontaneous conversation or a philosophical musing. According to Bråten (2004) this degree of reciprocity distinguishes the interview sharply from dialogue and conversation in the ordinary sense of these terms. Those who participate in a dialogue do so with mutually complementary perspectives. This mutuality is found to a moderate degree in interviews. The Norwegian child researcher Per Olav Tiller describes the interview as a verbal process of interaction where reciprocity is found to a certain degree. The answers that are given affect what follow-up questions are posed, and the manner in which this is done. However, this mutuality cannot be understood as the interviewee having the ability to put questions to the interviewer. It consists of the interviewee having some ability to guide the process through the answers given. Thus, there is some influence in both directions (Tiller, 2006). However, there is room for the asymmetry of power to be adjusted somewhat. Both the interviewer and the interviewee have some counter-manoeuvres at their disposal. For instance, the interviewer may refrain from answering, or change the subject. It is also possible for the interviewee to ask questions. When it comes to the potency of such strategies, child interviews and elite interviews are at opposite ends of a continuum. The interviewer can, for example, allow the informants to read the interpretation of the interview to see if they agree (Kvale, 2014). These strategies in the struggle for a more even distribution of power may be understood as resistance. Vitus, Thuesen and Tanggaard (2014) cite studies where informants express their resistance through lying or refusing to cooperate with the interviewer, by being evasively polite, or through body language and laughter.

In interviews where the informants are children, the question of power relations becomes especially important. Children are particularly vulnerable in asymmetrical power relations, heightening the researcher's responsibility to safeguard the child ethically and methodologically, e.g. through the use of supplementary materials. The role of adults towards children in society should be one of protection, care and nurture, but also collaboration and participation (FNs Barnekonvensjon, 2003). This role is in many ways unchanged at the micro-level, such as when interviewing children. The researcher cannot discard the role of an adult when faced with a child. Morrow and Richards (1996) emphasise this inequality of power and status as being the greatest challenge for a researcher working with children. Power is, according to Weber (2000), one's ability to impose one's will in social life, even if the others participating in the collective should resist. In power relations, conflict and resistance occur readily. Between the researcher and the child, who should decide what? Who should get their way? The Danish child researcher Hanne Warming writes that inequalities in power relations between adult and child frame conversations with children. Thus, the adult has the greatest responsibility to make room for and facilitate the child's perspective (Warming, 2011).

Supplementary Tools and Activities

Tiller (2006) recommends that the children who have difficulties in expressing themselves verbally should be asked to draw what they are trying to say. Greig, Tylor and MacKay (2007) have reviewed childhood studies utilising participatory methods or tools such as drawing, photographs, pots of beads, vignettes, images of faces showing various emotions, etc. They conclude that the tools in themselves don't provide innovation, but rather the way in which they are utilised by the researchers. They have used these tools in a qualitative and participatory way in an attempt to understand and empower the children's voices. Clarie O'Kane (2000) used such methods and techniques in a study of children's participation in decision-making in the English Children's Services. Randi Juul used paper dolls in conversations with children for her doctorate on the Norwegian Child Welfare Services (Juul, 2010). According to Warming (2011) the possibilities are endless. A child's tongue may be loosened by a car trip with music the child likes. Other children prefer to be kept physically active. Within professional practice, there are numerous books concerning tools and activities for conversing with children (Drugli & Engen, 2004; Eide & Rohde, 2009; Holmsen, 2011; Mæland & Hauger, 2008). Such supplementary tools are not mandated in child interviews, but they are options that should be considered. Some children are content simply sitting and talking, but others might find this intimidating. They clam up. What is conducive to good communication depends on the child's individual skills and preferences and the topic that is to be discussed (Warming, 2011).

The child interview method, with or without supplements, is still under development. In a recent book on conversations with children Kinge (2006) writes that experience is pivotal in the use of supplementary aids. When it comes to the development of methodology, I concur with Tiller (2006, p. 38), who states: *"We can only learn through trial. Within this perspective, each interview with a child becomes important knowledge about the method itself"(my translation).*

This article is about child interview methodology as it pertains to children in difficult life circumstances. I have interviewed children as part of my own PhD-project. Based on two interviews with one of these children, whom I call Peter, I will show the methodological choices that contributed to the child opening up and sharing. The data I present shows how resistance and power struggles play out in dialogue between researcher and child, becoming a turning point for how the researcher handles power relations and conducts interviews.

In this article the aim is to show that resistance and power struggles in interviews may be a source of new knowledge about tools and activities in children interviews. My research question is: how can tools and activities can assist in the progression of interviews with children in difficult life circumstances?

Method

This article is based on empirical material taken from interviews with children as part of my own study. I use Peter as my example, as the interviews with him demonstrate methodological experiences with the use of supplements, experiences that may be valid in conversation with other vulnerable children. There are also examples of resistance in interviews with the other children, but only in the interviews with Peter are the struggles over what shape the interviews should take so clear. What is interesting about the interview process with Peter is the struggle over his video games and the result of the struggle. The solution reveals itself when I allow Peter to assert his own wishes. The case is one of positive knowledge production contributing to the positioning of the child as a resource.

Ten children in all participated in my study, aged 9–17, and the data collection took place during the spring of 2014. All the children were recruited from Child Welfare Services in three small municipalities in central Norway. Most live with their parents and receive benefits, while three live in foster homes. All the families are monitored by one or more public agencies in addition to Child Welfare Services. This study concerns interaction practices between children and professionals in childcare and social services.

The interviews are qualitative and have a low degree of structuring (Kvale, 1997). I converse openly with the children guided by four introductory topics: – like, appreciate, – struggles and difficulties, – experiences with participation and cooperation with professionals regarding assistance and – own solutions. With grounding in a narrative (Riessman, 2008) and active interview form (Holstein & Gubrium, 1995), I invite the children to cooperation and co-creation of thematic life accounts on experienced social life, both here and now, and retrospectively. I emphasise the mutual influence that occurs in dialogue between researcher and child. The study has constructivist and interactionist leanings (Järvinen & Mik-Meyer, 2005).

I use a visual conversation board as an interview supplement. This is an A4 sheet of paper with an emoticon for each of the four guiding topics. While interviewing the youngest children (aged 9–12), I also give them crayons. In addition, I utilise paper dolls. These were useful in mapping the professionals and other persons with whom the child was in contact, and in making stories. The child was first asked to find himself among the dolls, and then to find the other actors in their accounts.

Analysis

I have conducted a narrative analysis with the intention of creating a methodological account of the child interview (Riessman, 2008). The analysis has consisted of several steps, from analysis during the interviews, to analysis of transcribed text (Kvale, 1997). The methodological account focuses on resources and shows how children in difficult life circumstances: i) have the resources and agency to stand up for themselves and ii) can suggest methodological choices that make the interview more child-friendly. Theoretically, the analysis was inspired by a power perspective on interviews, as well as the importance of power, resistance and conflict in qualitative research, and the potential of these phenomena to provide new insights and generate knowledge (Kvale, 2014; Vitus et al., 2014).

I will give a brief description of the steps of the analysis. Step 1: I keep a re-search log. One of the questions in this log concerned the factors that could affect the interview process. When the log is subsequently reviewed, it becomes clear that video games play a prominent role in the struggles arising between Peter and myself. Step 2: I listen to the recordings, transcribe and write memos. I almost finish the transcription and memo writing before conducting the second interview. I follow the same routine for this second interview; listen to the recording, tran-scribe, and write memos. At this stage of the analysis, it becomes increasingly clear that the way in which Peter uses video games alters the interview consider-ably. Step 3: I review the transcribed texts from both interviews with Peter in order to gain perspective. It is now clear that video games are the bone of contention in the interaction. The first and second interviews differ strongly. Resistance and power struggle is the order of the day in the first interview, being replaced by co-operation for the second. I re-read the parts of the interview where resistance and power struggles are expressed. I attempt to understand how these phenomena are expressed in the interaction. It seems to me that the text expresses fear and stress, negotiation and protest. After this, I read the second interview in order to under-stand how cooperation was initiated, and what it means for the dialogue. I realise that the collaboration begins by Peter taking the initiative to cooperate regarding his video games. Concerning the dialogue, cooperation leads to co-creation of life accounts. In this way, I distinguish between four topics, a) fear and stress, b) ne-gotiation and confrontation, c) cooperation becoming the order of the day, and d) life accounts being created. This topical division is done to bolster the method-ological account of the child interview. I use various metaphors such as combat gear to describe how resistance and power was expressed within the interaction.

The data and analysis yield reliable findings of the way in which Peter profited from an interview form with activities rather than a purely verbal conversation. The data and analysis do not, however, give grounds for generalisation, but rather show that some children prefer to have something to do while being interviewed. Face to face interactions can seem laboured and paralysing.

Findings

In this section, I present my findings. An impression based on the analysis is that in the first round, the researcher and Peter enter into a power-play, with manoeu-vres and counters. Rather than being a supporting partner for the child, listening to his wishes and ideas, the researcher becomes an antagonist. Simultaneously, the resistance and power struggle are what spurs the researcher on to change strategy. The researcher then experiences Peter as a "team player". Below is the methodological account structured according to the four topics which I distinguished in the analysis.

a) Fear and Stress

As I was about to start the interview, before I had asked the opening question, Peter already seems antagonistic, proclaiming:

> Peter: I don't have much to talk about.

Peter is seated in the sofa, hunched and talking softly into his chest. He seems sluggish and lethargic. What is Peter attempting to convey, and how should I receive this message? One interpretation could be that Peter is afraid of the questions and afraid that his answers should be insufficient. Another interpretation would be that Peter is announcing at the start that there is a limit for what and how much he is prepared to tell. He might also have "secrets". Resistance is clad in fear, stress and emotional tension. Peter is challenging my emotional equilibrium. I become both disappointed and annoyed that he is being contrary and reserved. Rather than acknowledge the resistance as well as the child's fear and tension, I attempt to conceal my reactions behind excessive comfort and encouragement to the point where it almost becomes invasive. I tell him that I'm sure he has a lot to tell me, and that he shouldn't worry about that.

b) Negotiation and Confrontation

The week before going to Peter's home to interview him for the first time, I visited him in order to get to know him. During this visit, Peter and I agreed that he would show me his video games the next time we met. As I was preparing the interview, Peter reminds me of this "agreement". I was in a quandary as to what would be best, playing first and talking after, or vice versa. Without discussing this with Peter, I make the decision that we should do the interview first. Peter seems displeased with this, and offers resistance throughout the interview "dressed up" as invitations to negotiate. When this leads nowhere, he metaphorically "straightens up", and the resistance is now dressed in combat gear. Peter repeatedly confronts me, without gaining the advantage. My own resistance, however, is clad in laughter and "friendliness". I choose to fight back.

> Interviewer: .... Is there anything else you like to do?
> Peter: no
> (Pause)
> I: OK, but these are very exciting interests.
> Peter: Is the hour over yet?
> I: No (laughs), the hour isn't over.

(.........)
Peter: Check out the Play Station?
I: Huh?
Peter: Should we check out the Play Station now?
I: I don't know, I think it's a bit early.
(.........)
I: .... Do you miss your old school?
Peter: Yes.
I: Yes, you simply miss it, yes. It's almost as if I can see you getting
     a little sad when you think about it.
Peter: Bored.
I: Oh, so you're bored (laughs), mmm.
Peter: I want to go upstairs and play.
I: You want to play, ok, we're going to.
I: But I wanted to hear a little about.........

Early in the interview, another situation conducive to negotiation is created. Peter attempts to get me to agree to him playing video games during the interview.

Interviewer: .... How do you like to spend your time most days?
Peter: Playing.
I: Ok, couldn't you tell me a little about that .... Ok, but you
     really need to tell me about that, this is the kind of thing I want to
     hear about, games (short break)
Peter: It's much easier just to show you.
I: Sure, but you can show them to me afterwards, um, games, right,
     in that case it's easier to show it.
Peter: Yes.
I: Are they computer games?
Peter: (shakes his head)
I: That's right; you said it was on the Xbox.
Peter: Yes (softly).
I: Yes, the Xbox .... it would be easier to show it, but can't you
     tell me a little, tell me a little about it?
Peter: I can't explain it.
I: Ok, you can't explain it (laughs), perhaps it is difficult to explain
     (pause). In that case, my suggestion is that you explain it to me
     afterwards when you show me, because then I think we'll have a
     really nice time together.
Peter: Star Wars or Minecraft (brightens up)?

Faced with the arguments in this "negotiation" I once again become doubtful, wondering if I should have gone along with his request. But this time, I feel Peter has the advantage over me. Should I go along with his wish? It feels like I'm about to be checkmated. I essentially agree with him that gaming is best demonstrated visually and practically. The Xbox is, perhaps, more suitable as a supplementary aid than the crayons or conversation board when the topic is video games. However, should I give in, my concern is that the time we have at our disposal will be eaten up by games and entertainment. Instead I choose to resist, to fight, and Peter's game will have to wait until later. I complete, practically force, an hour's interview. Peter, on his part, is reluctant to answer or to participate. These forms of resistance, clad in "diplomatic attire" and "combat gear" challenge the relations of power between me as researcher and Peter. I am in a position to allow Peter more power and influence over the framework of the interview, but I choose to fight. In my roles as adult and researcher, I am more powerful than Peter. I apply pressure to get the "interview" concluded my way, and fail in producing thematic life accounts. Unwittingly, I assume the role of an interrogator, and the opportunity to establish a partnership with Peter is missed. The dialogue is put on hold.

> Interviewer: But, what about when you are at school? Couldn't you
>   tell me a little about what you do, what you like?
> Peter: I think it's boring.
> I: Are you bored at school?
> Peter: (coughs)
> I: What about when you arrive at school in the mornings?
> Peter: Bored.
> I: So, you're bored right from the start?
> Peter: Yes, school is so boring. . . . .

c) Cooperation becomes the order of the day

In the second interview, I change strategy, resolving to afford Peter more power and agency in deciding for himself if he wishes to play before or after he is interviewed. Peter decides to begin with playing his video game.

> Interviewer: So what am I doing now? Are we playing against each
>   other, or are we on the same side, or what?
> Peter: We're cooperating.
> I: We're cooperating how?
> Peter: You're Robin and I'm Batman
> (. . . . . later in the game)
> Peter: You have to press the blue button.
> I: Is that the one you attack with?

Peter: Yes, but you mustn't hold it in.
I: OK, I have to press it.
Peter: Yes, pay attention now!

I feel quite uncomfortable joining in the game, but I resolve to use this opportunity
to acquire gaming skills. Peter obviously accepts this challenge. Taking charge,
he places me in a chair with a controller in my hands. He swings himself into
the top bunk, this being his habitual spot for relaxing with his games, and we're
off. Peter attempts to play co-op, but I take it more competitively. I struggle with
coordination, which is clear to us both. I have problems keeping up. We continue
this way for almost half an hour, but then Peter doesn't have much energy left to
play with me. Surprisingly, he seems quite positively disposed towards starting
the interview. I think about how Peter preferred to play cooperatively, while I saw
it as a competition. In the role of partner in an unknown and unsafe situation, I
relax and the performance anxiety lessens. This situation of learning the game
changes the power-relations between Peter and me. Our roles are reversed. In the
interview, I have the power and control, in the game it is him. He takes charge
and invites the researcher to cooperate. I feel in good hands, and am suddenly
conscious of how I behaved during our first interview. I relive it, and realise how
I could have taken better care of Peter through cooperation rather than fighting. In
the first interview I showed Peter little confidence as a partner. I used the power
of my position to make the decisions. The experience of learning to play the game
and my new-found acknowledgement of the importance of teamwork, leads to an
increased respect and confidence in Peter as a partner in dialogue. I feel I owe
Peter more power and authority.

d) Life accounts are created

After half an hour of gaming, Peter is ready for the interview. He swings himself
down from the top bunk, and hops into the chair next to me. He surprises me
with a positive and cooperative attitude towards getting started. Peter changes
discs in the Xbox to play a racing game while I fetch soft drinks, chocolate, paper
dolls and sheets of paper. His video gaming has become part of the interview.
Peter takes the lead, and I let it happen. I leave to Peter the task of regulating the
focus between the game and the topic of the interview. With the first interview
fresh in my mind, I risk doing this. In the first interview, Peter is more willing
to talk after it was concluded and we went to his room to play. I now feel that
we both are more relaxed. The atmosphere is less tense and forced. Peter seems
more happy and energetic. He enters and leaves his game, helps prepare the dolls,
answers questions and participates actively with creating the accounts. Peter can
draw social support from the familiar driver in his racing game, and thus feels

more secure in entering into dialogue with the researcher. In a way, we are on a road trip, with Peter driving and me as the passenger. The gaming is brought into the dialogue, which oscillates between the topics at hand and what is happening on the screen. To the accompaniment of revving motors and screeching tires, as well as the sound track from the pause menu, accounts are created collaboratively, including those regarding Peter's difficulties at school. In the first interview, Peter answered vaguely and deceptively on questions pertaining to school: "bored". In this dialogue, Peter is given the opportunity to open up, including on these difficult topics:

Interviewer: How are the free periods?
Peter: Pretty good.
I: What do you get up to?
Peter: Dodge ball and that kind of thing.
I: Ok.
Peter: (Racing sounds from the Xbox)
I: Ok.
Peter: We have to be careful on this track (referring to the game)
I: Sure.
Peter: It's very narrow.
I: But, hmmm. I'm wondering, if something was difficult and prob-
    lematic at school, is (the teacher) willing to help you with it?
Peter: Sometimes.
I: Can you remember a time when she was?
Peter: No.
I: Ok, do you remember if something has happened at school that
    wasn't very nice?
Peter: No, I just get bullied a little.
I: Hmm, you get bullied (short pause) that's not very nice.
    Peter: It's not fun being bullied. (Sounds from the racing game)
I: No.
Peter: You're never the same again.
I: No (with firm agreement).
Peter: Because I get bullied.
I: Yes?
I: Is it the big boys who bully you? (Sounds from the game)
Peter: It's (someone) in my class.
I: It's someone in your class?
Peter: Yes.
I: Ok.

Peter: I don't really want to tell you their names (sounds of racing)

A way into the second interview, another account is created concerning how professionals can interpret children's signals when they are in distress.

> Interviewer: I think there could be children at school who get bullied
> without saying anything. And they (the adults) think the kids are
> fine, when they're not?
> Peter: I know how you can tell. You kind of see it in his face when he
> speaks (sounds of racing in background)
> I: That's very smart. Then, these people (I point to the paper dolls
> representing the teacher and the caseworker) could have seen it!
> Peter: It's like this, like this (the boy makes a pained grimace), so it's
> almost suspicious.
> I: Yes, isn't it, that your face is kind of sad or something like that.
> Peter: Or a little red maybe.
> I: A little red in the face, yes.
> (......) (Peter continues, expanding on the account)

Discussion

A central finding is that gaming as an activity influences the dialogue between the researcher and Peter. Peter becomes more open, sharing and accommodating with a controller in his hands. When this activity is fitted into the interview, the difference is considerable.

The qualitative interview is primarily a verbal interaction process. It is reasonable to inquire as to how suitable a purely verbal interview is in child research. In a manual on rights-based research with children, compiled by the Norwegian Centre for Child Research (NOSEB) in collaboration with researchers from around the world, it is stated that interviewing is not a recommended method: *"These are not good methods to use with children, who are likely to be intimidated by being asked direct questions by a researcher, and to search for the correct answer, or simply lie"* (Manual-5, 2009, p. 35). Such manuals recommend participating methods such as drawing, photography, videos and visual tasks. Role playing and dramatization are also recommended methods, as is getting the children to complete short sentences, either verbal or written. These techniques have been developed from the methodology of Participatory Rural Appraisal (PRA). This was a method developed to improve cooperation between social scientists and the people in poor, agrarian societies. The goal was to get local knowledge and expand on it in development work. In this manual, the goal is essentially the same; to draw out children's knowledge.

The goal of the researcher is to facilitate the children, making it easier for them to volunteer their own perspectives and analyses (Manual-1, 2009; Manual-5, 2009).The manual expands on the UN Convention on the Rights of the Child, and in my opinion represents a rather radical view on children's participation in research. What is interesting in this regard is what the tools of PRA contribute to situations involving power and power distribution in a dialogue between child and researcher. These tools, which in Norway go by the name of Participatory Learning and Action (PLA), are regarded as suitable for creating egalitarian dialogue between professional and participant. Participants are given influence and power while traditional power-relations are set aside (Aune, Skåra, & Foss, 2001; Sanner & Brattvåg, 2000).

The purpose of research interviews is to bring out the subject's views and opinions. This was challenging in the first interview with Peter. The researcher made a display of power, allowing Peter little influence. The dialogue became a battle over video gaming rather than responding to questions. The researcher dominates the conversational space, deciding the premises of both the form and content. Bråten developed a theory which describes this kind of power-relation in dialogue: the theory of model power. The ideal in dialogues is where both parties are allowed to express their perspectives on their own terms. When one party is subordinated to the other's point of view, the dialogue is superficial. One party is the model-strong participant, while the other is the model-weak (Bråten, 2004). Superficial dialogues have a repressive effect, preventing the opinions and experiences of the child from emerging, and thus only allowing the researcher's preconceptions to be confirmed. In the second interview with Peter we see more reciprocity in the interaction. Peter is allowed more space. He gets to demonstrate and teach something he's good at, video gaming. He experiences himself as competent and more empowered in this situation. He also becomes bold enough to instruct the researcher to pay attention. The researcher and Peter interact over two simultaneous projects, "the interview project", controlled by the researcher, and the "gaming project" ruled by Peter. Both are in their own way empowered in the dialogue, smoothing the inequalities of power and making the dialogue more egalitarian. With regard to the many challenges which the interview represents for relations of power, I have to agree with the child researchers who produced the manual on rights based research. Interviewing children is difficult (Manual-5, 2009).

Other researchers take the opposite route, having developed interview techniques specifically with child research in mind (Andenæs, 1991). In a recent Norwegian project on children's participation in everyday and professional practice, the researchers emphasise conversations with children. They use variants of life form interviews. This interview was originally developed and used by Hanne

Haavind in a project on the everyday life of mothers (Haavind, 1987). Since then, others have evolved the method to be used in research on a variety of informant categories. An example is Agnes Andenæs who developed a variant which she used in conversation with 4–5 year olds on their everyday lives (Andenæs, 1991). Ulvik studied children in foster homes. She used a variant of this method when talking to foster children and foster parents (Ulvik, 2007). In the life form interview the researcher talks to the informant about the previous day, week or their whole life history. Events embedded in the life course structure the content of the conversation. Andenæs has also used space to structure the interview. She interviews the child about a typical day as she moves with the child from room to room in the home, kindergarten or playground (Andenæs, 1991; Ulvik, 2014). In the aforementioned project, the researchers used the life form interview in dialogue with children. The children they interviewed were disabled, and therefore the researchers supplemented the interviews with photographs of children engaged in activities at school (Gulbrandsen, Øien, & Opsahl, 2014).

When it comes to child interviews as a research method, this literature reveals that some scientists engaged in child studies emphasise verbal investigation, while others prefer activities, tasks, play and words. A similar bifurcation appears in professional practices in Norway. There is growing interest for conversations with children, which *we* can see in relation to the UN convention on the rights of the child and its stipulation about children's right to participation. The Norwegian Child Welfare Services is constantly working to better hear and inform children. In recent years, methods for professional child conversations have been specially developed for children in the welfare system and others in difficult life situations (Gamst, 2011; Øvreeide, 2009). An example is the dialogue-based conversation method (DCM). It was first developed to be used with children in courtroom settings, later it was adapted for children in the welfare system, and now, in book form, this method is recommended for all those working with children professionally. The method is primarily verbal, and supplementary aids should only be used with children who need support in expressing themselves, especially younger children. The tools that are suggested are crayons, plasticine, visual materials and ordinary dolls. These tools should only be used after the child has started talking, and even then only used instructively, so as to avoid the child initiating free play. Such supplements can be a considerable distraction with regard to the conversation between child and adult, unless the adult comes prepared for this (Gamst, 2011). Eide and Rohde (2009), whose backgrounds are in therapeutic work with children and families, use a different approach when conversing with vulnerable children. They focus on method within conversation. As opposed to Gamst, who has developed a distinct conversational method, they describe how it is possible to use various supplements in various types of discourse with children. They describe a range of tools, such as visual expressions which may be conducive in conversation with children; the river of life, various task sheets, hand puppets, drawing and conversation pictures. They emphasise creativity, activity and play when dealing with children. From their perspective, the use of these tools may be planned or spontaneous and spur of the moment. Both the topic of conversation and its methodology are often developed as the interaction proceeds, and therefore it is good to have a great many ideas to hand, as well as developing new ones.

It is interesting to note how some conversational methods emphasise activity and play, while others don't. Bearing in mind that children's interaction is more play than conversation, it is reasonable that the role of activities and supplementary aids should be questioned in the methodology of child conversations. My experience is that integrating the activity into the interview itself, giving the child something to do during the interview, yielded positive results. Jensen discusses child interviews in research. She recommends that such activities that the children can do during the interview, such as drawing or clay modelling, should be accommodated. This may help the child regulate the pace of the conversation and give the interviewer a clear way to see when the child needs a break (Jensen, 2012). Warming (2011) writes that children may need to take their time in presenting their experiences and examples. Children need more time and space to give shape to their thoughts. She suggests pauses in the conversation, letting the child listen to music, or do some other activity. Others are more in tune with the use of supplements suggested by DCM. Eide and Winger (2003) who describe how dolls, toys and pictures may be used consciously during interviews with children. What is presented above is a variety of ways in which tools and activities may be used in an interview. Regardless of how it is done, the child is given mental space to rest from the ordeal of face to face interaction. This kind of dialogue, answering questions, may be quite stressful for children in challenging life circumstances. The child can come to feel gawked at, and may come to fear that some secret might be revealed inadvertently through facial expressions. Activities give the child room to think and decide which accounts that he/she feels comfortable sharing.

The use of supplemental tools brings both advantages and disadvantages. I have focused mostly on the advantages in my discussion. Children's credibility is a topic that is often discussed when such aids are concerned, but I have let this discussion lie. Here at the end though, I should mention that such activities and supplements can present ethical challenges. The child might misunderstand the situation, thinking it to be fun and games, and thus be more forthcoming than might otherwise have been the case (Warming, 2011). Another hazard concerning the use of games etc. is that the child might become more engrossed in the game than the topic under discussion (Kinge, 2006).

This discussion gives us a glimpse into various attitudes and practices concerning the use of supplements and activities when conducting child interviews. In the interviews with Peter, the activity made a clear difference. This doesn't mean that activity is a necessary condition of successfully carrying out child interviews, as there are many other relevant factors. Trust is such a factor, as are the child's cognitive and linguistic development, the child's communicative skills, and not least, the experience and attitudes of the researcher.

It isn't easy for children in challenging life circumstances to relay their thorny emotional experiences. In my study it became possible for Peter to abandon his defences and open up when I stopped struggling, and allowed Peter more influence over the form and pace of the interview.

Concluding Reflections

In this article, I have attempted to show the importance of understanding children's communicative styles, adjusting the shape and use of activities and supplements. The traditional face to face interaction worked well when interviewing the older children. The interview with Peter was different. This experience served as a wake-up call and a reminder that children require different forms of communicative support. When the interaction with a dialogue becomes antagonistic, devolving into a game of manoeuvring and countering, it is all too easy to place the blame on the child's circumstances; he/she has had a difficult upbringing, he/she is unaccustomed to attentive adults, etc. In an interactional perspective, the question is rather whether or not the researcher perceives the child's signals and attempts at dialogue, as well as what the researcher does with them.

After having interviewed children for my PhD project, I have experienced power and resistance in interaction as a demonstration of the importance of being more responsive to the child's own initiatives. The way in which I wanted the interviews to proceed, was one that felt safe for me. However, this doesn't mean the child felt safe. Peter taught me something about humility and daring to let a child lead me by the hand.

References

Andenæs, A. (1991). Fra undersøkelsesobjekt til medforsker? Livsformsintervju med 4–5 åringer [From object of research to co-ressearcher? Life mode interview with 4–5 year old children]. *Nordisk psykologi, 43*(4), 274–292.

Aune, L., Skåra, B. B., & Foss, N. (2001). *Fellesskap for utvikling: PLA – medvirkning i praksis[Fellowship for development]*. Oslo: Kommuneforl.

Bråten, S. (2004). *Kommunikasjon og samspill: fra fødsel til alderdom [Communication and interaction: from birth to old age]* (2. utg. ed.). Oslo: Universitetsforl.

Drugli, M. B., & Engen, M. (2004). *Spør barn få svar!: samtaler med barn om sosiale relasjoner [Ask children get answers !: conversations with children about social relationships]*. Oslo: Damm.

Eide, B., & Winger, N. (2003). *Fra barns synsvinkel: intervju med barn – metodiske og etiske refleksjoner [From the perspective of children: interview with children – methodological and ethical reflections]*. Oslo: Cappelen akademisk forl.

Eide, G., & Rohde, R. (2009). *Sammen så det hjelper: metoder i samtaler med barn, ungdom og familier [Together so it helps: methods in conversations with children, youth and families]*. Bergen: Fagbokforlaget.

FNs Barnekonvensjon. (2003). *FNs konvensjon om barnets rettigheter: vedtatt av De forente nasjoner 20. november 1989, ratifisert av Norge 8. januar 1991: revidert oversettelse mars 2003 med tilleggsprotokoller[UN Convention on the Rights of the Child: passed by the United Nations 20th November 1989, ratified by Norway 8th January 1991: revised translation with addenda march 2003]* Oslo: Barne- og familiedepartementet Norge

Gamst, K. T. (2011). *Profesjonelle barnesamtaler: å ta barn på alvor [Professional conversations with children: about taking children seriously]*. Oslo: Universitetsforl.

Greig, A., Taylor, J., & MacKay, T. (2007). *Doing research with children* (2nd ed. ed.). Los Angeles: Sage.

Gulbrandsen, L. M., Øien, I., & Opsahl, K. (2014). Utforskende fremgangsmåter i forskning og profesjonell praksis [Exploratory methodologies in research and professional practice] In L. M. Gulbrandsen (Ed.), *Barns deltakelse i hverdagsliv og profesjonell praksis: en utforskende tilnærming [Children's participation in everyday life and professional practice: An exploratory approach]* (pp. 75–99). Oslo: Universitetsforl.

Haavind, H. (1987). *Liten og stor: mødres omsorg og barns utviklingsmuligheter [The big and the little one: maternal care and the developmental possibilities for children]*. Oslo: Universitetsforlaget.

Holmsen, M. (2011). *Samtalebilder og tegninger: en vei til kommunikasjon med barn i vanskelige livssituasjoner [Conversation Photos and drawings: one way of communication with children in difficult life situations]* (2. utg. ed.). Oslo: Cappelen Damm akademisk.

Holstein, J. A., & Gubrium, J. F. (1995). *The active interview* (Vol. vol. 37). Thousand Oaks, Calif: Sage Publications.

Jensen, T. (2012). Intervjuer med barn og unge i spesielt vanskelige livssituasjoner – kan vi snakke med barn om alt? [Interviews with children and youth in particularly difficult life situations-can we talk to children about everything?]. In I. Frønes & E. Backe-Hansen (Eds.), *Metoder og perspektiver i barne- og ungdomsforskning[Methods and perspectives in child and youth research]*. Oslo: Gyldendal akademisk.

Juul, R. (2010). *Barnevernets undersøkelser av bekymringsmeldinger: diskursive praksisformer og barneperspektiver i den kommunale barneverntjeneste, og konsekvenser i forhold til barna [The Child Welfare Services' investigation of concerned reports. Forms of dicursive practice and children's perspectives in the municipal Child Welfare Services, and their consequences for the children's conditions]* (Vol. 2010:199). Trondheim: Norges teknisk-naturvitenskapelige universitet.

Järvinen, M., & Mik-Meyer, N. (2005). Indledning: Kvalitative metoder i et interaktionistisk perspektiv[Introduction: Qualitative methods in an interactionist perspective]. In M. Järvinen & N. Mik-Meyer (Eds.), *Kvalitative metoder i et interaktionistisk perspektiv: interview, observationer og dokumenter[Qualitative methods in an interactionist perspective: interviews, observation and documents]* (pp. 9–24). København: Reitzel.

Kinge, E. (2006). *Barnesamtaler: det anerkjennende samværet og samtalens betydning for barn med samspillsvansker[Child conversations: the acknowledged togetherness and the importance of conversation for children with interative deficits]* Oslo: Gyldendal akademisk.

Kvale, S. (1997). *Det kvalitative forskningsintervju [An Introduction to Qualitative Research Interviewing]* (T. Anderssen & J. Rygge, Trans.). Oslo: Ad notam Gyldendal.

Kvale, S. (2014). Hvordan kan konflikter være en vidensgenerator? [How can conflict generate knowledge?]. In L. Tanggaard, F. Thuesen & K. Vitus (Eds.), *Konflikt i kvalitative studier [Conflict in qualitative studies]* (Vol. 3). København: Hans Reitzels Forlag.

Manual-1. (2009). *The right to be properly researched: how to do rights-based, scientific research with children: Manual 1: Where do we start?* Bangkok: Black on White Publ. Norwegian Centre for Child Research and World Vision International

Manual-5. (2009). *The right to be properly researched: how to do rights-based, scientific research with children: Manual 5: How are we going to find out?* Bangkok: Black on White Publ.Norwegian Centre for Child Reserach and World Vision International

Morrow, V., & Richards, M. (1996). The Ethics of Social Research with Children: An Overview1. *Children & society, 10*(2), 90–105. doi: 10.1111/j.1099–0860.1996.tb00461.x

Mæland, I., & Hauger, B. (2008). *Anerkjennende elevsamtaler: metoder for reell elevmedvirkning i arbeidet med karriereplanlegging og forebygging av frafall i opplæringen[Acknowledging conversations with pupils: methods for real pupil participation in career planning work and the prevention of dropping out]* Drammen: Buskerud fylkeskommune Sareptas.

O'Kane, C. (2000). The Development of Participatory Techniques Facilitating Children's View about Decisions wich affect Them. In P. Christensen & A. James (Eds.), *Research with children: perspectives and practices* (pp. 136–159). London: Falmer Press.

Riessman, C. K. (2008). *Narrative methods for the human sciences.* Los Angeles: Sage Publications.

Sanner, M., & Brattvåg, H. (2000). *Vi sa vi [We said we]* (2. utg. ed.). Oslo: Redd barnas rettighetssenter Press – Redd barna ungdom.

Tiller, P. O. (2006). Barn som sakkyndige informanter Om forholdet mellom barnets verden og den voksne intervjuer [Children as expert informants in the relation between the child's world and the adult interviewer]. *Norsk Senter for barneforskning, Barn nr. 2*, 15–39.

Ulvik, O. S. (2007). *Seinmoderne fosterfamilier: en kulturpsykologisk studie av barn og voksnes fortellinger[Late modern foster families: a study of children's and adults' accounts in cultural psychology].* Oslo: Unipub.

Ulvik, O. S. (2014). Å utforske barns deltagelse i hverdagslivet: metodologiske refleksjoner [Exploring children's participation in everyday life: methodological reflections]. In L. M. Gulbrandsen (Ed.), *Barns deltakelse i hverdagsliv og profesjonell praksis: en utforskende tilnærming[Children's participation in everyday life and professional practice: an exploratory approach]* (pp. 56–74). Oslo: Universitetsforl.

Vitus, K., Thuesen, F., & Tanggaard, L. (2014). Konflikt i kvalitative metoder – hvorfor og hvordan? [Conflict in qualitative methods – why and how?]. In L. Tanggaard, F. Thuesen & K. Vitus (Eds.), *Konflikt i kvalitative studier* (Vol. 3, pp. 15–36). København: Hans Reitzels Forlag.

Warming, H. (2011). *Børneperspektiver: børn som ligeværdige medspillere i socialt og pædagogisk arbejde[Children's perspectives: children as equal participants in social and pedagogical work]* København: Akademisk forlag.

Weber, M. (2000). *Makt og byråkrati: essays om politikk og klasse, samfunnsforskning og verdier[Power and bureocracy: essays on politics and class, social science and values]* (D. Østerberg, Trans. 3. utg. ed.). Oslo: Gyldendal.

Øvreeide, H. (2009). *Samtaler med barn: metodiske samtaler med barn i vanskelige livssituasjoner [Conversations with children: methodological conversations with children in difficult life situations]* (3. utg. ed.). Kristiansand: Høyskoleforl.

Author

Inger Sofie Dahlø Husby
PhD Fellow at Norwegian University of Science and Technology (NTNU)
Faculty of Social Sciences and Technology Management
Department of Social Work and Health Science Trondheim, Norway
Research area is interdisciplinary work and partnership with children and families in child welfare